Rethinking the man question

Jane L. Parpart & Marysia Zalewski | eds

Rethinking the man question
sex, gender and violence in international relations

Zed Books
LONDON | NEW YORK

Rethinking the man question: sex, gender and violence in international relations was first published in 2008 by Zed Books Ltd, 7 Cynthia Street, London N1 9JF, UK and Room 400, 175 Fifth Avenue, New York, NY 10010, USA

www.zedbooks.co.uk

Editorial copyright © Jane L. Parpart and Marysia Zalewski, 2008
Copyright in this collection © Zed Books, 2008

The rights of Jane L. Parpart and Marysia Zalewski to be identified as the editors of this work have been asserted by them in accordance with the Copyright, Designs and Patents Act, 1988.

Cover designed by Andrew Corbett
Set in OurType Arnhem and Futura Bold by Ewan Smith, London
Index: ed.emery@thefreeuniversity.net

A catalogue record for this book is available from the British Library.
Library of Congress cataloging in publication data are available.

ISBN 978 1 84277 979 8 hb
ISBN 978 1 84277 980 4 pb

Contents

Acknowledgements

We have accumulated many debts in the course of putting this volume together; not least to the authors in this book, who have met and corresponded across time and place, contributing to an extended conversation about gender, sex, violence and international politics. The authors first presented their papers at two panels at the annual convention of the International Studies Association in 2006 in San Diego and then in Chicago in 2007 as well as at the annual conference of the British International Studies Association in 2005 (St Andrews, Scotland). We also met in smaller groups at the University of Bristol, sponsored by the politics department; at a conference on hegemonic masculinities organized by Juanita Elias and hosted by the University of Manchester; and at numerous other gatherings primarily in the UK and North America. The editors and the book as a whole benefited enormously from these meetings and discussions. The varied audiences raised important critical comments that kept sending us back to the drawing board. We are particularly grateful for input from Jindy Pettman, Maria Stern, Anne Sisson Runyan, Laura Shepherd, Christina Rowley, Moya Lloyd, Juanita Elias, Craig Murphy, Spike Peterson, Judith Squires, Jutta Weldes, Helen Kinsella, Jacqui True, Cynthia Enloe, Sandra Harding and members of the Bristol Gender Reading Group, and to Sandy Livingston for editorial assistance.

We are also indebted to a number of key institutions. Jane has been particularly peripatetic during this book's gestation, and could not have managed without the support of Dalhousie University's Department of International Development, the Gender Institute at the London School of Economics and Political Science and, currently, the University of the West Indies (St Augustine) Centre for Gender and Development Studies. She is especially grateful to the administrators of those departments: Marian MacKinnon, Hazel Johnstone and Glenda Ottley, all of whom provided crucial assistance at key points. Jane (and the book) also benefited enormously from discussions with many colleagues, including Rebecca Tiessen, Pauline Gardiner Barber, Diane Perrons, Clare Hemmings, Silvia Posocco, Sadie Wearing, Rosalind Gill, Rhoda Reddock, Patricia Mohammed and Gabrielle Hosein. She also extends thanks to numerous colleagues and students around the world who have participated in discussions about *Rethinking the Man Question*. Most importantly, Jane wants to thank her husband, Tim Shaw, and her co-editor, Marysia Zalewski, for her patience, tenacity and insights as we struggled to find common ground for thinking through and framing the book.

Marysia particularly wants to thank Maria Stern and Jindy Pettman for their unwavering support and help while collating this volume. She also extends warm thanks and gratitude to Margaret Jolly, Tamara Jacka, Michelle Antoinette and Janet Beard at the Gender Relations Centre in the Research School of Pacific and Asian Studies at the Australian National University for providing a welcoming and intellectually stimulating environment while she was a visiting fellow there from November 2007 to January 2008 – a beautiful and colourful space which enabled the completion of this book. Thanks are due to the University of Aberdeen for financial support and to the Gender Institute at the London School of Economics and Political Science for providing physical and intellectual space in the summer of 2007. Marysia is especially grateful to her co-editor, Jane Parpart, for her patience, diplomacy, hard work and energy, without which the book would not have been completed. She also wants to express her deep appreciation to Bernie Hayes for unstinting care and support.

Finally we would like to thank the fine team working with us at Zed Books, especially Susannah Trefgarne and Ellen McKinlay for their enthusiasm for the project and for their patience during the process of getting the book into press.

The editors and Zed Books would like to express their gratitude for permission to reprint the following poems in the book: 'How the Children Were Born', 'How a Long Way Off Rolled Itself Up' and 'How the Answers Got Their Questions' from Moniza Alvi, *How the Stone Found Its Voice* (Bloodaxe Books, 2005); 'The Butterfly Farm' from Medbh McGuckian, *The Flower Master* (1982), by kind permission of the author c/o The Gallery Press, Loughcrew, Oldcastle, County Meath, Ireland; 'At The Sex Frontier' from Fiona Sampson, *Common Prayer* (Carcanet, 2007); 'Mending the Helicopter' from Robert Crawford, *Selected Poems* (Jonathan Cape, 2005), reprinted by permission of The Random House Group Ltd. All reasonable efforts have been made by the authors to contact the copyright holders of all poems reproduced in this volume. The publishers would be pleased to hear from any copyright holder it was not possible to contact before publication.

Preface: the man question, gender and global power

We usually think of gender as an issue of personal life and close relationships. This is true, but incomplete. Gender certainly concerns our bodies, emotions and intimacy. Gender is also an aspect of public, institutional life, of the way companies, governments, education systems and mass media function. This book and its predecessor (Zalewski and Parpart 1998) demonstrate an even wider scope. To identify the 'man question' in international relations is to recognize that gender is an integral, not an accidental, feature of the worldwide structure of diplomatic, military and economic relations.

Nearly forty years ago, theorists of the women's liberation movement saw gender inequalities spread across the world, and evolved a concept of global patriarchy. This meant a common structure of domination by men and subordination of women, with consequences in human degradation, war and environmental destruction. Robin Morgan, a prominent women's liberation writer in the United States, drew the logical conclusion: 'More and more, I begin to think of a worldwide Women's Revolution as the only hope for life on the planet' (1970: xxxv).

Since she wrote those words, the state of the planet has certainly changed. The United States was defeated in Vietnam and withdrew for a while from military adventures. Its client state in Iran collapsed and was replaced, after violent struggles, by a new religious state. The Soviet Union was defeated in Afghanistan and a few years later collapsed, replaced by a kleptocracy and increasingly authoritarian secular states. A huge debt crisis engulfed Latin America, and military dictatorships or neoliberalism took over most governments in the region. Many of the post-colonial states in Africa imploded and civil wars became endemic in west and central Africa.

At the same time, the dictatorship in China began to reintroduce capitalism and returned to the international scene as a great power. Nuclear arms proliferated, the Atlantic/European nuclear powers being joined by Israel, Pakistan, India and China, with others waiting in the wings. The remaining superpower, the United States, cashed in its post-cold-war dividend for a new wave of military and surveillance technology, and increasingly took the shape of a security state, a process accelerated by the 'war on terror' and new military adventures under the Bush administrations. Every one of these shifts was led by groups of men.

This does not look much like a women's revolution. Yet there have been undeniable gains for gender equality. Women's labour force participation, and therefore access to wages and to the other resources that come with money, has risen in most parts of the world. Underpinning that is the education revolution that in some ways is the greatest gender change of all on a world scale. The provision of elementary education for girls and literacy rates among women have risen massively across the developing world. Gender balances in secondary and advanced education have also changed, with a growing presence of women in professional training and then in professional occupations.

Women have, accordingly, been appearing in greater numbers at senior levels of professions, for instance as judges. And unevenly, but persistently, this has included the senior levels of government. Women, always a large part of the public sector workforce, are now more present in public sector management. Gender equality units have appeared in the policymaking apparatus of many states. The first woman head of government in a modern state came to office in 1960 – in Sri Lanka – and though this is still exceptional, it is no longer extraordinary. The list of countries that have had women elected heads of government now includes India, Indonesia, Pakistan, Chile, Argentina, Nicaragua, Britain, Germany, New Zealand and Norway, the home of the famous 'cabinet of women'. In the Nordic countries as a group, women now make up 42 per cent of elected members of national parliaments.

These statistics tell us about a broad effect, but not about the processes that produced it. The census-takers' categories 'men' and 'women' are themselves produced by fine-grained social processes in which gender meanings and group memberships can be redefined – as some of the chapters in this book demonstrate. Popular understandings of how political authority should work are also subject to change. The assumption that a hierarchical gender order is unchangeable and unquestionable has been crumbling in many parts of the world. Gender orders were massively disrupted by colonialism; continuing change in gender relations is difficult to deny; and the diversity of gender identities and groupings is increasingly acknowledged.

The historicity of gender is now plain. Increasingly the cultural assumption is *for* gender equality, rather than against it. Ali Shariati, the thinker who did much to inspire the Islamic revolution in Iran, reflected this in his theological argument that women and men, being created with the same nature, have the same entitlement to respect – which led him to defend women's education and women's presence in the public realm.

Passing this cultural horizon has allowed the growth of gender-related rights regimes, such as equal opportunity rules, anti-discrimination laws and changed rape laws. Since 1979 the UN convention on the elimination of all forms of discrimination against women (CEDAW) has made gender equality normative in international arenas. Genuinely equal employment opportunity is not yet a reality anywhere, but a movement towards it has happened, even in the security apparatus – an increasing number of states now recruit women into police and military forces. Through civil rights struggles, a lesbian and gay presence in the public realm has developed in cities from London to São Paulo, and in many authoritarian states lesbian and gay communities are also present, though half underground. The contestation of gender arrangements and the possibilities of debate and change in gender relations are now familiar in most parts of the world.

Contestation still does not amount to revolution. Women as a group have increased their presence in the paid labour force, but men as a group have *not* substantially increased their role in housework or infant care. There are honourable exceptions, to be sure, and they are important in establishing the possibility of change; yet large-scale change in the gender division of domestic labour in heterosexual households is stalled. The group of men who do most unpaid housework is gay couples. In the paid workforce, equal opportunity may be official policy but new forms of gender segregation constantly appear. This is startlingly true in terms of new technologies, for instance in the computer industry. It is also true in old technologies being reorganized under neoliberalism, for instance in light manufacturing in poor countries' export processing zones, and in the international trade in domestic labour which brings women from poor countries – from the Philippines to Moldava – into middle-class homes in wealthier countries as maids, cooks and cleaners.

There is also a cultural refurbishing of men's authority. Ali Shariati may have rejected the veil and the seclusion of women, but it was Ayatollah Khomeini's followers who came out on top in Iran. In the United States, neoconservative Protestantism has flourished, alongside secular pseudosciences such as sociobiology, evolutionary psychology and Jungian depth psychology. All of these purport to show that gender division and masculine domination are natural. Spectacles of aggressive masculinity, such as football, motor racing and 'action' movies and video games, have a large presence in mass media and have acquired huge popular followings. While equal rights regimes have taken root in some parts of the world, the position of women has deteriorated in the countries of the former USSR – which had once pioneered the public commitment to gender equality, despite the privileging of men in communist practice.

For all the change documented above, women who make it to the elite level of politics remain vastly outnumbered by men. Men make up 82.5 per cent of members of national parliaments worldwide, and a higher proportion of cabinets. In some parts of the world there are no women in the top leadership group at all – as shown by the Chinese leadership's televised curtain call at the end of the 2007 Communist Party congress, showing a line of men in dark suits surrounded by flowers. In most large-scale religions there are no women in senior leadership positions – no women popes, archbishops, patriarchs, ayatollahs, muftis or chief monks. Even in those military forces that recruit women, the generals and admirals are overwhelmingly men. Military leadership at lower levels is still constructed through social definitions of powerful masculinity, nuanced and changing as this undoubtedly is.

In the corporate world, women make up a large fraction of the workforce, a significant minority of professional and middle administrative positions, and a trivially small proportion of top management – where power and wealth are increasingly concentrated, in a neoliberal economy. In 2007, for instance, of the top 200 corporations listed on the Australian Stock Exchange, just five have women as CEOs. That is to say, 97.5 per cent of the top executives in my country are men. Patriarchy seems decidedly resilient.

Again, the statistics give us only a bare outline of gender realities. Closer examination shows that these hierarchies are neither uniform nor static. The studies in this book build on research from the last two decades that has documented, very richly, the multiplicity of masculinities and their capacity for change. Change is visible even in dominant forms of masculinity, where there is struggle for hegemony as the circumstances for the maintenance of social power themselves change. The form of masculine authority that was effective in the era of steam power and elaborate bureaucracy is not likely to work well in an era of computers, nuclear weapons and lean organizations. In the constant struggles for influence and power at the elite levels of politics and business, gender practices and identities may and sometimes do shift.

Nor do all men share equally in the dividend of benefits, services and income that flows to men collectively from patriarchal gender arrangements. Some gain great benefits – and in no period of history have the rewards for the privileged been so great. Other groups of men pay heavy costs – in unemployment, violence, prejudice, exclusion and injury. In the mixed civil wars and military interventions that seem characteristic of the post-cold-war international order, men from poor, working-class or peasant backgrounds fire most of the guns and stop most of the bullets.

The costs to men and boys from the existing gender order have increasingly been publicized. Media storms have raged about a supposed crisis in boys' education, and more credibly about men's health problems. The emotional consequences of rigid, violent or work-driven masculinities have also been debated – for instance, the Japanese controversy over white-collar corporate warriors who work themselves to death. These concerns, together with feminist criticism of domestic violence, rape and war, have fuelled searches for new and more peaceable forms of masculinity. Both utopian visions and practical reform programmes have resulted. There is certainly no unified 'men's movement'. Many progressive movements and initiatives have, however, sprung up in the last generation. They range from the anti-violence 'White Ribbon' movement in Canada, to self-help and support groups for teenage fathers in Brazil, to men's groups in many countries mobilizing for care and prevention in the HIV/AIDS epidemic.

Since the pioneering efforts of the Pinochet regime in Chile, neoliberalism has spread dramatically, and now provides the meta-policy framing of government and economy in most parts of the world. Market 'reforms' have impacted welfare states, education systems and mass media as well as finance, taxation and international trade. This has had gender consequences. The neoliberal market agenda has shifted resources into institutions controlled by men, especially corporations and finance markets; and it has undermined the capacity of exploited social groups to achieve change and redistribution by collective action, promoting instead an ethic of individual 'choice'. Apparently gender-neutral, the market often reinstals gender divisions, in deregulated labour markets, in segregated private schools, in the untrammelled marketing of sexist toys, videos and other consumer goods. Yet the market agenda has also produced gender change. For instance, capital's search for a cheap and flexible labour force has translated into neoliberal 'welfare reforms' pressuring women to enter the labour market. This in turn has triggered a reworking of the social meaning of motherhood, in both rich and poor countries.

Neoliberalism is closely connected with the expansion of international trade, international investment and managerial power, and with the growth of worldwide electronic communication and migration – the patterns that have come to be called (rather misleadingly) 'globalization'. These processes have many effects on existing gender orders. They have also created new social arenas: transnational corporations, international markets (e.g. currency, share and derivative markets), international media, and supranational state institutions (including military and intelligence apparatuses). In each of these arenas, a gender order is being constructed, carrying forward the gender hierarchies of earlier and more local institutions but also showing features of its own.

If gender hierarchy is resilient, then, it has also been forced to transform itself. I would suggest that the world is now best understood as the scene of competing market patriarchies, linked antagonistically through the arenas of media, commodity and finance markets, diplomacy and war. The core power holders are the elites of transnational corporations and major states, overwhelmingly men, who embody variations on a technocratic, power-oriented masculinity. The patriarchal dividend from innumerable local gender economies is concentrated in their hands, manifest in the unprecedented wealth of the contemporary super-rich and their almost unbelievably wasteful lifestyle.

Around this core revolve the allied groups on whom the stability of their privilege actually rests: the comprador masculinities of middle management, the politicians of client states, the wives of the corporate elite, the exemplars of muscular masculinity in commercial sports, the mercenaries of the security services (who have replaced the citizen-soldiers of earlier regimes) and the organic intellectuals of the market world – the advertising agents, fashion gurus and entertainers who fill the media with an apparently ever-changing but deeply repetitive gender display. Specific patriarchal networks very often struggle against each other – within a nation-state such as South Africa, in a regional context such as the struggle in south-west Asia between the Iranian and the US regimes, or in a global context, as we see with the rise of the new Chinese version of state capitalism.

The historic resistances to patriarchal power have to a large extent been contained, some of them smashed by repressive states (feminist organization in Indonesia, for instance, crushed by the Suharto regime). Public sector feminism, social-movement feminism, gay activism and intellectual radicalism do not have much purchase in this historical moment.

Yet they are not dead; and new resistances have kept appearing, some of them documented in this book. They include queer activism, women's activism against HIV/AIDS and violence, anti-violence activism among men, feminist environmentalism, gender-aware trade unionism, maternal feminism (in the face of patriarchal dictatorships), movements for engaged fatherhood, contestation about gender and sexuality within religious organizations, and cultural changes among youth which have produced, in some social milieux, an informal but systematic practice of gender equality. I think of these, on a world scale, as forming an archipelago of resistances rather than a coherent social movement. There are, nevertheless, connections among them, sometimes making creative use of new media such as the Internet or events such as the World Social Forum.

How far their pressure will be able to transform the formidable new market patriarchies of the post-cold-war world remains to be seen. Potentials for change in the global gender order are easy to see: the unintended consequences of neoliberalism, the tidal effects of women's education on the global periphery, gender egalitarianism among youth, new forms of resistance and new connections among them. We still do need a worldwide women's revolution; if we are to have one, it will be wonderfully colourful and variegated, with many men waving the banners of change on the barricades too.

Raewyn Connell, University of Sydney

References

Morgan, R. (1970) *Sisterhood is Powerful: An Anthology of Writings from the Women's Liberation Movement*, New York: Random House.

Zalewski, M. and J. Parpart (eds) (1998) *The 'Man' Question in International Relations*, Boulder, CO: Westview Press.

In remembrance of his warm
expressions of masculinity, this book is
dedicated to Marysia's father,
Stanley (Stanislaw) Zalewski (1925–2005),
and to Jane's father,
Elbert Payson Little (1912–1983),
for his generous, loving and flexible
interpretation of masculinity.

How the Answers Got Their Questions

The most difficult task of all was not
finding new questions or harder questions,
dipping your wrists into the blood of questions.

It was finding questions for the answers
which had none, prising them out of the earth,
catching them before they burst into flames.

Moniza Alvi (2005)

Introduction: rethinking the man question

MARYSIA ZALEWSKI AND JANE L. PARPART

Rethinking the Man Question is inspired by the challenge of studying gender and sex in the context of contemporary international politics. We present this as a twofold challenge. First, we try to understand the impact of the deadly mix of fear, humiliation and wounded masculine pride which marks the post-9/11 international political landscape. Second, this is an attempt to produce responsible and politically effective knowledge about gender and sex through an academic discipline traditionally marked by rigorous, even violent, methodological policing of its epistemological and ontological borders. Here, we outline the contours of this dual challenge and contextualize each of the subsequent chapters. Before moving on to do this, we will make some introductory remarks on the links and disjunctures between this book and *The 'Man' Question in International Relations* (1998),[1] whose impact on the field provided both the motivation and the framework for analysis which inspire and inform this new book.

The 'man' question

When we first asked the 'man' question, our view was that the global political landscape was very much a man's world – one seemingly overwhelmingly populated by men and dominated by masculine aspirations (Zalewski and Parpart 1998). Not only did governments continue to look like 'men's clubs' (Enloe 1989: 6) but also the theories and practices of the discipline of international relations seemed largely untouched – really unmoved – by feminist insights about gender and the international. Given this, we decided to collate *The 'Man' Question* as we judged it necessary to move from asking the feminist-inspired 'woman question' – as this seemed to be proving simultaneously insufficient (not changing the gender order in significant ways) and reactionary (presenting woman as a 'problem to be solved') – to asking the 'man' question. Consequently, our feminist strategy in *The 'Man' Question* was to interrogate the constituted subject of man and his varied masculinities in order to offer an alternative, gendered exposé of the study and practice of international politics.[2]

Given that the discipline of international relations, which purports to offer a comprehensive analysis of international politics, had largely proved stubbornly immune to the impact of feminism, this approach seemed a creative move, intellectually, politically and pedagogically.

In *The 'Man' Question*, the sexed bodies of men and the injuries of masculinity emerged as significant sites of enquiry in our investigations into relationships between power, gender and violence. Yet asking the 'man' question was (and is) always about attempting to dislocate the 'male-orderedness' of enquiries about gender and crucially about interrupting the stability of the terms 'men' and 'women' as a way to loosen the hold gender has on meaning and life (Ferguson 1993: 7). Interrupting this stability while at the same time invoking its terms – man, woman, femininity, masculinity, gender, sex – is, however, tricky. Notwithstanding this, our decision to move the gender spotlight to the constructed subject of man was made partly in order to interrupt the stability and normality of focusing on woman as a kind of gender problem. The focus on man drew attention to the way masculinities, in their variable forms (which includes the simultaneous evisceration and inclusion of the feminine), structure the theories and practices of international politics but also – crucially – signalled quite clearly that the whole of international politics was gendered; a point more easily, if wrongly, missed when the gender focus remains on woman.

Though moving the gender spotlight to man might be perceived as a democratic remedy for the apparent singular focus on woman, recent critical scholarship demonstrates that the move to men or indeed masculinities does not overcome the constitutive production of gender as a heteronormative binary (Wiegman 2002). This again raises questions about how to responsibly and effectively ask questions about gender, an issue that has long preoccupied feminist scholars. Kathy Ferguson articulates this as puzzling over the 'proper way' to frame questions about gender (1993: 1). In *The 'Man' Question* the framing of our question about gender involved a challenge to essentialist understandings of gender and sex indicated by encasing 'man' in inverted commas. In this book the inverted commas seem unnecessary given the profound impact of performative understandings of identity on feminist scholarship. The strength of this impact is demonstrated in Susan Hekman's claim that Judith Butler's performative understanding of identity and subjectivity has become the baseline from which all subsequent feminist discussions engaging these issues must proceed (2004: 8). Though this view may be contentious, Butler's work has indeed been 'pivotal in shifting the terms of the debate away from a unified conception of [the subject] woman' (Lloyd 2007: 7), casting radical deconstructionist doubt on the theoretical credibility and integrity of such an (im)position.

Though the issue of how best to ask questions about gender remains an issue of much debate within the broad range of feminist scholarship, there is no doubt that gender[3] continues to saturate our cultural, political, personal and international imaginations and daily lives. Indeed, gender has proven to be impressively malleable, adapting to new circumstances rather than withering away in response to demands for change (Weston 2002: 2). Feminist activists and scholars[4] have produced prodigious amounts of information and analysis on the intricacies and devastations of gender's effects. This work has resulted in some undeniable gains stated by Raewyn Connell in the preface to this book. In *Rethinking the Man Question* leading scholars re-engage with the man question in order to rethink the potent contemporary connections between violence, power and sex in the light of increasingly complex understandings of sex, gender and sexuality, particularly in this post-9/11 'manly moment' (Eisenstein 2004: 161). Working with the productive character of sex and gender, the authors draw on a mix of contemporary critical feminist theory, masculinity studies and post-colonial theories to investigate the diverse and often understated ways in which gender/sex functions in international politics, particularly in relation to violence. *The 'Man' Question* was merely the beginning, not the end. It was our intention then, manifested here, to keep open and to reopen debates about how sex, gender, masculinity and femininity are implicated in one another (Lloyd 2007: 27); and how these continue to make and remake the world of international politics and moreover how we re-produce and recirculate gender/sex in our educative, intellectual and policymaking practices in the context of the international. We believe these rethinkings are always necessary and will, it is hoped, be productive for the reader as well as for the discipline of international relations and the practices of international politics.

The structural and material violences associated with and structured by gender were a central concern in *The 'Man' Question*; they remain an issue of concern to the contributors to this book. The World Health Organization has labelled violence a global pandemic,[5] with a multitude of causes and manifestations; from the arms race, small and large, to the international corporate commodification of almost every human activity, to the HIV/AIDS endemic and the unyielding grinding poverty and concomitant ill health which blights the lives of millions of people. It is currently estimated that 600 million people worldwide are chronically undernourished, while 40,000 children die each day as the result of malnutrition (Vestlesen 2005: 291). Yet another example is the 875 million illiterate people in the world, two-thirds of whom are women; a proportion practically unchanged since 1990 (Sharma 2004: 4). Some of these acts and manifestations of violence are of concern to governments and international bodies such as the United Nations, if never quite enough; though it is often only the more conventionally obvious violences that appear to be of interest in the mainstream academic study of international politics. But these glimpses of suffering are not an accidental feature of international politics, but are 'embedded in the patterns of politics and order that regulate global life' (Burke 2007: 1). We refer to these violences as toxic, as this invokes a sense of the poisonous and insidious character of international violences which show no real signs of abating, with new kinds emerging alongside depressingly familiar ones. As such, a key but newly energized point of connection with *The 'Man' Question* is that we remain intensely interested in the power, particularly the gendered power – most particularly that with a 'masculinized face' – that recirculates and makes invisible the constitutive evidence of violence in the everyday and in the international. It remains vitally important to keep interrogating the question of why relations of gendered power are so intractable and so enduring, even in the face of collective resistance (Ahmed 2004: 12).

Rethinking the Man Question engages both the practices and the study of international politics as sites of empirical and theoretical analysis, though necessarily selectively. We argue that both these sites are worthy of investigation given that we are interested in illuminating both obvious and less obvious forms of violence, epistemological and methodological as well as material and structural. In this context all the chapters are presented as case studies, even if the latter chapters seem more recognizably so. We began by identifying part of the contemporary challenge in studying gender and sex in international politics as connected to the possibilities of producing responsible and effective knowledge in an international environment marked by a deadly mix of fear, humiliation and wounded masculine pride; we will now move on to clarify and discuss this.

Knowledge in 'dark times'

Wendy Brown uses the imagery of 'dark times' to refer to anxieties about the production of critical knowledge and the possibilities of political action consequent to the attacks on the USA on 11 September 2001 (2005). The ensuing war on terror, and concerns about national security, specifically US national security, continue to dominate Western-inspired understandings of what counts as internationally and politically significant (Burke 2007). These events, coded globally as 9/11, have helped to reinvigorate the Western study of international politics as well as reorganize the practices of international politics more in line with traditional masculinist and imperial concerns lethally refracted through the current prism of neoliberalism. Consequent to 9/11, leading governments of the world, most especially that of the USA, immediately began to develop tougher interventionist, 'no-nonsense attitudes' to eliminate what George W. Bush emphatically called 'evil' (Vestlesen 2005: 295). The reinvigoration of traditional categories of 'good versus evil' nurtures, and is nurtured by, simple but highly effective rhetorics of wounded national pride; an injury which goes right to the heart of ideals of 'heroic manhood'. Moreover, the reassertion of these appealing and familiar dualistic logics – us/them, good/evil, protector/protected – is, as always, overlaid with ideologies of gender. The cluster of post-9/11 US films – some rather belatedly being released[6] – is a useful means of monitoring the reassertion of these traditional categories. Oliver Stone's *World Trade Center*[7] uses quite staggeringly traditional gendered tactics to make the story of the film work and really tug at the heartstrings of the American public. Without a wife and pregnant girlfriend waiting at home for the two Port Authority cops trapped in the rubble of the World Trade Center, the film would not work at all.[8] The film is 'rather comforting', one reviewer remarked;[9] while another claimed it as 'one of the greatest pro-American, pro-family, pro-faith, pro-male, flag-waving, God Bless America films you will ever see'.[10]

The mix of fear (insecurity/war on terror), humiliation (a brutal attack on the literal heart of corporate America)[11] and wounded masculine pride (this devastating attack was carried out so simply and for all America and the world to see as it happened – by 'othered' men) consequent to 9/11 is playing a significant part in refiguring the international landscape. And as Raewyn Connell notes in the preface to this volume, it is groups of men who are still making most of the deadly decisions in the global arena. It is therefore important to be vigilant in relation to this gendered remapping of international politics and maintain a passionate and critical re-engagement with texts, in all their varied forms. Critical analysis insists on a persistent questioning of hegemonic forms of truth-making (Burke 2007: 12).

Intellectual and pedagogical space for critical interrogation is not, however – and never is – secure. The institution of the university is not exempt from the overwhelming domination of the values of the neoliberal market, where profitability is fast becoming the sole justification for just about everything (Vestlesen 2005: 291); indeed, it wholeheartedly endorses it.[12] As such it is our view in this book that it is vitally important to reconsider or 're-pose questions' (Shaw and Walker 2006: 158) about the production of knowledge in an institutional environment that does not welcome too much critical interruption, given the permeation by the consumer mentality and brand-name courses (Brown 2005: 43). With the commercialization of universities in a global market and the commodification of knowledges as priced options, the 'devaluation of critical thinking seems inevitable' (Kirby 2007: 129). Moreover, the global competition for students and the drive to increase profitability will necessarily have a significant effect on this site of institutional knowledge production, suggesting that it is an important location to critically analyse; the 'neoliberal takeover bid for the world has epistemic consequences as well as economic and political' (Connell 2007: 207). Feminist scholars have always viewed knowledge production as an important terrain for gendered investigation, as the authoritative accounts of the world accredited by academic disciplines have profound effects on people's lives (Hawkesworth 2006). The need for feminist-informed critical enquiry has simply increased.

This book, like The 'Man' Question, is inspired by and indebted to feminism. In this newly virile moment we consider feminism – in its varied pluralities and (dis)guises, manifestations and metamorphosing identities and practices – to be crucial in our investigation into the man question. Our feminist curiosities about gender/sex may well – and do – lead us to corporeal reconfigurations and manifestations of femininity and masculinity. But the feminism we engage with and draw upon in this book is not a parsimonious one. Overlaid as it is with a sense of the philosophical and concerned with asking open-ended, exploratory questions, we understand feminism to be interested in 'how we organize life, how we accord it value, how we compel the world' (Butler 2004: 205). What form these philosophically inflected questions take, what relationship they have to the bodies of women (or men), or to transformative practices, or to knowledge projects, changes. As Robyn Wiegman suggests, 'feminism as an intellectual and political project is not finally bound to any prescribed domain of gender's complex universe' (2002: 52).

The impact of performative understandings of identity and subjectivity on contemporary scholarship investigating sex and gender has clearly shifted the ways in which we think about how gender works and the kinds of questions we might ask. Moreover, the work emanating from post-colonial and masculinity studies has both challenged and deeply enriched investigations into the relationships between sex/gender, violence and the international. Working with multilayered and intersecting understandings of gender/sex, each contributor in this volume maintains that it is imperative to work with manifestations of gender/sex in order to have some critical understanding of the re-production of violence and power in international politics, but also, crucially, of the re-production of gender/sex.

Yet how to produce responsible and politically effective knowledge about gender and international politics has preoccupied many of the contributors to this book; not least because our students constantly raise similar concerns and questions.[13] If *The 'Man' Question* demonstrated a measure of confidence in a rather conventional relationship between analysis, theory and social change,[14] one that assumed, or at least hoped for, an effectual relationship between academic work and social and political change, we adopt a more cautious and methodologically eclectic approach in these 'dark times'. The faith in sure-footed connections between agency and action, with theory and the writing of it acting as some kind of active interlocutor between them, has been subject to much critical enquiry, drawing us into greater doubt about conventional methodological approaches.[15] These traditional approaches are often stringently parsimonious, usually in a relentless quest for the 'essence' of a subject (Doty 2000: 137), its truth. In contrast, for critical scholars, the epistemological challenge is not so much about the difficulties encountered on the way to achieving true knowledge – 'in an ideal world we would know everything' (Nicholson 2000: 186). Rather, it is to work with the idea that 'we don't like not knowing, so we pretend that we do' (Edkins 2003: 13).

Consequently, questioning the character of the relationship between theory and practice is integrally connected to the vital issue of how we produce responsible knowledge, if such knowledge is possible, particularly through academic disciplines. As suggested, this issue has been of persistent concern within feminist scholarship, and more regularly so of late within international relations (IR). Recent discussions in the field imply that the discipline is 'as much a problem as a solution ...

rarely producing students capable of querying the relevance of categories' (Shaw and Walker 2006: 160, 161). Students/citizens often emerge with limited understanding of the power and politics involved in deciding which categories count and which do not, assuming that the exclusions are somehow 'natural'. Shaw and Walker's damning conclusion is that the discipline of IR is inadequate to the task of educating its students. This is a serious charge, making it even more important to investigate the silences surrounding gender and their attendant deadly practices. Studying silences is difficult and hard to grasp, especially using traditional methdological tools (Cohn 2006; Kronsell 2006). Yet given that silences are integral to knowing (Eisenstein 2004: 37) it is the task of critical scholars to weave alternative paths through the narratives that traditional methodologies create. A sense of this task is lyrically evoked in the poem that preceded this Introduction.

In order to weave alternative paths and to help access the silent violences surrounding gender, we have included poetry in *Rethinking the Man Question*. The poems are intended to act as a creative/imaginative methodological intervention, ventilating the text to generate a kind of epistemological breathing space. Most mainstream education, perhaps starkly illustrated in the conventional teaching of international politics, scarcely equips us with the skills needed to be critical thinkers; and indeed critical thinkers are struggling to both comprehend and resist those powerful forces that are currently reshaping the world (Brown 2005; Mullen 2006: 283). We offer the poems in this book as challenges to conventional ways of reading, seeing and understanding. By injecting this measure of methodological plurality in the book we hope to tangentially illustrate the complexity of gender's work and to simultaneously problematize the 'turn toward certainty' (Edkins and Zehfuss 2005: 451) evident in both the study and practices of international politics in a post-9/11 environment. Of course, the more complex things are or begin to appear, the less certain the outcome seems to be, something of an anathema in an international political environment dominated by 'certainties of voice' (Shaw and Walker 2006: 157); but this also leaves more room 'for inventing ourselves out of this mess' (Keller 2006: 229). And it is surely true that 'this world of ours is not in a very good shape – witness not only the war on terror but the deeply troubling causes producing as well as constantly reproducing it' (Vestlesen 2005: 298).

In his chapter, Terrell Carver addresses the metonymical linkages that 'work discursively to erase the inherent hypocrisies and license mass destruction'; poetry also works with metonymical linkages – rendering strange that which is familiar, and thus encouraging readers to make connections they might not otherwise make. Thinking about political puzzles through and with poetic methodological imaginations can help to articulate those forces, languages and structures that appear dormant or ineffectual when using traditional analytic tools; this is especially significant as looking at what is unsaid is important, 'as what is unsaid … carries (like a membrane) all that is said' (Hunt 1990: 30). The latter is perhaps a poetic articulation of the postmodern idea that discursive power functions by concealing the terms of its fabrication (Brown 2001: 122). The poems we include in this volume all address, in different ways, practices of power, knowledge, gender and sex in a form that simple prose cannot access, offering a more 'daring, more socially critical and creative work of metaphor and imagination' (Burke 2007: 58). We have therefore included poetry to aerate the text, and simultaneously to help readers to see that it is all too easy to accept the authority or competence of conventional, familiar forms of producing knowledge (Sampson 1997: 254).

Rethinking the man question

In *Rethinking the Man Question* we tangentially work with Wendy Brown's idea that for 'theory to live it must keep moving' (2001: 123) and Kathy Ferguson's idea of 'loosening the hold of gender on meaning and life' (1993: 4). The authors in this book investigate variable venues and sites through which gender operates and functions; some through the sexed body, some not. By loosening the attachment of gender and sexed bodies, or rather by illustrating the unstable connections between gender and bodies, we reconsider ways in which gender/sex disciplines, reconstitutes and organizes power in international politics. We are also interested in how power becomes persistently coded as masculine outside the location of the sexed bodies usually assigned this identity. Moreover, we illustrate how the unstable link between gender and sexed bodies gives masculinism the flexibility to take on different modalities, practices and performances. These may include variably sexed bodies and exclude some male-identified bodies, all without radically disturbing the connections between masculinism and power.

Kimberly Hutchings interrogates one of the reasons for the ongoing marginalization of feminist/gender concerns in the academic study on international relations. She claims that a fundamental reason for this relates to the legitimizing function played by masculinity discourses. To illustrate her claim, she investigates two influential accounts of international politics, Mearsheimer's *The Tragedy of Great Power Politics* (2001) and Hardt and Negri's *Empire* (2000). She concludes that masculinity operates as a resource for thought in theorizing international politics, working as a kind of shorthand for processes of explanatory and normative judgement, and thereby as one of the crucial ways in which our social scientific imagination is shaped and limited. Ultimately, Hutchings argues, without the logic of masculinity, grand theorists of international politics would be required to work a great deal harder in order to persuade us of the accuracy of their diagnosis of the times we are in and their historical antecedents.

In a similar philosophical vein, Terrell Carver argues that metaphors act as motors of discourse which work to frame and naturalize masculinist assumptions within international politics. He suggests that masculinities are commonly delineated through metaphors, which do the discursive work of telling us 'what a man is'. Animals are popular, but mechanical and mechanistic metaphors are also effective shorthands for framing modern masculinity. For Carver, militarization constitutes a machine-like masculinity. The current focus of militarization has, however, shifted from individualized warrior-males to 'human systems' and technologies of indiscriminate violence (see Masters, this volume). Individualized warfare with limited technology has become 'othered' as 'guerrilla fighting' and 'terror'. A crucial point to note here is that the constituent metaphors in this process masquerade as factual categories, thereby working discursively to erase inherent hypocrisies and license mass destruction.

As the licensing of mass destruction regularly passes unnoticed except in its more obvious guises, in *Rethinking the Man Question* we are curious to interrogate the 'conceptual architecture of our world' (Kirby 2007). In her chapter, Cristina Masters considers a particular kind of conceptual architecture, the bio-political architecture of power. She investigates this in the context of debates about the ethico-political possibilities of technology and associated claims that advanced technology is both liberatory and transgressive. Her chapter explores this question: does/can technology liberate us from gendered regimes of knowledge and consequently from the deadly politics of war? In considering this, she interrogates the representative practices at work in the interface between man and machine in the military and their ethico-political implications by tracing the constitution of the cyborg soldier in the US military through both techno-scientific and masculinist discourses of power. She explores how masculinity – and gender writ large – is being rearticulated within this particular context. By grafting masculinity on to technology and by unhinging male subjectivity from the physical male body, she demonstrates how masculinity no longer need coincide with the bio-male body. Her discussion may help elucidate why the destruction of flesh-and-blood bodies in conflict receives little attention or is so easily written off as collateral damage or acts of terrorists/'others'.

Feminism's critical turn towards unleashing masculinity from its assumed natural attachment to corporeal bodies highlights the need to re-explore ways in which masculinist power and male bonding deny various forms of masculinity and produce social hierarchies (Wiegman 2002). This raises the issue of how feminist analysis relates to the rapidly growing field of masculinity studies (Connell 1995, 2005; Connell and Messerschmidt 2005; Alsop et al. 2002; Kegan Gardiner 2002; Seidler 2005; Kimmell 2005), particularly since in this volume we all draw upon feminist scholarship to some extent. While largely focused on men, the work of Raewyn Connell has been important in challenging assumptions that all men wield similar masculinist power. Connell claims that the link between men and power is reinforced and maintained by its foundation in a very specific form of masculinity, hegemonic masculinity. This form of masculinity is associated with practices, discourses and institutions linked to hegemonic male power, which, while continually contested and reconfigured, is designed to maintain the link to masculinist power, rather than its mere content. Those who threaten this link through sexuality, race, ethnicity or behaviour are excluded from the charmed circle[16] of hegemonic male bonding and become comprehensible only as subordinate and marginalized masculinities/men. But the façade of hegemonic masculinity requires constant vigilance and 'constant cultural work in order to appear the effortless attributes of a privilege simultaneously justif[ied] and disguise[d]' (Kegan Gardner 2002: 17). Also required is a willingness – indeed obligation[17] – to expunge those who interfere with maintaining the commonsense belief that men are the natural power brokers in the world of international politics. Linking this argument to the critical feminist separation of gender from sexed bodies, we can begin to see that hegemonic masculinity does not simply relate to biologically sexed men; it might also include women and 'other' men as well as the non-corporeal and the non-human (see Carver and Masters, this volume).What seems to persistently emerge is the maintainence of an authoritative link between power and hegemonic masculinity; this encourages us again to reflect on Sara Ahmed's question: 'why are relations of power so intractable and enduring even in the force of collective forms of resistance?' (2004: 12).

Investigating some of the enduring characteristics of the discipline of international relations is the focus of Kevin Dunn's chapter. Like Kimberly Hutchings, Kevin Dunn is intrigued by the lack of interest in feminist analysis in the academic study of the subject. This leads him to be particularly curious about the ongoing domination of white men in the academic study of international politics. To more adequately examine and remedy discrimination and oppression, he claims we must make systems of power and privilege visible. He does this by illuminating the manifestation of white male privilege in the academic study of international politics. Dunn's chapter provokes us to reconsider what profound institutional changes might be required to dislodge this privilege's turgidly familiar raced and sexed landscape. As Raewyn Connell suggests in the context of her exploration of masculinities, 'moving toward a gender-equal society involves profound institutional change as well as change in everyday life and personal conduct' (2005: 1801).

Sandra Whitworth's chapter on Post-Traumatic Stress Disorder (PTSD) demonstrates the disciplinary force required to maintain the hegemonic position in the context of militarized masculinity and its racist and sexist constitution. Ostracized and marginalized soldiers suffering from PTSD have quickly experienced the limits of the mythology of the warrior brotherhood. Moreover, a disproportionate number of PTSD sufferers were women and soldiers of Hispanic and African descent, owing largely to the sexist and racist behaviour of their white male colleagues. This is another story shoved under the rug; another story that must be silenced to maintain the fiction of a tolerant and inclusive military. Yet the necessity for secrecy and masquerade demonstrates the ongoing fragility of militarized masculinity and the ruthless behaviour regarded as 'necessary' to protect the masculinist credentials of the warrior brotherhood.

Recent post-colonial and critical scholarship on masculinities further complicates our analyses of gender/sex and the international, calling for a more complex, fluid and situated understanding of gendered assumptions and practices over time and place.[18] Post-colonial writings have highlighted the need to understand the impact of historical forces such as colonialism and imperialism on international politics writ large (Chowdhry and Nair 2002; Ling 2002). While often preoccupied with the way in which colonial and post-colonial racial hierarchies have continued (and continue) to shape and limit people's lives around the world, recently scholars such as Paul Gilroy have begun to call for the need to move beyond the 'brutal dualistic opposition between black and white' (2001: 28). The critiques of essentialist binaries, and the focus on complexity and fluidity within and across difference, resonate with the scholarship on intersectionality, particularly the need to understand the 'multiple dimensions and modalities of social relations and subject formations' in the making of gendered life, particularly class, ethnicity, race and age (McCall 2005: 1771; Salime 2007). This attention to complex, intersecting factors in the international arena raises important questions. Eurocentric notions of masculinity are no longer seen as sufficient for explaining and analysing an increasingly global world. Indeed, Ouzgane and Morrell (2005) question the tendency to equate hegemonic masculinity with a Western-dominated global capitalism that is inevitably opposed to homosexuality, racial difference and the feminine, arguing (with others) for the need to pay attention to the complex, often hybrid relations between various constructions of masculinity in an increasingly global world (Beasley and Elias 2006; Cornwall and Lindisfarne 1993; Demetriou 2001; Lindsay and Miescher 2003). These arguments raise critical concerns for the study and practice of international politics, and are threaded through many of the chapters (see particularly Anand, Conway, Dunn, Munn and Parpart).

Paying attention to post-colonial scholarship has deepened our understanding of the way in which Western colonial constructs continue to dominate and shape our lives today by defining certain groups of people outside and others inside the circle of masculinist power (Ling 2002; Mohanty 2003). In his chapter, Daniel Conway demonstrates the lengths to which the apartheid state in South Africa was willing to venture in order to counter challenges to its militarized masculinist order. Supporters of the End Conscription Campaign (ECC), largely white males and females, were jailed and vilified as cowards and queers. Neither their race nor their sex saved them, again exposing the masquerade of sex and race as 'real' or stable categories. Moreover, the ferocity of state reaction demonstrates both the central role of militarized masculinity in the construction of masculinist power in South Africa and the fragility of that bond. Thus, Conway illustrates the power of masculinist disciplinary actions to constrain behaviour while also highlighting the transgressive potential of alternative masculinities at particular junctures.

Jamie Munn's chapter also focuses on the transgressive potential of alternative masculinities/sexualities to destabilize hegemonic masculinity in post-conflict societies. Given the intricate, fluid and contested world of post-conflict Kosovo, Munn questions Raewyn Connell's link between hegemonic masculinity and heterosexuality. He argues that homosexual discourses and practices, along with other forms of masculinity, present challenges to the dominant trope of militant warrior masculinity. While acknowledging the power of militant warrior mythologies of nation and the limited transgressive potential of alternative embodied practices, he argues that the narrative performances of homosexuality have the potential to undermine and complicate the connections between nation, nationalism and masculinity.

The issue of nation, nationalism and hegemonic masculinity/ies also preoccupies our final two chapters. Through ethnography, Dibyesh Anand discovers that male Hindu nationalists idealize a controlled, ascetic heterosexuality, while vilifying Muslim men and women for their impetuous hyper-sexualized behaviour. Like Munn, he argues that this complicates Raewyn Connell's too-easy equation between hegemonic masculinity and heterosexuality, and highlights the importance of paying attention to context and self-understandings. Indeed, the Hindu version of hegemonic sexuality intensifies nationalist identity, brings women into the fold or expunges them as traitors, and projects Hindu male insecurities and desires on to the enemy 'other', both male and female. Thus, porno-nationalism[19] reminds us that multicultural, contested political arenas are often framed and understood through masculinist sexualized discourses, but not always in easily recognized forms.

Parpart is also concerned with the role of masculinist discourses and practices in a multiracial, multi-ethnic struggle over national power in colonial Zimbabwe. Interrogating sources from all sides of this complex, fluid and violent struggle, she discovers that masculine metaphors and tropes played a central role in legitimizing the conflict, vilifying enemies, celebrating allies and defining gender regimes on both sides. While the struggle opened spaces to challenge established gender practices and hierarchies, ultimately the victors managed to silence opponents and to reaffirm a triumphant militant masculinism. A war-weary population welcomed the new regime, with its promise of progress and order, little realizing that the institutionalization of a militant masculinist nationalism would enable ruthless surveillance and intolerance towards dissenting voices and alternative visions for the nation – depressingly resonant of colonial practices.

Concluding thoughts: feminist leaps of imagination?

We include the poem 'The Butterfly Farm', to draw the Introduction towards its close. Medbh McGuckian's poem has incredible 'surface beauty', yet is riddled with gendered violence, its poetic construction a passionate methodological example of the critical approaches we try to engage in this book.

The Butterfly Farm

The film of a butterfly ensures that it is dead:
Its silence like the green cocoon of the car wash,
Its passion for water to uncloud.

In the Japanese tea house they believe
In making the most of the bright nights:
That the front of a leaf is male, the back female.

There are grass stains on their white stockings;
In artificial sun even the sounds are disposable;
The mosaic of their wing is spun from blood

Cyanide in the killing jar relaxes the Indian moon moth,
The pearl-bordered beauty, the clouded yellow,
The painted lady, the silver-washed blue.

Medbh McGuckian (1982)

There is surely sex and gender in this poem;[20] and we do think we can 'see' gender/sex, we claim to 'know' how sex/gender functions to produce specific forms – bodily, emotionally, intellectually – and specific violences. Kath Weston's observation that this tells us very little about what sustains these arrangements suggests there is a constant need to rethink how we conceptualize and re-create gender, sex and the violent international. In *Rethinking the Man Question* we are interested in investigating some of the obvious and subtle ways in which gender functions and the varied sites through which gender and sex emerge. Though gender remains significant and constant (Branaman 2007: 119) it also remains slippery and elusive. The ability to *see* gender, to document its effects and to *know* that gender relations could be different, perhaps does not tell us enough about their reinvention or what might be done to '*make* them otherwise through anything other than leaps of imagination' (Weston 2002: 131). Perhaps unfortunately, leaps of imagination are not likely to figure highly on many undergraduate or postgraduate courses in international politics as an appropriate methodology for understanding the intricacies of international political practices. Yet feminist and other critical scholars of gender have always had to work with something akin to leaps of the imagination in order to find new questions and to work out how the answers that become so familiar in international politics 'got their questions'.[21]

This book is vital, eclectic and exploratory. It makes no claim to meta-theoretical coherence; rather the tensions and paradoxes inflected throughout the volume are offered to readers as an opportunity to reflect on the toxic, violent and relentless reproductions of gendered power to which we pay attention.

Notes

1 Subsequently referred to as *The Man Question.*

2 In general, 'international politics' invokes international political practices; while international relations refers to the academic study of international politics.

3 Recognizing and working with the performative constitution of gender, we use the words gender and sex interchangeably or utilize a slash between the two – gender/sex, sex/gender – to indicate that we do not assume that sex is prior to gender or vice versa.

4 See the special issue of *Millennium* (vol. 35, no. 1, 2006) for discussions on the relationship between activism and academia.

5 See <www.ucgs.yorku.ca/ Y-File%20item%20on%20Cukier% 20seminar.asp.html>, accessed 2 December 2007. See also Gruffydd-Jones (2006) and Barkawi and Laffey (2006) on the violences that structure international politics.

6 Other more recent films include *Rendition* (2007) and *Lions for Lambs* (2007).

7 *World Trade Center* (2006), Paramount Pictures.

8 Try imagining the two central characters as lesbians with wives or girlfriends waiting at home to see just how far we have (not) advanced in relation to gender/sexuality. The reassertion of religion, in specific forms, is also crucial to the telling of the story in this film.

9 <www.bbc.co.uk/ films/2006/09/06/world_trade_ centre_2006_review.shtml>, accessed 2 December 2007.

10 <www.townhall.com/ Columnists/CalThomas/2006/07/20/ world_trade_center_is_a_world_ class_movie>, accessed 2 December 2007.

11 See Saurette (2006) and Vestelen (2005) on humiliation and international politics/violence.

12 Particularly the contemporary Western/US university system. See Readings (1996); Evans (2004).

13 Panel discussion at the International Studies Association Convention, Chicago, February 2007.

14 See Stanley and Wise (2000)

for a discussion of feminism and 'transferable knowledge'.

15 See Rengger and Thirkell-White (2007); Hawkesworth (2005, 2006); Ackerly et al. (2006).

16 See Gayle Rubin's influential essay on the 'charmed circle' in relation to 'good' and 'bad' sexual practices (1993).

17 See Cockburn (1991).

18 Sinha 1997; Hooper 2001; Reddock 2004; Connell 2005; Kimmel 2005; Hearn and Connell 2005a; Ouzgane and Morrell 2005.

19 This is a term invented by Anand to describe the level of sexualization involved.

20 We will not offer close readings of the poems in this book; we leave that up to readers.

21 We refer readers to the poem that preceded the Introduction.

References

Ackerly, B., M. Stern and J. True (eds) (2006) *Feminist Methodologies for International Relations*, Cambridge: Cambridge University Press.

Ahmed, S. (2004) *The Cultural Politics of Emotion*, Edinburgh: Edinburgh University Press.

Alsop, R., A. Fitzsimons and K. Lennon(2002) *Theorizing Gender*, Cambridge: Polity Press.

Alvi, M. (2005) 'How the answers got their questions', in *How the Stone Found Its Voice*, Tarset, Northumberland: Bloodaxe Books, p. 11.

Barkawi, T. and M. Laffey (2006) 'The postcolonial moment in security studies', *Review of International Studies*, 32: 329–52.

Beasley, C. and J. Elias (2006) 'Situating masculinities in global politics' (mimeo).

Branaman, A. (2007) 'Gender and sexualities in liquid modernity', in A. Elliot (ed.), *The Contemporary Bauman*, New York: Routledge, pp. 117–35.

Brown, W. (2001) *Politics out of History*, Princeton, NJ: Princeton University Press.

— (2005) *Edgework: Critical Essays on Knowledge and Politics*, Princeton, NJ: Princeton University Press.

Burke, A. (2007) *Beyond Security, Ethics and Violence: War against the Other*, New York: Routledge.

Butler, J. (1990) *Gender Trouble: Feminism and the Subversion of Identity*, New York: Routledge.

— (2004) *Undoing Gender*, London: Routledge.

Chowdhry, G. and S. Nair (eds) (2002) *Power, Postcolonialism and International Relations*, London: Routledge.

Cockburn, C. (1991) *In the Way of Women: Men's Resistance to Sex Equality in Organizations*, London: Palgrave Macmillan.

Cohn, C. (2006) 'Motives and methods: using multi-sited ethnography to study US national security discourses' in B. Ackerly, M. Stern and J. True (eds), *Feminist Methodologies for International Relations*, Cambridge: Cambridge University Press.

Connell, R. W. (1995) *Masculinities*, Cambridge: Polity Press.

— (2002) 'Long and winding road: an outsider's view of US masculinity and femininity', in J. Kegan Gardiner (ed.), *Masculinity Studies and Feminist Theory*, New York: Columbia University Press.

— (2005a) 'Change among the gatekeepers: men, masculinities, and gender equality in the global arena', *Signs*, 30(3).

— (2005b) *Masculinities*, Cambridge: Polity Press.

— (2007) *Southern Theory: Social Science and the Global Dynamics of Knowledge*, Cambridge: Polity Press.

Connell, R. W. and J. Messerschmidt (2005) 'Hegemonic masculinity: rethinking the concept', *Gender & Society* 19(6): 829–59.

Cornwall, A. and N. Lindisfarne (eds) (1993) *Dislocating Masculinity: Comparative Ethnographies*, London: Routledge.

Demetriou, D. (2001) 'Connell's concept of hegemonic masculinity: a critique', *Theory and Society*, 30(3).

Doty, R. (2000) 'Desire all the way down', *Review of International Studies*, 26(1): 137–9.

Edkins, J. (2003) *Trauma and the Memory of Politics*, Cambridge: Cambridge University Press.

Edkins, J. and M. Zehfuss (2005) 'Generalising the international', *Review of International Studies*, 31(3): 451–72.

Eisenstein, Z. (2004) *Against Empire: Feminism, Racism and the West*, London: Zed Books.

Enloe, C. (1989) *Bananas, Beaches and Bases: Making Feminist Sense of International Politics*, London: Pandora Books.

Evans, M. (2004) *Killing Thinking: The Death of Universities*, London: Continuum.

Ferguson, K. (1993) *The Man Question: Visions of Subjectivity in Feminist Theory*, California: University of California Press.

Gilroy, P. (2001) 'Debating "race" in South African scholarship', *Transformation*, 76.

Gruffydd-Jones, B. (ed.) (2006) *Decolonizing International Relations*, London: Rowman and Littlefield.

Hardt, M. and A. Negri (2000) *Empire*, Cambridge, MA: Harvard University Press.

Hawkesworth, M. (2005) 'Engendering political science: an immodest proposal' *Politics and Gender*, 1(1): 141–56.

— (2006) *Feminist Inquiry*, New Brunswick, NJ: Rutgers University Press.

Hekman, S. J. (2004) *Private Selves, Public Identities: Reconsidering Identity Politics*, Pennsylvania: Pennsylvania University Press.

Hooper, C. (2001) *Manly States: Masculinities, International Relations, and Gender Politics*, New York: Columbia University Press.

Hunt, E. (1990) 'Notes for an oppositional poetics', in C. Bernstein (ed.), *The Politics of Poetic Form: Poetry and Public Policy*, New York: Roof Books.

Kaplan, A. E. (2003) 'Feminist futures: trauma, the post 9/11 world and a fourth feminism?', *Journal of International Women's Studies*, 4(2): 46–59.

Kegan Gardiner, J. (ed.) (2002) *Masculinity Studies and Feminist Theory*, New York: Columbia University Press.

Keller, J. (2006) 'Language as visible vapor: skywriting through Lyn Hejinian's *Happily*', in J. Retallack and J. Sphar (eds), *Poetry and Pedagogy: The Challenge of the Contemporary*, New York: Palgrave Macmillan.

Kimmel, M. (2005) *The Gender of Desire: Essays on Male Sexuality*, Albany, NY: State of New York Press.

Kimmel, M., J. Hearn and R. W. Connell (eds) *Handbook of Studies on Men and Masculinities*, Thousand Oaks, CA: Sage.

Kirby, V. (2007) *Judith Butler: Live Thinking*, London: Continuum.

Kronsell, A. (2006) 'Methods for studying silences: gender analysis in institutions of hegemonic masculinity', in B. Ackerly, M. Stern and J. True (eds), *Feminist Methodologies for International Relations*, Cambridge: Cambridge University Press.

Lindsay, L. and S. Miescher (2003) *Men and Masculinities in Modern Africa*, Portsmouth, NH: Heinemann.

Ling, L. H. M. (2002) *Postcolonial International Relations*, London: Palgrave Macmillan.

Lloyd, M. (2007) *Judith Butler*, Cambridge: Polity Press.

McCall, L. (2005) 'The complexity of intersectionality', *Signs*, 30(3).

Mearsheimer, J. (2001) *The Tragedy of Great Power Politics*, New York: Norton.

Mohanty, C. (2003) *Feminism without Borders: Decolonizing Theory, Practicing Solidarity*, Durham, NC: Duke University Press.

Mullen, H. (2006) 'Between Jihad and McWorld: a place for poetry', in J. Retallack and J. Sphar (eds), *Poetry and Pedagogy: The Challenge of the Contemporary*, New York: Palgrave Macmillan.

Nicholson, M. (2000) 'What's the use of International Relations?', *Review of International Studies*, 26: 183–98.

Ouzgane, L. and R. Morrell (eds) (2005) *African Masculinities*, London: Palgrave Macmillan.

Readings, B. (1996) *The University in Ruins*, Cambridge, MA: Harvard University Press.

Reddock, R. (ed.) (2004) *Interrogating Caribbean Masculinities*, Trinidad: University of the West Indies Press.

Rengger, N. and B. Thirkell-White (2007) 'Still critical after all these years? The past, present and future of Critical Theory in International Relations', *Review of International Studies*, 33: 3–24.

Rubin, G. (1993) 'Thinking sex: notes for a radical theory of the politics of sexuality', in H. Abelove et al. (eds) *Lesbian and Gay Studies Reader*, New York: Routledge, pp. 3–44.

Salime, Z. (2007) 'The war on terrorism: appropriation and subversion by Moroccan women', *Signs*, 33(1): 1–25.

Sampson, F. (1997) 'Poetry and the position of weakness: some challenges of writing in health-care', in V. Bertram, *Kicking Daffodils: Twentieth-Century Women Poets*, Edinburgh: Edinburgh University Press.

Saurette, P. (2006) 'You dissin me? Humiliation and post 9/11 global politics', *Review of International Studies*, 32: 495–522.

Seidler, V. (2005) *Transforming Masculinities*, London: Routledge.

Sharma, U. (2004) *Gender Mainstreaming and Women's Rights*, New Delhi: Authorspress.

Shaw, K. and R. B. J. Walker (2006) 'Situating academic practice: pedagogy, critique and responsibility', *Millennium*, 35(1): 155–65.

Sinha, M. (1997) *Colonial Masculinity*, New Delhi: Kali for Women.

Stanley, L. and S. Wise (2000) 'But the empress has no clothes! Some awkward questions about the "missing revolution" in feminist theory', *Feminist Theory*, 1(3): 261–88.

Stern, M. and M. Zalewski (forthcoming) 'Feminist fatigue(s): reflections on feminist fables of militarization', *Review of International Studies*.

Sylvester, C. (2002) *Feminist International Relations*, Cambridge: Cambridge University Press.

Vestelsen, A. J. (2005) *Evil and Human Agency: Understanding Collective Evildoing*, Cambridge: Cambridge University Press.

Weston, K. (2002) *Gender in Real Time*, London: Routledge.

Wiegman, R. (2002) 'Unmaking: men and masculinity in feminist theory', in J. Kegan Gardiner (ed.), *Masculinity Studies and Feminist Theory*, New York: Columbia University Press, pp. 31–59.

Zalewski, M. (1998) 'Introduction: from the "woman" question to the "man" question in International Relations', in M. Zalewski and J. Parpart (eds) (1998) *The 'Man' Question in International Relations*, Boulder CO: Westview Press.

Zalewski, M. and J. Parpart (eds) (1998) *The 'Man' Question in International Relations*, Boulder, CO: Westview Press.

At the Sex Frontier

[...] the holy show
that models how the world should be
and could be, shared, glittering in near focus.

Les Murray

On a warm evening
breath and body-moisture
steam the glass,
making what should be clear
                         mysterious –
a blur of spoiled film.

But here I am, in Arrivals,
pressing my hand on the pane
to greet you.
                When I take it away –
spy-holes,
a spatter of dots
clear as landing lights on the white surface;
and something I know must be you
shifting in them –
sleeve, eyebrow, wink of a button.

... Imaginary *noir*. Behind steam
you seem an emanation –
                  of the density of walls, doors,
surveillance cameras;
precipitated along corridors
with thunderclap footsteps and slams.

Meanwhile, water sets itself down
on convenient glass,
                such as this pane:
stitch by plump stitch
tacking together hot
                and cold –
which can't simply be folded
                into each other
as if *this* were *that* –

My finger-holes spread and weep
in glittery water-mesh
which catches the outside world
and holds it back
           from this strip-lit foyer.

Obscurely *beyond*,
you're waiting for a kiss –
           semblable, frère –
but when I search the glass
I don't feel you. Only damp mineral shine,
dissolving cold.
           And yes, it's odd
to reach forward, cuff in fist –
making smears
           which fade like Döppler notes –
to where you hang
in the window's two-way mirror:

an icon on a screen
with your hand raised.

When your face
comes puckering up,
so that I lean across the shiny space between us
towards the image of me
floating in you
           like a palimpsest –

raising the banner of my lipsticked mouth –

it's to a familiar;
smudged blue and silver by these lights.

Fiona Sampson

ONE | Cognitive short cuts

KIMBERLY HUTCHINGS

Since the end of the cold war, there has been a flowering of theoretical debate about the frameworks through which contemporary international politics should be understood. This has included the narratives of 'end of history' and 'clash of civilizations', reassertions of mainstream liberal and realist paradigms in the study of international relations, and optimistic and pessimistic accounts of globalization.[1] It has also included the development of feminist approaches to understanding international politics.[2] Although the latter have developed in parallel with the rest, they have had little impact on the ways in which international politics is framed when it comes to the 'big pictures' through which we make sense of politics, both in academic debate and at a more popular level. In 1998, in the precursor to this volume, Peterson and True called for international relations theory to engage in 'new conversations' adequate to 'new times' by taking seriously feminist contributions to the field (1998: 15). Non-feminist mainstream and critical approaches to international politics have not by and large, however, been persuaded that gender has anything other than a marginal relevance for grand theories of the post-cold-war world.[3]

The purpose of this chapter is to examine one of the reasons for this ongoing marginalization of feminist/gender concerns. I will argue that a key reason for the ongoing invisibility of women and gender in the theoretical frames through which post-cold-war international politics is grasped is the legitimizing function of masculinity discourses within those theories. My central claim is that masculinity operates as a resource for thought in theorizing international politics. That is to say, masculinity operates as a kind of commonsense, implicit, often unconscious shorthand for processes of explanatory and normative judgement, thereby as one of the crucial ways in which our social scientific imagination is shaped and limited. I will explore how this works in two very influential but different accounts of contemporary international politics: the 'offensive' realism of Mearsheimer (*The Tragedy of Great Power Politics*, 2001) and the post-Marxist story of 'empire/multitude' in the work of Hardt and

Negri (*Empire*, 2000). In conclusion, I will argue that one can hope, to paraphrase Ferguson, to loosen the hold of *masculinity* on meaning and life only once one has first appreciated how much intellectual work is accomplished by masculinity's logical structure (Ferguson 1993: 29). Without the logic of masculinity, grand theorists of international politics would be required to work a great deal harder in order to persuade us of the accuracy of their diagnoses of the times.

What is 'masculinity' in international politics?

The concept of masculinity has always been a focus of concern for feminist international relations scholars (Zalewski 1998). In this section, my aim is to analyse the ways in which masculinity has been understood within feminist work on international relations, including work that adopts the notion of 'hegemonic masculinity' as a key analytical tool. I will argue that there are two predominant narratives of masculinity within this literature, which are analytically distinguishable but usually intertwined within particular feminist arguments. Crudely speaking, one of these narratives focuses attention on what masculinity *is* as a condition for what it *does*; the other focuses attention on what masculinity *does* as definitive of what it *is*. The former directs us to causal or constitutive links between the ways in which international politics is practised or theorized and the qualities associated with masculinity which can be seen as aggression, instrumental rationality or objectivity. The latter directs us to the rhetorical work of valorization, denigration and exclusion done by the formal, relational properties of masculinity as a concept, regardless of the substantive qualities in question. Compare, for instance, Tickner's account of the constitutive role of masculinity in the understanding and conduct of world politics discussed below with the argument of Ashworth and Swatuk. They show how identification of one's own position with masculinity and that of one's opponents with femininity operates as a way of trumping the opposition in debates between 'realists' and 'liberals' about the nature of international politics (Tickner 1991, 1992; Ashworth and Swatuk 1998).

As mentioned above, it is rare to find feminist work on international relations that operates with only one of the above accounts of masculinity; in most cases they are combined.[4] For instance, if we look at pioneering feminist arguments such as those of Cohn (1989), Elshtain (1995 [1987]), Enloe (1989) and Tickner (1991, 1992), then we find that the analysis of masculinity appears in both guises. In her analysis of the discourses of nuclear defence intellectuals, Cohn identifies masculinity with a specific set of attributes, which are shown to be efficacious for the kind of reasoning necessary for thinking about operating weapons of mass destruction (Cohn 1989: 115–19). She also points, however, to the ways in which masculinity operates as a marker of value across its association with qualities that are by no means consistent with one another (strategic rationality, God-like powers of creation, risk taking). Regardless of its substantive association in any given instance, masculinity is always valued; and its value is associated with the denigration and exclusion of the feminine (ibid.: 121). Similarly, Elshtain's argument elaborates a set of masculine qualities that, along with their feminine counterparts, sustain the social institution of war and demonstrates how the same value hierarchy, in which masculinity trumps femininity, subsists across different aspects of masculinity in different contexts (Elshtain 1995 [1987]: 194–225).

From a feminist point of view, masculinity poses a problem in two different ways. It is a problem insofar as masculine identities have concrete effects, for instance in the perpetuation of nuclear deterrence and war. In addition, masculinity is a problem because it incorporates a hierarchical logic of exclusion of women and the feminine. What remains unclear is the relation between the two problems: does the hierarchical logic of exclusion depend on the nature of masculine identity or does the efficacy of masculine identity depend on the hierarchical logic of exclusion? Cohn, for example, points to the ways in which using ordinary speech, as opposed to technical acronyms, was dismissed and denigrated as feminine by defence intellectuals (Cohn 1989: 128). But is technical speech masculine as such; or is it masculinized as an uncontentious way of signalling its positive value?

Tickner and Enloe address a broader canvas than Cohn and Elshtain in their work on feminism and international relations. In their contributions to the literature, they deal with issues of nation-states, nationalism, diplomacy, international political economy, and international relations theory and methodology, as well as war and militarism. Again, however, the engagement with masculinity in their work moves between masculinity as a particular form of substantive identity, with real effects on the theory and practice of international relations, and masculinity as a mode of hierarchical exclusion of the feminine. In Tickner's well-known interrogation of Morgenthau's international relations theory, we are offered an account of how these two narratives of masculinity are interrelated, so that what masculinity does, to the world in general and women in particular, appears to depend on what masculinity *is*: 'I have suggested that Morgenthau's attempt to construct an objective, universal theory of international relations is rooted in assumptions about human nature and morality that, in modern Western culture, are associated with masculinity' (Tickner 1991: 32).

Tickner's critique of Morgenthau focuses attention on the link between particular masculine qualities and modes of theorizing international politics. Sovereign individuality, objectivity, instrumental rationality and 'power over' are argued to be implicit within models of masculinity entrenched in the Western tradition. This leads to the shaping of the principles applied to making sense of the international realm. The ways in which these principles exclude the feminine is grounded in their substantive meaning, which excludes feminine qualities associated with relationality, contextualism, emotion and 'power to' (ibid.: 29–32). These alternative feminine qualities provide the ground for Tickner to articulate an alternative *feminist* set of principles for understanding international politics which provide a corrective to Morgenthau's masculine bias (ibid.: 37). Elsewhere, Tickner argues that masculine gender identity is crucial to how international politics is practised as well as how it is understood, though she is also careful to note that the category of 'masculinity' is neither trans-culturally nor transhistorically stable and certainly cannot be identified with men in general (1992: 6).

In her essay 'Nationalism and masculinity', Enloe suggests the masculine experiences of and responses to oppression have dominated the ideologies and strategies of national liberation struggles. This means that substantive characteristics of masculinity explain, at least in part, the fact that outcomes of struggles for national liberation do not tend to produce a different kind of state, either as an international actor or in terms of domestic gender policies (1989: 64). At the same time, she also demonstrates how the meaning of masculinity is essentially invested in the denigration and exclusion of the feminine. Therefore, on Enloe's account, it is impossible to disentangle substantive qualities associated with nationalist masculinity from the imperative to keep the feminine at bay; but the nature of the link still remains a puzzle. Does keeping the feminine at bay necessarily correlate to particular qualities and modes of behaviour and to particular sorts of outcomes in international politics; or are substantive qualities or behaviours irrelevant except insofar as they are endowed with a masculine or feminine meaning? Either way, Enloe points to the difficulty, even for women freedom fighters, of being dissociated from the feminine and the effects of exclusion on women in emergent nation-states who find themselves, after the wars of liberation, being once more confined to the private sphere (ibid.: 44–5, 63).

In common with most feminist scholars, Cohn, Elshtain, Tickner and Enloe do not think of gender in simplistically causal terms. Nevertheless, each of them argues that masculinity and the theory and practice of international politics are in some sense mutually constitutive. In all cases, this mutual constitution is tied up with commonalities between qualities, modes of behaviour and norms associated with masculinity, and with the theory or practice of international politics. The standards governing what it means to be a man are also identified as governing, at least in part, the practices of nuclear defence, war, theorizing and practising international politics, and struggles for national liberation. At the same time, however, this picture is complicated by the fact that, even though the norms of masculinity are treated as invariable in terms of their exclusionary effects, they are variable in their content. The highly rational, technologically skilled nuclear intellectual (unemotional, rational, calculating) discussed by Cohn is a very different archetype from the 'just warrior' (chivalrous, protective) presented in Elshtain's work. Thus, the continuum of masculine qualities appears not only to be flexible but also to contain significant tensions between different elements, for instance risk-taking and rationality or discipline.

One response of feminist international relations scholars to the difficulties involved in theorizing the link between masculinity and the theory and practice of international politics is to make use of the notion of 'hegemonic masculinity', pioneered by R. W. Connell[5] (Connell 1995; Tickner 1992; Zalewski and Parpart 1998; Hooper 2001; Cohn and Enloe 2003; Whitworth 2004). Connell suggests that 'hegemonic masculinity', a type of culturally dominant masculinity distinguished from other subordinated masculinities, is a socially constructed cultural ideal. It does not correspond to the actual personality of most men; however, it sustains patriarchal authority and legitimizes a patriarchal political and social order. Thus hegemonic masculinity is sustained through maintaining pre-eminence over various subordinated and devalued masculinities, such as homosexuality, along with its dominance in relation to various devalued femininities (Tickner 1992: 6).

Many feminist international relations scholars find the notion of hegemonic masculinity useful because it allows an account of the mutually constitutive link between masculinity and international politics, which operates at two levels. On the one hand, the shifting characteristics of hegemonic masculinity are seen to correspond to shifts in the challenges raised by practices of international politics such as war, trade and diplomacy. On the other hand, the inculcation of these characteristics in international actors can be explained by the way in which the idea of masculinity embeds hierarchies of value that permit discrimination between different masculinities, while maintaining a clear logic of denigration and exclusion in relation to the feminine. Hooper, for instance, argues that the requirements of economic restructuring in the global political economy produce struggles between different masculinities for hegemony, in particular between those of warrior masculinity and the masculinity of the rational, bourgeois individual (Hooper 2001: 221–3). The idea of hegemonic masculinity can also explain how the meaning of warrior masculinity becomes stretched to encompass new kinds of qualities needed by the modern war machine or extends its meaning beyond war-related activities as a label for a new kind of global traveller, the 'road warrior' international businessman, forever hooked up to his computer or BlackBerry (Niva 1998; Barrett 2001; Der Derian 2002).

Nevertheless, it is not clear that the puzzles we have already raised as to the nature of the link between what masculinity *is* and what it *does* are resolved by the concept of hegemonic masculinity. On the one hand, substantive qualities and characteristics are posited as fundamental to the workings of international politics. On the other hand, the ways in which masculinity operates, as a means through which values are embedded, are posited as key to how any particular set of qualities and characteristics becomes identified as hegemonic or subordinate or as incommensurate with masculinity altogether. If the effects of masculinity are rooted in what it is, then the task of the feminist theorist must be to identify and challenge the particular form taken by hegemonic masculinity within world politics in any given context. If what masculinity *is* is rooted in what it *does*, then it is not any particular instantiation of masculinity which feminist scholarship needs to challenge but the work of evaluation and exclusion that it accomplishes regardless of its referential meaning.

Much of the feminist scholarship engaging with the question of masculinity in relation to international politics is caught between these two different ways of challenging masculinity. The problem is that these two ways of thinking about the task of feminist critique are not compatible with one another once the notion of masculinity being a stable and coherent substantive meaning is abandoned. There may be a whole range of feminist reasons for objecting to the uncritical valorization of some qualities and attributes as opposed to others in world politics, from physical courage to instrumental rationality. But to the extent that *masculinity* plays an independent part in such arguments, it is in its role in 'uncritical valorization', not because of some necessary connection between physical courage or instrumental rationality and the nature of masculinity. This is borne out by Hooper's argument, which points to the emptiness of 'masculinity' as a signifier and suggests that negotiation over the meaning of masculinity in a changing world order provides opportunities for feminism.

> Masculinity appears to have no stable ingredients and therefore its power depends entirely on certain qualities constantly being associated with men. Masculine spaces are precisely the places where such associations are cemented and naturalized. Therefore, even the marginal appearance of women ... together with feminist ideas, and/or other self-conscious references to gender issues, may sufficiently alter the overall ambience of such spaces that their masculine associations become weakened. (Hooper 2001: 230–31)

Hooper confirms that the feminist quarrel with masculinity is concerned only with the various and inconsistent ways in which masculinity *is* because of the invariable and consistent work that masculinity *does*. But even though she points to strategies for disrupting masculinity's denigration and exclusion of the feminine, the largest part of her analysis is devoted to documenting how 'resilient and sophisticated hegemonic masculinity is' (ibid.: 230). This 'resilience' may be explained in a variety of ways, including in terms of how it legitimizes the behaviour of particular elite male and female actors. Another reason for masculinity's resilience, however, has less to do with the ways in which it serves specific interests and more to do with the ways in which it operates as a cognitive short cut in our frameworks for understanding the world.

At the beginning of this chapter, I stated that the ways in which the 'big picture' of post-cold-war international politics is understood tend to ignore and marginalize gender and the ideas and insights of the feminist contribution to the study of international relations celebrated by Peterson and True (1998: 23–4). Now I want to suggest that the persistence of masculinity as the lens through which international politics is viewed has much more to do with the formal than with the substantive properties with which it is associated. The meaning of the concept of masculinity is simultaneously embedded in the logics of contrast and contradiction. The logic of contrast gives masculinity its flexibility and malleability and enables changes in dominant modes of masculinity to make sense in terms of familiar contrasts between higher and lower, normal and deviant and hegemonic and counter-hegemonic modes. The logic of contradiction embedded in masculinity is complementary to the logic of contrast. The crucial characteristic shared by all masculinity discourses is that they are not feminine. It is the fixed-value hierarchy ascribed to masculine and feminine which provides the means through which discrimination between different forms of masculinity becomes possible. It also is the fixity of the masculine/feminine distinction which enables the differentiation of things such as courage, rationality and discipline as different aspects or gradations of masculinity; that is to say, as having something in common as well as being hierarchically differentiated. In other words, making a link between a given social or political practice or institution with masculinity provides a stable ground for a range of cognitive operations through which we can discriminate between the inside and outside of particular phenomena (what counts as international politics and what does not) and between good or bad instances of particular phenomena (good statecraft and bad statecraft, the heroes and villains of world politics).[6]

To argue that we need to think about masculinity as a resource for thought is not in any sense new. This has always been a crucial theme within feminist theory and philosophy; and as we have seen, all the feminist international relations literature discussed so far also identified the symbolic and rhetorical work accomplished by masculinity as crucial to its significance.[7] Much of the time, the focus of feminist arguments concentrating on masculinity as a logic has been on the ways in which it operates so as to exclude the feminine and by implication women from participation in the public world and in the ways in which that world is made intelligible.[8] This is argued to result in the reproduction of masculinist hegemony, in distorted accounts of the world and in the ongoing marginalization of women and other feminized groups. Ashworth and Swatuk, for instance, show how, in the study of international politics, the identification of both realist and liberal paradigms with masculinity shores up their status in relation to each other and reproduces a binary and exclusive world order (1998: 87). Although such arguments are persuasive in many respects, what gets overlooked, however, is one important reason why masculinity, whether hegemonic or not, exerts hegemony on our modes of theorization. It is not necessarily that theorists, whether consciously or unconsciously, fear emasculation or denigrate the feminine or women; rather, it is utilizing masculinity as a resource for thought which saves a great deal of work in rendering arguments persuasive. I will now go on to illustrate this by looking at two recent influential attempts to trace the big picture of post-cold-war international politics: Mearsheimer's *The Tragedy of Great Power Politics* (2001) and Hardt and Negri's *Empire* (2000).

Masculinity and grand theories of international politics

The two works on which I have chosen to focus occupy very different positions in the spectrum of 'big picture' theorization about international politics. Mearsheimer's work is firmly located in the discipline of international relations and neo-realism, and represents an influential post-cold-war restatement of this paradigm. It remains grounded in an account of international politics as interstate politics, in particular the politics of great powers. Therefore, it denies or marginalizes the relevance of non-state actors, of structural relations of power such as class or gender, and of socio-economic processes such as globalization for the understanding and explanation of contemporary world politics. In contrast, Hardt and Negri's work emerges out of Marxism and a variety of postmodernist theoretical positions, Foucault and Deleuze being influential in particular, and takes globalization and the overcoming of the significance of interstate politics as the starting point for analysis. Ideologically, Mearsheimer represents a kind of conservatism, at least in relation to foreign policymaking; whereas Hardt and Negri identify themselves with a revolutionary tradition and various forms of radical anti-globalization political movements. These are very different sets of arguments, and they are made in very different ways. But one thing they have in common is their utilization of the logic of masculinity as a way of rendering their arguments persuasive. I will argue that they do this within the specific context of their own theoretical account by setting up a hegemonic masculinity which enables discrimination between what counts and does not count and what is good and bad within the practice of international politics and in terms of how the practice should be explained and judged. I will look at each theorist in turn; first, I will outline the substance of their 'big picture' before moving on to illustrate how they position their own discourse in relation to it.

Mearsheimer's narrative in *The Tragedy of Great Power Politics* reflects the standard parsimony of neo-realist accounts of international politics. Within such accounts, a limited number of assumptions enable explanation and prediction of the behaviour of states in the international domain. Mearsheimer's five key assumptions are: an anarchical international system, the offensive military capability of great powers, the uncertainty of any state about the intentions of any other, the goal of state survival, and that states are rational actors (Mearsheimer 2001: 30–31). On the basis of these assumptions, he argues that we know that all states will struggle for relative advantage in relation to all others: great powers will aim for hegemony, multipolar balances of power are more unstable than bipolar ones, and so forth. The key issue for grasping the presence of international politics, for Mearsheimer, is working out the dynamics of the contemporary balance of power and accordingly identifying the likely distribution of threats. From the point of view of the USA, he concludes that the key threat is a rising China; and this means that the current policy of engagement with China on the part of the USA is fundamentally mistaken (ibid.: 401–2).

Mearsheimer treats states as agents whose behaviour is structured by systemic aspects of their situation and their rational struggle towards the goal of survival. Within this political imaginary, the hegemonic position is occupied by a particular vision of the rational actor who is presented to us in two ways: first, as the strategic thinker or the card player who knows how to do the trick (ibid.: 40) and second, as the actor capable of using violence in a controlled and intelligent way (ibid.: 37). These figures are male in the straightforward sense that Mearsheimer's rhetorical personifications of the state are gendered male, although they also clearly call upon familiar archetypes of masculinity. In addition, however, they are dynamically implicated in the logic of masculinity with which we are already familiar. Thus, a particular understanding of masculinity provides the standard for thinking about international politics according to a logic of contrast and a logic of contradiction. The way in which this works is simple. Standards are specified for what it means to be a proper state (man) in the context of international politics. These standards provide the parameters for what can count as a state (man) but enable discrimination between more or less stately (manly) attributes and actions. In addition, they provide a means for identifying when a state is being or behaving in a way that contradicts its 'stateness' (becoming unmanly or emasculated). For example, the key contrast between great powers and weak powers is presented along the continuum of masculinity: all states are men but great powers are the 'real men' in international politics. It may be necessary for weak states to use the feminized strategy of 'bandwagoning'; but when this is used by great powers, it signifies a degeneration into 'unstately' (unmanly) behaviour, given that they do have the wherewithal to 'put up a decent fight' (ibid.: 163). Similarly, the use of 'appeasement' is 'fanciful and dangerous' and is a literal contradiction of what it means to behave like a great power (real man) in the international system (ibid.: 163–4).

There are two ways in which the logic of masculinity helps Mearsheimer underpin discrimination between inside and outside and good and bad in his analysis. One of these ways relies on invoking the line between pathological and normal stateness (manliness), the other on invoking the line between having and lacking stateness (manliness): 'In short, great powers are not mindless aggressors so bent on gaining power that they charge headlong into losing wars or pursue Pyrrhic victories. On the contrary, before great powers take offensive actions, they think carefully about the balance of power and about how other states will react to their moves' (ibid.: 37). The contrast between what great powers do (or should do) and 'mindless' aggression is explained through the contrast between bad masculinity out of control and the good masculinity of the man who is capable of strategically directing his violence. The discrimination between appropriate and inappropriate great power behaviour is rhetorically anchored through a familiar value-laden contrast between healthy and pathological masculinities. The way in which the contrast between healthy and pathological masculinity works illustrates the interconnection between the discriminatory logic of masculinity and the equally entrenched logic, within the Western political imaginary, of the distinction between 'civilized' and 'barbarian'. State violence, from Machiavelli to Clausewitz and Weber, is justified within realist political theory through a distinction between 'good' and 'bad' violence along the lines suggested by Mearsheimer. Traditionally, 'good' violence is associated with the controlled and civilized violence of the state and 'bad' violence with the supposedly uncontrolled violence of the racialized tribal or barbarian 'other'. Clearly, the contrast between good and bad violence is secured in part by the logic of masculinity. Bad masculinity is, to some extent, feminized by being associated with the irrational; but it is not sufficiently feminized to take it out of the continuum of masculinity established by Mearsheimer's hegemonic standard in which the attachment to violence is a crucial marker. Again, we are taken into a set of deeply familiar distinctions that act as a short cut for thought (Frazer and Hutchings 2007).[9] These distinctions tell us that the irrational use of violence does not necessarily contradict what it means to be a state, even though it is behaviour unworthy of a great power. In Mearsheimer's case, the contrast between healthy and pathological masculinity reflects the link between violence and rationality in his account of great power behaviour. It is possible for such a state to irrationally use violence; but even so, as long as the state is aggressive, it remains 'stately', just as a barbarian man is still a man.[10] What genuinely undermines the meaning of great power is to abandon the means of violence altogether; this latter form of irrationality takes the analysis from a logic of contrast to one of contradiction.

In his analysis, Mearsheimer is clear that he is both describing how great powers behave and prescribing how they should perform in light of his assumptions. As we have seen, he argues that states, especially great powers, are and should be rational and do and should use violence in a rational way. For this reason, irrationally aggressive great powers are condemned. There is, however, a much more profound mistake that great powers can make on Mearsheimer's account; a mistake that effectively means they are not behaving like a state, let alone like a great power. Any state or great power may misread the dynamics of a particular balance of power. The fundamental mistake, however, is to read international politics as anything other than an ongoing struggle for survival in a context of anarchy. To do this is to abandon both rationality and reliance on relative advantage in the instruments of violence that are the only ultimately effective way of securing one's own survival. Liberal states seeking to institutionalize liberal foreign policies, as the USA tried to do under the Clinton administration on Mearsheimer's account, are in effect behaving like a woman (ibid.: 402).[11] In other words, they are contradicting the masculine core of what international politics means. Such behaviour spells disaster.

Mearsheimer implicitly relies on the logic of masculinity in order to set up his categories and render his account of international politics intelligible and plausible.[12] In addition, we find the logic of masculinity at work in the ways in which Mearsheimer positions his own discourse. He contrasts his theory of international politics with other versions of realism (defensive neo-realism, classical realism) and with liberal and constructivist theories. From his point of view, he needs the reader to see how his account is related to and improves upon other versions of

realism; he also needs to express its incommensurability with liberal
and constructivist alternatives. Thus, we find Mearsheimer, the theorist, positioned as more masculine than other realists in relation to the
rational actor's controlled use of a violent hegemonic model. Classical realists put too much emphasis on aggression as a characteristic
of human nature. In contrast, defensive realists have not quite got the
balance right between rationality and aggression; and they occupy a
somewhat feminized, slightly lacking, position on the continuum of realist thought. Liberal and constructivist theories are so far away from the
assumptions of realism, however, that they scarcely count as theories
of international politics. Mearsheimer ends the book with a warning
to US foreign policymakers to beware of the extension of liberal values
to the international stage because to do so would to put the survival of
the USA in peril. Theorists of international politics cannot afford to be
feminine any more than foreign policymakers can; it is their duty to
join the company of men and embrace the hegemonic ideal of rational
action and controlled violence.

It would be hard to find a greater contrast than between the parsimonious great power theory of Mearsheimer and the eclectic, ambitious and
sometimes inconsistent theoretical framework of Hardt and Negri. In
contrast to Mearsheimer, Hardt and Negri rely on multiple theoretical
sources and see complexity rather than parsimony as a requirement for
understanding international politics. It is impossible to do justice to all
aspects of their argument. Therefore, I will focus on certain key contrasts
through which their argument is ordered and which set up the ways in
which, according to Hardt and Negri, contemporary international politics
should be understood and judged.

Hardt and Negri's argument takes inspiration from two main sources:
Marx's materialist theory of world-historical development and the theorization of bio-political power in the work of Foucault, Deleuze and Guattari.
From Marx, they draw on the argument that 'relations of production'
condition class struggle and the possibility of revolutionary, progressive
change in different eras. From Foucault, Deleuze and Guattari, they take
the idea that contemporary relations of production are bio-political. That
is to say, relations of production are now structured through the globalization of Foucauldian governmentality in which the production of particular
kinds of subjects is central. In broad terms, Hardt and Negri's argument
is that the nature of international politics has fundamentally changed
in the closing decades of the twentieth century. It has shifted from an

imperialist, capitalist, Westphalian order to a condition of globalized capitalism in which all life is biopolitically produced and ordered in the service of sustaining globalized capitalism (empire) (Hardt and Negri 2000: 32). In the new global situation of empire, there is no centre of power; instead, power relations are systemically produced and reproduced at all levels of social, economic and political life. This situation creates different possibilities for revolutionary politics than were embedded in the old imperialist order. The revolutionary subject is no longer the proletarian class with its distinctive relation to the means of production; rather, the 'multitude' of bio-politically produced subjectivities sustain the complex network of flows of technology, production, service, trade, finance and information that make up global capitalism. The plausibility of Hardt and Negri's argument depends on making analytic and normative distinctions between *imperialism, empire* and the *multitude*. I will go on to suggest that these distinctions are, at least in part, secured through drawing on the logic embedded in discourses of masculinity.[13]

Hardt and Negri's argument places empire between a previous historical phase of imperialism and the future of the 'multitude'. This historical distinction is also a normative distinction between a past of oppression, in which revolutionary action utterly failed to transform the conditions of world politics, and a future of liberation in which the productive power of the 'multitude' will literally make a new world. Empire occupies both a transitional, historical position and an ambivalent normative position in Hardt and Negri's narrative. On the one hand, empire is the logical culmination of imperialism, the victory of the oppressive forces of capitalism in a global, systemic form. On the other hand, empire is the condition of possibility of a different, more promising kind of revolution. Therefore, empire is both praised and condemned within the text. In order to make their argument for the revolutionary potential of the multitude, Hardt and Negri have to render intelligible claims about the nature of empire and its normative status. One way in which they do this is by integrating the logic of contrast and contradiction inherent in masculinity discourses into their analysis.

In Hardt and Negri's case, the ideal of masculinity, which is hegemonic for their analysis, is associated with the multitude. The multitude is described as specifically masculine by using metaphors of war-making, male sexual potency or monstrosity (ibid.: 213–18, 411–13; Hardt and Negri 2006: 194–6; Quinby 2004: 234–5). Unlike Mearsheimer's masculine hegemon characterized by rationality and controlled violence, the hegemonic masculinity of the multitude is one of explosive creativity, the artistic genius rather than the responsible politician. Whereas Mearsheimer's hegemonic ideal depends on a 'civilized'/'barbarian' contrast that valorizes the former at the expense of the latter, Hardt and Negri's hegemonic ideal of masculinity taps into a romantic tradition in which this valorization is reversed. This is a move that recalls Rousseau's use of the figure of the 'noble savage' to illuminate the effeminacy and corruption of his own civilized times (Dunn 2004).[14] In a tradition of revolutionary political thought going back at least as far as Sorel's *Reflections on Violence* (1999), this creative masculinity embedded in an untrammelled productive energy is contrasted with the repressive masculinity of imperialism (Hardt and Negri 2000: 12).[15] The question for Hardt and Negri is how historically and normatively to make sense of empire as the middle ground between imperialism and the multitude. The paradoxical situation of empire is described through its being simultaneously positioned as the continuation and intensification of the masculinity of imperialism in which repressive power shifts into productive power *and* as the place in which masculinity is entirely evacuated. Empire is both more masculine than imperialism and entirely feminized (impotent).

The masculinity of empire is evident in the way the 'constitutive machine' of empire 'penetrates' all areas of life; produces 'master' narratives; and in the manner of Schmittian sovereignty, determines the exception (ibid.: 17, 32–4; Schmitt 1996). But empire does not accomplish these things through the exercise of repressive power, as was the case with imperialism; it accomplishes them by producing rather than controlling subjects. For example, it produces the subject as consumer and the subject as rights-bearer. This means the globalization of market relations, the expansion of human rights regimes, and practices such as humanitarian intervention are legitimized as projections of universal truths about what it means to be human as enacted in everyday life. Empire is more masculine than imperialism because masculinity does not need to constrain the behaviour of its subjects; it *makes* those subjects maintain and amplify empire's power.

> The great industrial and financial powers thus produce not only commodities but also subjectivities. They produce agentic subjectivities within the biopolitical context: they produce needs, social relations, bodies and minds – which is to say they produce producers. In the biopolitical sphere, life is made to work for production and production is made to work for life. (Hardt and Negri 2000: 32)

At the same time as describing empire as the epitome of the masculine ideal of creativity, however, Hardt and Negri also present empire as parasitical on the multitude, which is 'the real productive force of our social world' (ibid.: 62). On this account, empire lives off the blood of the multitude like a vampire (ibid.: 62–3); or alternatively, is simply the passive, feminized field upon which the productive power of the multitude acts. The productive power does not belong to empire but to an energy that is already in the hands of the multitude, even if they do not yet realize it. Hardt and Negri's argument clearly draws on the Marxist contrast between a class 'in' and 'for' itself and asserts that, over time, the multitude will recognize its own power and will transform its productive potential to overcome empire and create a new, radically democratic future.

> The ontological terrain of Empire, completely plowed and irrigated by a powerful, self-valorizing, and constituent labor, is thus planted with a virtuality that seeks to be real. The keys of possibility, or really of the modalities of being that transform the virtual into reality, reside in this realm beyond measure. (ibid.: 359)

Within Hardt and Negri's argument, it is necessary for empire to appear as both powerful and weak. This combination of power and weakness is difficult to explain in terms of the bio-political analysis of thinkers such as Foucault, Deleuze and Guattari. Since bio-power reaches into the most intimate aspects of life, it would appear that challenging the status quo is much more difficult than where power is presented in repressive terms. Hardt and Negri overcome this difficulty by appealing to the familiar contradictory logic of masculinity/femininity in order to render their argument intelligible. By asserting the masculine power of empire as properly belonging to the multitude, Hardt and Negri appeal to our commonsense knowledge that masculinity both contradicts and trumps femininity. According to the logic of masculinity, no machine can be both masculine and feminine; and since masculine is superior to feminine, it must be the masculine which will eventually triumph over the feminine in the machine of empire. Empire cannot last because empire is a woman being ploughed and irrigated by the masculinized multitude.

As with Mearsheimer, Hardt and Negri utilize a logic of masculinity in order both to characterize their object of analysis and its key determinations and to characterize their own analysis in relation to that logic. On the one hand, the superiority of their framework of analysis is demonstrated through a contrast with other perspectives on the masculine continuum, which are nevertheless inadequate in the sense of being less in tune with the productive power of hegemonic masculinity. On the other hand, they point to theoretical or ideological positions that fundamentally contradict appropriate ways of understanding and judging contemporary world politics. Included in the first category, on the continuum of masculinity, are Marx (Hardt and Negri 2006: 140–53), Foucault, Deleuze and Guattari (Hardt and Negri 2000: 22–30). The achievement of these theorists is their grasp of the centrality of productive power. In the case of Marx, his theory approximates most closely to the masculine ideal; but because times have changed with the growth of bio-political power and new sources of resistance, his analysis has become outdated. Foucault, Deleuze and Guattari, in contrast, have grasped the true, bio-political nature of empire; but they have not grasped the revolutionary potential of this new form of productive power.

> Deleuze and Guattari, however, seem to be able to conceive positively only the tendencies toward continuous movement and absolute flows, and thus in their thought, too, the creative elements and the radical ontology of the production of the social remain insubstantial and impotent. (ibid.: 28)

If, however, Deleuze and Guattari, like classical and defensive realists for Mearsheimer, do not live up to the manly potential of their own analysis, then liberal cosmopolitans (again, as in Mearsheimer's account) occupy a much more radically feminized position. One example of such a mistaken argument is that of Richard Falk, who argues for the radical potential of global civil society as a force for good in the post-cold-war world. Hardt and Negri argue that theorists such as Falk fail to appreciate productive power; thus, they read the politics of NGOs and human rights regimes in mistakenly benign terms without recognizing that these are techniques of bio-political power in the service of empire (ibid.: 36–7). Whereas Foucault, Deleuze and Guattari remain on terrain in which debate is possible and potentially useful, Falk occupies the position of the feminine other who simply does not understand how international politics works. In contrast to all of the above, Hardt and Negri's own analysis emerges as equivalent to their own hegemonic masculine ideal; an ideal in which the 'postcolonial' hero gets his hands dirty and identifies with the life forces that will make the world anew.

Our analysis has to descend into the jungle of productive and conflict-
ual determinations that the collective biopolitical body offers us. The
context of our analysis thus has to be the very unfolding of life itself,
the process of the constitution of the world, of history. The analysis
must be proposed not through ideal forms but within the dense complex of experience. (ibid.: 30)[16]

Conclusion

In their influential texts, Mearsheimer, Hardt and Negri aim to do two
things through their arguments: first, they aim to paint a big picture of
what international politics is like, how it works, and what is likely to happen to it; and second, they aim to establish the credentials of their particular mode of analysis in relation to other possibilities. I have suggested in
both cases that drawing on a logic of masculinity helps accomplish these
aims. It is likely that these theorists would argue that the use of masculine
language and logic is a matter of rhetorical decoration and does not affect
the validity of their substantive inductive or deductive arguments. On this
account, these theorists could make the same arguments either without
rhetorical decoration altogether or by using another set of rhetorical
tropes to make the same case. I would argue, however, that the logic of
masculinity provides a powerful incentive against raising questions about
the substantive assumptions and inductive and deductive moves made in
the arguments of theorists such as Mearsheimer, Hardt and Negri. The
framing of contemporary international politics in terms of masculinity
logic locks our social scientific imagination into a very familiar world in
which we already understand how things ontologically work in terms of
value hierarchies. But it also provides a massively efficient short cut for the
cognitive tasks of categorization and analysis and for the evaluative tasks
of judgement with which Mearsheimer, Hardt and Negri are concerned.
Of course, it is the case that the formal characteristics of the logic of
masculinity are intertwined with other conceptual schemes grounded
in binary oppositions. We have, for instance, seen how the distinction
between 'civilized' and 'barbarian' operates to help sustain the logic of
contrast and contradiction essential to Mearsheimer, Hardt and Negri's
arguments. Nevertheless, we have also seen, at least in the context of these
particular theories of world politics, the logic of masculinity providing a
particularly stable reference point for rendering the cognitive operations
of contrast and contradiction intelligible, regardless of referential meanings assigned to practising or theorizing international politics.[17]

Feminist scholars have long pointed out that the logic of masculinity, as a mechanism for framing our understanding of international politics, renders the thinking of the feminine and the feminized impossible other than in terms of lack or absence. Quite rightly, much feminist analysis has been devoted to tracing the practical effects of this logic for the ways in which international politics is practised and understood and as a precursor to challenging masculine hegemony in its many different forms. As this chapter has demonstrated, however, the resilience of masculinity as a mode of making sense of world politics reflects the amount of analytic and normative work that it accomplishes. Therefore, it raises the question of what kind of politics and theory would be possible without the work accomplished by gendered logics. This also suggests that disentangling the operations of thought from the operations of gender is a profoundly difficult task.

Notes

1 All these narratives present a 'big picture' of the nature of the present in world politics. For overviews of these competing theories see: Paul and Hall (1999); Held et al. (1999); Lechner and Boli (2004). The 'end of history' argument was put forward by Fukuyama (1992) and is contested in Huntington's account of the 'clash of civilizations' (1998). One influential example of a reassertion of realist theories of international politics is Mearsheimer (2001), discussed below. Also discussed below is Hardt and Negri's path-breaking *Empire* (2000).

2 Feminist approaches to studying international politics pre-date the end of the cold war (see, for instance, Cohn 1989; Elshtain 1995 [1987]; Enloe 1989, discussed below). Nevertheless, it is since 1989 that feminist perspectives have become explicitly acknowledged within the discipline of international relations, and there has been a flourishing of

feminist research, on both the theory and practice of international politics, in this time. See Steans (2003) and Youngs (2004) for overviews of feminist international relations scholarship and Ackerley et al. (2006) on feminist methodologies in IR.

3 Squires and Weldes make the point that there is a problem with feminist work that remains locked in the exploration of its own marginality. This is because such work ghettoizes feminism and confirms the hegemony of mainstream non-feminist work (Squires and Weldes 2007). I am sympathetic to this argument, but nevertheless consider that non-feminist mainstream theoretical frameworks are a legitimate focus for feminist analysis and, within that context, feminism's marginality remains a significant issue.

4 There are some exceptions to this – for instance, Hartsock's psychoanalytic account of masculinity as the root cause of war (1989). Examples

of unitary masculinity narratives
are most often found in analyses
in which masculinity figures as an
explanatory 'gender variable'. Such
analyses are not necessarily explicitly
feminist. See, for instance, Breines et
al. (2000) or Goldstein (2001).

5 Connell's notion of 'hegemonic
masculinity' draws on the Gramscian
notion of 'hegemony' as the
monopoly of consent. The concept
of hegemonic masculinity has not
gone uncontested. It has been argued
to be inapplicable in non-Western
cultural contexts (see Parpart on
African masculinities in this volume).
And it has also been criticized for
analytical weakness and failure to
explain the link between 'hegemonic
masculinity' and the 'hegemony of
men' (Hearn 2004).

6 My concerns within this
chapter are with the operations of
the logic of masculinity in theories of
international relations. My argument
should not be taken as an assertion
that this logic works in the same way
in all contexts, although its referential flexibility and formal stability
could explain how it is that masculin-
ity/femininity distinctions do such a
lot of work across a range of different
contexts within Western cultures. It
should also be noted that the logic of
masculinity is entangled with other
binary logics, such as those concerning race and sexuality. In the context
of theories of international politics
discussed below, the intersection of
gendered and racialized logics is of
particular interest.

7 For feminist critiques of binary
thinking in Western philosophical
and theoretical traditions, see: Garry
and Pearsall (1989); Malson (1989);
Gunew (1991); Tuana (1993); Lennon
and Whitford (1994); Tanesini (2002).

8 'Modernity's expression of
the metaphysics, positivist science,
(re)inscribes the identification of
masculinity – as objectivity, reason,
freedom, transcendence, and control
– against femininity – as subjectivity,
feeling, necessity, contingency, and
disorder. Women are thus excluded
from the authority of knowing,
and from authority more generally,
by the exclusion of "woman" from
privileged rationality (objectivity,
transcendence, autonomy)' (Peterson
1992: 13).

9 The most obvious recent
illustration of the entanglement of
gendered and racialized logics in
relation to uses of political violence
is in the rhetoric surrounding the
so-called 'war on terror' (Hunt and
Rygiel 2006).

10 Mearsheimer separates his
historical analysis of great power
behaviour into two chapters, one
devoted to Japan, Germany, the
Soviet Union and Italy, the other to
Great Britain and the USA. In his
account of Japan, Germany and
the Soviet Union, he is concerned
to demonstrate that, on the whole,
the behaviour of these states was
consistent with the requirements of
offensive realism and therefore not
pathological or irrational (2001: 224),
but the contrast between the rational,
healthy (real man) behaviour of
a great power and the irrational,
unhealthy (hyper-masculine barbaric
man) is crucial to how the analysis
works (ibid.:168–233). It is a contrast
that illustrates the interconnection between the discriminatory
logic of masculinity and the equally

entrenched distinction, within the Western political imaginary, between 'civilized' and 'barbarian'.

11 The tendency to signify weakness in states or statesmen by linking them to femininity is obviously one that is widespread beyond Mearsheimer's analysis. See Cohn on 'War, wimps and women' (1993) and Zalewski's reference to descriptions of Carter's foreign policy (1998: 2).

12 See Ashworth and Swatuk (1998) for a similar analysis of the way in which theoretical debates in international relations are conducted.

13 I am not alone in making this claim; see Quinby (2004).

14 The way in which Hardt and Negri's analysis draws on the figure of the 'barbarian' in the Western imagination testifies to the ways in which gendered and racialized logics intersect within that imagination. On a superficial reading it also suggests that patterns of valorization are less stable in the case of the invocation of the barbarian other than of the feminine other, given, as we shall see, that Hardt and Negri counterpose the barbarian positivity of the multitude to the feminine negativity of empire. On closer inspection, however, it is clear that the role of the 'barbarian', whether positively or negatively perceived, draws on stereotypes that have standardly legitimized racialized patterns of exclusion and discrimination.

15 See Frazer and Hutchings (2007) for a discussion of argument and rhetoric surrounding traditions of theorizing revolutionary violence. For this tradition, which can be traced back to the French Revolution

and Romanticism, hegemonic masculinity is associated with the creative genius of the artist, or the capacity for 'male birth' famously rendered in Mary Shelley's *Frankenstein*. In Hardt and Negri's follow-up book to *Empire*, *Multitude: War and Democracy in the Age of Empire*, there is an extended discussion of the link between the multitude's revolutionary potential and the monsters of the eighteenth- and early nineteenth-century Western imagination: 'Scientific method is defined increasingly in the realm of indetermination and every real entity is produced in an aleatory and singular way, a sudden emergence of the new. Frankenstein is now a member of the family. In this situation, then, the discourse of living beings must become of theory of their construction and the possible futures that await them' (Hardt and Negri 2006: 195–6).

16 The descent into the 'jungle' in this quotation conjures up visions of Western explorers, tapping into another racialized trope of masculinity and again testifying to the instability of the pattern of valorization in Hardt and Negri's rhetorical imaginary when it comes to the 'barbarian' other. This forms a contrast with the positive invocation of the 'new barbarian' discussed above. Once more, however, it is interesting to note that the valorization of masculine/feminine remains stable – whether as 'great white hunter' or as 'noble savage', the hegemonic ideal is always masculinized in contrast to a feminine other.

17 As feminist philosophers have pointed out over the past half-century, the binary logic of

masculinity/ femininity is particularly powerful and pervasive, and provides a commonsense anchoring point for other sorts of binary distinctions, such as mind and body, ideal and real, reason and emotion, which are at work in other binary oppositions such as civilized/barbarian (Garry and Pearsall 1989).

References

Ackerly, B. A., M. Stern and J. True (eds) (2006) *Feminist Methodologies for International Relations*, Cambridge: Cambridge University Press.

Ashworth, L. M. and L. A. Swatuk (1998) 'Masculinity and the fear of emasculation in International Relations theory', in M. Zalewski and J. Parpart (eds) (1998) *The 'Man' Question in International Relations*, Boulder, CO: Westview Press.

Barrett, F. J. (2001) 'The organizational construction of hegemonic masculinity: the case of the US Navy', in S. M. Whitehead and F. J. Barrett (eds), *The Masculinities Reader*, Cambridge: Polity Press, pp. 77–99.

Breines, I., R. W. Connell and I. Eide (2000) (eds) *Male Roles, Masculinities and Violence: A Culture of Peace Perspective*, Paris: UNESCO.

Cockburn, C. and D. Zarkov (eds) (2002) *The Postwar Moment: Militaries, Masculinities and International Peacekeeping in Bosnia and the Netherlands*, London: Lawrence and Wishart.

Cohn, C. (1989) 'Sex and death in the rational world of defense intellectuals', *Signs*, 12(4): 687–718.

— (1993) 'War, wimps and women',
in M. Cooke and A. Woollacott (eds), *Gendering War Talk*, Princeton, NJ: Princeton University Press.

Cohn, C. and C. Enloe (2003) 'A conversation with Cynthia Enloe: feminists look at masculinity and the men who wage war', *Signs*, 28(4): 1187–208.

Connell, R. W. (1995) *Masculinities*, Cambridge: Polity Press.

Der Derian, J. (2001) *Virtuous War: Mapping the Military-Industrial-Entertainment Network*, Boulder, CO: Westview Press.

Dunn, K. C. (2004) *Africa's Ambiguous Relation to Empire*, London: Routledge.

Elshtain, J. (1995 [1987]) *Women and War*, 2nd edn, Chicago, IL: Chicago University Press.

Enloe, C. (1989) *Bananas, Beaches and Bases: Making Feminist Sense of International Politics*, London: Women's Press.

Ferguson, K. (1993) *The Man Question: Visions of Subjectivity in Feminist Theory*, Berkeley, CA: University of California Press.

Frazer, E. and K. Hutchings (2007) 'Argument and rhetoric in the justification of political violence', *European Journal of Political Theory*, 6(2): 180–99.

Fukuyama, F. (1992) *The End of History and the Last Man*, Harmondsworth: Penguin.

Garry, A. and M. Pearsall (eds) (1989) *Women, Knowledge and Reality: Explorations in Feminist Philosophy*, Boston, MA: Unwin Hyman.

Goldstein, J. (2001) *War and Gender*, Cambridge: Cambridge University Press.

Grant, R. and K. Newland (eds)
(1991) *Gender and International
Relations*, Milton Keynes: Open
University Press.

Gunew, S. (ed.) (1991) *A Reader in
Feminist Knowledge*, London:
Routledge.

Hardt, M. and A. Negri (2000) *Empire*,
Cambridge, MA: Harvard University Press.

Hardt, M. and A. Negri (2006)
*Multitude: War and Democracy
in the Age of Empire*, London:
Penguin.

Hartsock, N. (1989) 'Masculinity,
heroism and the making of war',
in A. Harris and Y. King (eds),
*Rocking the Ship of State: Towards
a Feminist Peace Politics*, Boulder,
CO: Westview Press.

Hearn, J. (2004) 'From hegemonic
masculinity to the hegemony of
men', *Feminist Theory*, 5(1): 49–72.

Held, D. et al. (eds) (1999) *Global
Transformations*, Cambridge:
Polity Press.

Hooper, C. (2001) *Manly States:
Masculinities, International
Relations and Gender Politics*, New
York: Columbia University Press.

Hunt, K. and K. Rygiel (eds) (2006)
*(En)Gendering the War on Terror:
War Stories and Camouflaged
Politics*, Aldershot: Ashgate.

Huntington, S. (1998) *The Clash of
Civilizations and the Remaking of
World Order*, New York: Touch-
stone.

Lechner, F. J. and J. Boli (eds) (2004)
The Globalization Reader, 2nd
edn, Oxford: Blackwell.

Lennon, K. and M. Whitford (eds)
(1994) *Knowing the Difference:
Feminist Perspectives in Epistemo-
logy*, London: Routledge.

Malson, M. R., J. F. O'Barr,
S. Westphal-Wihl and M. Wyer
(eds) (1989) *Feminist Theory in
Practice and Process*, Chicago, IL:
University of Chicago Press.

Mearsheimer, J. (2001) *The Tragedy
of Great Power Politics*, New York:
W. W. Norton.

Niva, S. (1998) 'Tough and tender:
new world order masculinity and
the Gulf War', in M. Zalewski
and J. Parpart (eds), *The 'Man'
Question in International
Relations*, Boulder, CO: Westview
Press.

Passavant, P. A. and J. Dean (eds)
(2004) *Empire's New Clothes:
Reading Hardt and Negri*, New
York and London: Routledge.

Paul, T. V. and J. A. Hall (eds) (1999)
*International Order and the Future
of World Politics*, Cambridge:
Cambridge University Press.

Peterson, V. S. (ed.) (1992) *Gendered
States: Feminist (Re)visions of
International Relations Theory*,
Boulder, CO: Lynne Rienner.

Peterson, V. S. and J. True (1998)
'"New times" and new conversa-
tions', M. Zalewski and J. Parpart
(eds), *The 'Man' Question in
International Relations*, Boulder,
CO: Westview Press.

Quinby, L. (2004) 'Taking the
millenialist pulse of *Empire*'s
multitude: a genealogical feminist
diagnosis', in P. A. Passavant
and J. Dean (eds), *Empire's New
Clothes: Reading Hardt and Negri*,
New York and London: Routledge,
pp. 231–51.

Schmitt, C. (1996) *The Concept of the
Political*, Chicago, IL: Chicago
University Press.

Sorel, G. (ed.) (1999) *Reflections on*

Violence, Cambridge: Cambridge University Press.

Squires, J. and J. Weldes (2007) 'Beyond being marginal: gender and international relations in Britain', *British Journal of Politics and International Relations*, 9(2): 185–203.

Steans, J. (2003) 'Engaging from the margins: feminist encounters with the "mainstream" of International Relations', *British Journal of Politics and International Relations*, 5(3): 428–54.

Tanesini, A. (2002) *An Introduction to Feminist Epistemologies*, Oxford: Blackwell.

Tickner, J. A. (1991) 'Hans Morgenthau's principles of political realism: a feminist reformulation', *Millennium*, 17(3): 429–40.

— (1992) *Gender in International Relations: Feminist Perspectives on Achieving Global Security*, New York: Columbia University Press.

Tuana, N. (1993) *The Less Noble Sex:*

Scientific, Religious and Philosophical Conceptions of Women's Nature, Bloomington: Indiana University Press.

Whitworth, S. (2004) *Men, Militarism and UN Peacekeeping: A Gendered Analysis*, Boulder, CO: Lynne Rienner.

Youngs, G. (2004) 'Feminist International Relations: a contradiction in terms? Or: why women and gender are essential to understanding the world we live in', *International Affairs*, 80(1): 101–14.

Zalewski, M. (1998) 'Introduction: from the "Woman" Question to the "Man" question in International Relations', in M. Zalewski and J. Parpart (eds), *The 'Man' Question in International Relations*, Boulder, CO: Westview Press.

Zalewski, M. and J. Parpart (eds) (1998) *The 'Man' Question in International Relations*, Boulder, CO: Westview Press.

TWO | Interrogating white male privilege*

KEVIN DUNN

What does it mean that world politics has largely been theorized by white men? Asking the man question has caused me to critically think about how *privilege* is linked to gender and race in the study and practice of international relations. This chapter does not provide an answer, as such. Rather, it is largely a polemical intervention seeking to provoke and challenge entrenched privilege. As with most polemics, it is my hope that this intervention will foster critical self-reflection among theorists and practitioners of international relations, which will, it is hoped, encourage developing new ways of analysing and 'doing' world politics.

Thinking about privilege

I begin with the observation that the social world is produced by intersecting material forces and discursive practices which are deeply gendered and raced. In my own life, the most 'clear' manifestation of the racist and sexist worlds I inhabit is the *privileges* bestowed upon me as a member of the privileged social categories – white and male. I place 'clear' in quotation marks because it often is not. Peggy McIntosh has referred to privilege as an invisible package of unearned assets (2005: 109). This invisible package needs to be unpacked largely because we live in a world that is so multilayered when it comes to the privileges and discriminations involved in gender, sexuality, race and class.

Yet to speak uncritically of a mythical white male ignores the complexities of race and gender that people across the globe daily navigate. I do not mean to imply that the privileges and discriminations associated with race and gender are either uniform or evenly distributed. Our lives are shaped by global economic and political dynamics, and different groups of people are very differently positioned in these processes. While race and gender relations have an international dimension, there are multiple dimensions; and the patterns of inequality and privilege can often be qualitatively different. Yet certain groups enjoy unearned invisible assets from the systems of power underpinning social life. More often than not, those people are white middle/upper-class males from North

America and western Europe. I will merely refer to this social group as white males for the sake of simplicity, though I am well aware of the problems involved in such simplification.[1] As a white middle/upper-class North American male, I am simultaneously writing from, to and about my subject position. I am particularly interested in how processes of privilege are part of my academic discipline.

Drawing upon the work of Peggy McIntosh, Allan Johnson stipulates that there are two types of privilege: unearned entitlements and conferred dominance (2001: 25–6). The first form refers to those unearned assets that give the dominant group a competitive edge over others; the second grants one group power over another. These two forms work together to create and sustain white male privilege in today's society and in the field of Western IR. As a white male, I was oblivious to this package of unearned assets for most of my life. Of course, silence in the face of privilege sustains its invisibility. To paraphrase James Baldwin, being white and male means never having to think about it. But once the package of unearned assets became visible to me, its existence seemed so utterly obvious and huge.

I know I did not get where I am today by my own personal accomplishments alone. I benefited from white male privilege, among other things. When I sought admission to college and graduate school, was interviewed for a professional job, applied for a grant, stood for tenure, almost all the people evaluating me looked like me; they were mostly white males. For the most part, I presented them with a reflection of themselves-to-be. And they were, after all, merely bearers of gendered and racialized structures. Reflecting on her own career, Raewyn Connell notes: 'My path into academic jobs involved learning certain gendered practices (such as ferocious concentration on writing tasks at the expense of human relationships) and rejecting others (including such conventional masculine items as enthusiasm for sport and sexual aggressiveness)' (Connell 2002: 197). This is an apt description of my own trajectory; but of course, I learned, whether consciously or not, certain racial and class practices as well. As Connell also observes, 'There is truth in Dorothy Smith's account of the academic world as a sector of a patriarchal power structure producing abstracted knowledge through texts that substitute for concrete knowledge. Yet her imagery is too mild to capture the lunatic divisiveness of that world and the tangled dynamics producing academic masculinities as ways of surviving and operating in it' (ibid.: 197). Even though the image I presented/performed was often a slightly warped reflection, with my piercings, tattoos and kooky hair, it was an advantage in the racist and patriarchal world in which we live. In fact, it was the result of white male privilege that I could have an 'alternative' self-presentation, as the comfort zone was wide enough that earrings and tattoos did not fundamentally challenge the fact that I am white, heterosexual and male. Of course, the comfort zone has its limits, as I have frequently discovered when I have deviated too far from the expected norm of dominant discourses of masculinity (see Hooper 2000).

To more adequately examine and remedy discrimination and oppression, we must make the systems of power and privilege visible, which mean making the privileges they create part of our discourse. This chapter is an attempt to do this by illuminating the manifestation of white male privilege in my own field of study, international relations theory.[2] As Ferguson noted (1993: 8), we need to make these dominant configurations 'strange' by demanding explanations about their existence. There is a problem, however, as regards where to target one's analysis: at the individual or systemic level. In earlier incarnations of this chapter, I struggled with the tension between outing specific scholars and exploring the *systemic* impact of white male privilege. Most scholars working on privilege stress the systemic aspects of racism and sexism, rather than their individualistic expressions. For example, Allan Johnson argued that 'individuals aren't what is actually privileged. Instead, privilege is defined in relation to a group or social category' (2001: 34). Stephanie Wildman and Adrienne Davis have argued that 'calling someone a racist individualizes the behaviour and veils the fact that racism can only occur where it is culturally, socially, and legally supported. This charge lays the blame on the individual rather than the systemic forces which have shaped that individual and his or her society' (1996: 11). Yet I find the notion of a latent structure simply too deterministic; and I am deeply uncomfortable with what I see as a simplistic division between structure and agency, that is between systemic privilege and individual practice. Moreover, an exclusive focus on systemic forces allows individuals to escape responsibility for their actions.

As I grappled with the issues of structures and agency, particularly those understood in terms of individual responsibility, I found myself turning to some of social theorist Pierre Bourdieu's (1984, 1990) insights on structures, social/symbolic *capital*, *habitus* and practices. Bourdieu posited that the social world is divided into relatively autonomous subsystems, fields or markets that follow their own logic. While relatively autonomous, fields are dynamic arenas of struggle and are affected by the existence of other fields. How people operate within the multiple fields in which they find themselves is largely shaped by what Bourdieu refers to as social capital and *habitus*. *Habitus* is the condition of 'those pre-conscious, ingrained, structured dispositions which inform the multiplicity of actions and practices which individuals carry out in the production and reproduction of social life' (Elliott 1999: 10). These systems of dispositions are sets of generating principles for making practical sense of the world and one's place in society. Bourdieu argues that people have a variety of resources, which he refers to by the shorthand term *capital*, granting them a position from which to act. Also, however, they often have taken-for-granted understandings that guide how they act. The concept of *habitus* helps capture the interplay between structuring discourses and individual practices. Discourses produce preconditions for action, but they do not determine action.

While discourse (*doxa*) captures understandings at a structural level, *habitus* captures their meanings at the agent level. 'As an acquired system of generative schemes, the *habitus* makes possible the free production of all the thoughts, perceptions and actions inherent in the particular conditions of its production – and only those' (Bourdieu 1990: 54). Bourdieu stresses that the social system cannot be seen as determining the activities or choices of individual subjects. As Elliott notes, 'On the contrary, actors have a multiplicity of strategies or tactics at their disposal in the generation of social conduct; in this sense, human agents are purposive, reflective beings. But Bourdieu certainly wishes to emphasize the influence of specific social contexts (or what he calls the "field" or "markets" of the social domain) within which individuals act. In this connection, he speaks of both a "structuration of practices" and "structuring structures"' (Elliott 1999: 10).

For white male academics operating within the field of international studies, as for white male practitioners, their race and gender provide both resources (capital) and *habitus*. Being white and male provides a system of structuring dispositions, which are largely habitual and unreflective, to help guide how they act. These are essential elements for power relations and lead to practices that are generative in the sense that they create meanings, entities and power relations. As Bourdieu notes, 'The *habitus*, a product of history, produces individual and collective practices – more history – in accordance with the schemes generated by history. It ensures the active presence of past experiences which, deposited in each organism in the form of schemes of perception, thought and action, tend to guarantee the "correctness" of practices and their constancy over time, more reliably than all formal rules and explicit norms' (Bourdieu 1990: 54). For our consideration here, white male privilege is internalized through the *habitus* and reinscribed through constituted practices. Privilege is taken for granted and made invisible, even though individual actions regularly reify it.

The majority of authoritative IR theory (the canon's canon, if you will) has largely been produced by white males from North America and western Europe. Yet those in the field rarely acknowledge it as the white male North American/western European field of international relations. Rather, it is cast simply as IR; and those scholars writing from outside those positions of privilege frequently have their work labelled in ways that mark it as outside the norm: feminist, post-colonial, non-Western, and so forth. Thus, I believe it is important to recognize that the current academic discipline is built upon a foundation of white male privilege and that the process of privilege remains an active element in how the discipline continues to be constructed, reproduced, taught and practised. If one is committed to challenging existing hierarchies and opening up space for alternative voices and ideas, as I am, then addressing white male privilege is an important enterprise. But the act of illuminating white male privilege introduces what Robert Jensen refers to as the 'ultimate white privilege': 'the privilege to acknowledge that you have unearned privilege but to ignore what it means' (2005: 115). Thus, the project, then, is not just to illuminate white male privilege but to challenge it as well. As Tim Wise writes, 'If we recognize our privileges, yet fail to challenge them, what good is our insight? If we intuit discrimination, yet fail to speak against it, what have we done to rectify the injustice? And that's the hard part, because privilege tastes good and we're loath to relinquish it' (2005: 120). In the following section, I suggest some of the ways in which the systems of dispositions (*habitus*) and social capital enjoyed/employed by white males in the study of IR have affected the structure and content of that academic discipline.

Illuminating how white male privilege shapes IR theory

Defining 'normality' and 'abnormality' The first step in interrogating white male privilege is to *illuminate* white maleness. This may seem obvious, but most white males do not actively think of themselves in those terms. White males tend to think of themselves as *just* people. The dominant racial and gender discourses in Western societies tend to powerfully bind whiteness and masculinity to assumed claims of realness (Halberstam 2002: 353). For example, in his work on whiteness, Richard Dyer (1997) begins by examining how white people are imagined within white cultural production. He argues that while other people are raced, white people are self-represented as being just people. 'This assumption that white people are just people, which is not far off saying that whites are people whereas other colours are something else, is endemic to white culture' (ibid.: 2). The often unreflective claim to be just a person is an attempt to define the bounds of normality. Such self-representations are both a manifestation of power and an assertion to power. As Dyer notes, 'there is no more powerful position than that of being "just" human. The claim to power is the claim to speak for the commonality of humanity. Raced people can't do that – they can only speak for their race' (ibid.: 2). Often unreflectively, white males simultaneously seek to define what is normal and speak for humanity.

Admittedly, this is not a particularly novel insight. Simone de Beauvoir observed in *The Second Sex*: 'Representation of the world, like the world itself, is the work of men; they describe it from their own point of view, which they confuse with absolute truth' (1952: 161). This obliviousness to gender and, I would argue, race is achieved because white males often assume that whiteness and maleness have little meaning. To refer back to Bourdieu, the social capital white males enjoy given their race and gender is largely invisible. As Harlon Dalton claims, such a disposition is largely 'the natural consequence of being in the driver's seat' (Dalton 1995: 109). But this invisibility does not mean there is a failure to discuss white males as subjects. Most of the time white males speak about nothing else. Because white males frame the conversation in terms of people in general, however, they are everywhere in representation but rarely recognized as such (Dyer 1997: 3). This is a convergence of the simultaneous privileges of race and gender. Whites, in general, and males, in particular, often fail to recognize their own subject positions while seeking to represent all of humanity.

At its root, this particular manifestation of white male privilege is about the power to define and lay claim to normality. The normal is the product of discursive practices, and the discourses defining normal in world politics privilege the white male subject position as the human one. Within the academic discipline and practice of IR, one can see a lengthy tradition of North American and western European white males writing about world politics from their own subjective position.

In doing so, they are both drawing from the dominant discourses from which they are privileged and also actively reproducing and entrenching those discourses through their *habitus*. That is, they are both products of discursive systems and active agents in the maintenance of those systems. To take but one simple example, much of IR theory relies on assumptions about human nature. These assumptions about human nature are manifested in myriad ways: from the myth of the stag hunt to various imagined state-of-nature scenarios. But in virtually all these cases, the actors are expressions of idealized white male subject positions. Introducing race, gender or class into the mythical stag hunt narrative, for example, produces a much more complicated and open story and, as such, a more varied discussion of human nature.

Feminist theorists working within the IR discipline have done an excellent job of exposing the privileged yet hidden male subject positions in traditional IR texts. For example, J. Ann Tickner's engagement with Hans J. Morgenthau's *Six Principles of Political Realism* is an excellent study in how one IR theorist wrote from within a specific narrow structural/linguistic frame of masculinity, while claiming to generalize out to all people and humanity. As Tickner pointed out, the list of six principles 'is a partial description of international politics because it is based on assumptions about human nature that are partial and that privilege masculinity' (1988: 433). In some ways, the target is too easy, since Realists are so explicit in their claims to objectivity and universalism. There is a lack of self-awareness, since given the assumption that they are just people they can generalize from their own historical experiences and cultural values that are internalized and unquestioned. Thus, Realists like Morgenthau can claim to speak of and for people and humanity while other interpretations are characterized/categorized as being gendered, racialized, cultured and/or classed. This is not an exclusive characteristic of Realism but is representative of most IR theories in general, since Tickner's tactic could be reproduced in countless white male theorists, from Kant to Keohane, Machiavelli to Marx.[3]

The normalizing discourses of whiteness and masculinity have enabled definitions and concepts that privileged this narrow segment of the world's population to become accepted as the norm within IR theory and practice, such as power, the state, civil society, security, and so forth. These concepts are placed at the centre of our intellectual project, which often means that females and non-whites must employ them if they are to be taken as serious IR scholars. Moreover, the meanings and normative values attached to these concepts are discursively bound to and typically nurture the needs and interests of the privileged white male subject position and dominant norms of masculinity. While this clearly has important implications for the construction of theory, it also has significant methodological repercussions. That is, white male privilege is not only embedded in our structures of knowledge, it also delineates acceptable systems of inquiry (Ackerly et al. 2006; Cohn 1987).

Stephanie Wildman and Adrienne Davis observe, 'The characteristics and attributes of those who are privileged group members are described as societal norms – as the way things are and as what is normal in society. This normalization of privilege means that members of society are judged, and succeed or fail, measured against the characteristics that are held by the privileged. The privileged characteristic is the norm; those who stand outside are the aberrant or "alternative"' (1996: 14). This is extremely relevant for IR theory, particularly in its normative manifestations. For that reason, let me offer a few examples.

Given the privileging of white male subject positions in the dominant discourses (*doxa*), the *habitus* generated by many IR theorists, who are predominantly white males, tend to create a system of dispositions positing their historical experiences and cultural values as the norm for the international community. As such, an idealized image of the Westphalian state serves as the norm. This is clearly articulated in the vast literature on state failure and state capacity. Taking an idealized North American/ western European state as the norm, much ink has been spilled about how and why many non-white experiences with the state are aberrant. Rarely does this literature engage in critical self-reflection, exploring how the assumed norm is the product of subjective experiences, values and imaginations. Thus, we are presented with a towering mass of work on failed or failing *African* states, for instance, but rarely is the assumed norm troubled or its racial and gender underpinnings exposed (Dunn 2001).[4]

In its most pronounced manifestations, this body of literature contains dangerous policy prescriptions. Often policies are constructed to make the non-white, non-male other more like us – for their own good. As Peggy McIntosh has observed, 'whites are taught to think of their lives as morally neutral, normative, average, and ideal; thus, when we work to benefit others, it is seen as work which will allow "them" to be more like "us"' (2005: 110; see also Eng and Kazanjiian 2002). Of course, it would be a mistake to assume it is always the goal to make others like us. A good deal of energy has historically gone into the project of constructing and violently policing the boundaries between us and the deviants who challenge accepted understandings and practices of whiteness and masculinity. For example, during the nineteenth and early twentieth centuries, the racist and sexist discourses operating in western Europe engendered acts of colonial conquest and domination (McClintock 1995; Lindqvist 1992). Today, in its liberal humanitarian articulation, constructions of alterity have contributed to violent interventionist wars in Iraq and the Balkans. Informing these policies is a manifestation of white male privilege: white North American and western European male IR scholars and practitioners claiming to speak for all humanity because they believe their race- and gender-informed experiences and values are the norm.

One can see this pattern repeated throughout mainstream IR theory. Democratic Peace Theory is firmly constructed on an artifice produced by race-, gender- and class-informed subject positions. As Ido Oren (2002) argues in *Our Enemies and US*, American political science in general, and the scholars advancing the idea of democratic peace in particular, are informed by the dominant discourses in which their own subject positions are privileged; in the case of Democratic Peace Theory, this has resulted in a fluid and historically contingent understanding of democracy shaped by America's experience and its historical rivalries. The gap in Oren's otherwise damning critique is his failure to adequately expose the racial and gender components so clearly present in the political science scholarship he investigates. The development sub-field of IR is also representative of how scholars operate under the assumption that their subject position is the norm and that they can speak for all humanity. One can see this within the modernization school, with its explicit attempts to make the non-white world more like the white one. But it is equally true for the neoliberal approaches to development, with their subjective agendas obscured behind claims of universalism. While neoliberalism is in principle gender and race neutral, R. W. Connell notes there has been a 'sharp remasculinization [and racialization] of political rhetoric and a turn to the use of force as a primary instrument in policy' (2005: 1815–16). Neoliberalism functions as a form of masculinity politics, and '[m]any mainstream policies (e.g., in economic and security affairs) are substantially about men without acknowledging this fact' (ibid.: 1816).

What is at play here is not merely the ability of white males to define the parameters of normality, but also the inability of white male IR theorists to deal with the problems that arise in the way they construct difference.

Naeem Inayatullah and David Blaney eloquently explore what they see
as Western culture's ongoing inability to deal with cultural difference in
their *International Relations and the Problem of Difference* (2004). Drawing
on the work of Tzvetan Todorov (1984), Inayatullah and Blaney claim
that, since the discovery of the Americas, Western culture has engaged
the other through a double movement: 'difference becomes inferiority,
and the possibility of a common humanity requires assimilation' (2004:
10). In the first move, difference is regarded as the complete absence
of commonality, which opens up the possibility of conquest, enslave-
ment and eradication. The second move recognizes commonality, but
only as a precursor to assimilation. The possibility of recognizing the
other as both the same and different has yet to be realized. Inayatullah
and Blaney chart this inability to deal with cultural difference through
the foundational texts of IR to the neo-modernization approaches of
contemporary IR, most notably in the literatures on liberal peace theory,
global civil society and pluralistic global community (ibid.: 1116–21). The
protagonist in Inayatullah and Blaney's narrative is Western IR, but I
would suggest the that fact that all the theorists they cite are white males
is not immaterial.[5] While I wholeheartedly agree with their critique, I
would suggest that putting a finer point on Western IR's inability to deal
with cultural difference is both a manifestation of white male privilege
and a mechanism for obscuring and maintaining that privilege.

Inayatullah and Blaney's discussion of the problem of difference and
the double movement of conquest/assimilation brings to mind Herman
Melville's classic novella *Benito Cereno*. The protagonist is an American
male captain who stumbles on to a ship that, initially unbeknownst
to the American, has been taken over by the slaves it was transporting
for trade. The story unfolds as the captain gradually sees the blacks
he initially sees as docile and inferior childlike creatures who inspire
both his pity and a desire to uplift become, in his eyes, bloodthirsty
murderers and crazed killers. As Toni Morrison (1997) has pointed out,
it is precisely this transformation of slaves from simple, friendly and
childlike creatures deserving our help and sympathy into irrational violent
monsters which displays the full spectrum of the racist gaze. The first
impulse is one of assimilation (like contemporary neo-modernization
IR theories), while the second is one of conquest and eradication, like
traditional colonially informed understandings of power politics. Both
positions deny the possibility of strategic, rational, calculated and intelligent action by those believed to be different from us. Melville's narrator

is blind to his racism because it flows from his *habitus*, just as with most scholars. Like Melville's narrator, white male scholars fail to see that the structures of power, in terms of both the structuring structures and the structuration of practices highlighted by Bourdieu, leave them in a position of privilege, from which they define what is normal and judge others who fail to meet that norm.

Making decisions for everyone

In his examination of white privilege, Richard Dyer wrote, 'White people have power and believe that they think, feel and act like and for all people; white people, unable to see their particularity, cannot take account of other people's; white people create the dominant images of the world and don't quite see that they thus construct the world in their own image; white people set standards of humanity by which they are bound to succeed and others bound to fail' (1997: 12). Dyer could have been even more specific by referring to white males in particular. In many ways, Dyer's observations reflect the privileged ability to define normality, which I previously discussed. But there is more to it. Privilege is also manifested in the ability of certain people with social capital to make decisions that affect everyone without taking others into account. Given the racist and sexist world in which we live, many white males feel they are comfortably in the driver's seat. This obviously is not true of all white males, given that the privileges and discriminations associated with race and gender are neither uniform nor evenly distributed. Yet the dominant race and gender discourses in Western society have allowed some white males the ability to control the agenda and define the rules, while being able to ignore the opinions of others. Allan Johnson writes:

> ... privilege generally allows people to assume a certain level of acceptance, inclusion, and respect in the world, to operate within a relatively wide comfort zone. Privilege increases the odds of having things your own way, of being able to set the agenda in a social situation and determine the rules and standards and how they're applied. Privilege grants the cultural authority to make judgments about others and to have those judgments stick. It allows people to define reality and to have prevailing definitions of reality fit their experience. Privilege means being able to decide who gets taken seriously, who receives attention, who is accountable to whom and for what. And it grants a presumption of superiority and social permission to act on that presumption without having to worry about being challenged. (2001: 33–4)

This passage is about as apt a description of the discipline and practice of Western IR as any other I know.

In many ways, Johnson's observations about privilege relate to individual behaviour as much as systemic structures, which underscores my earlier discussion about Bourdieu and the intersection of structure and agency. bell hooks observed, 'In white supremacist society, white people can "safely" imagine that they are invisible to black people since the power they have historically asserted, and even now collectively assert over black people, accorded them the right to control the black gaze' (1992: 168). As such, the *habitus* of being a white male in IR provides me with the ability to decide whether I am going to listen to others, whether I am going to hear them, or whether I am going to do neither. I have the privilege of silencing others without intending to or even being aware of it. This advantage allows me not to see privilege in myself and to be angry, hurt or bemused at those who do. As white male IR theorists and practitioners, we have the privilege *and ability* to discount the worth of a non-white male, his comments and behaviour, and to alter his future, based on our assessment. This is true of non-white males as colleagues (that is, other IR theorists) and as subjects of enquiry (i.e. feminism, African IR, post-colonial critiques, and so forth).

One manifestation of privilege is the ability to determine inclusion and exclusion of oneself and others in a group. As white male IR theorists, many of us can exclude or include at our whim. For example, we can position ourselves in various scholarly camps, schools or fields of study far more easily than non-whites and women. For example, I can lay claim to inclusion in a number of groups: Africanist, feminist, post-structuralist, post-colonialist, environmentalist, and so forth. In those cases, the issue of my race or gender is rarely considered. Admittedly laying claim to two labels that are assumed to be at odds, such as Marxism and post-structuralism, can be problematic for numerous reasons, not the least being that some labels seem to exclude others. For women and non-whites, however, the discipline accordingly tends to categorize them. The adjective descriptor is far more difficult for them to shake off and often becomes the dominant exclusionary label. That is to say, they will be more readily categorized as female, feminist, 'African', Indian, and so forth, which limits their ability to claim inclusion in other labels and groups.

What this has meant in the field of IR, as mentioned above, is that white males can include and exclude more or less at our whim, functioning as de facto gatekeepers of the discipline. In many ways, this is related to Bourdieu's idea of viewing others in society as *capital*-bearing objects, rather than *capital*-accumulating subjects. Again, *capital* is understood as the variety of resources granting actors a position from which to act within a given social field. While I certainly do not agree with many of Bourdieu's thoughts on '*la domination masculine*' (1998; see also Lovell 2000 and Adkins and Skeggs 2005), in which he posits women's status in society as being only that of *capital*-bearing objects, I believe there is something to the fact that male scholars believe they can increase their social *capital* within the field by occasionally including those they see largely as *capital*-bearing objects. When editing a book or creating a symposium, white male scholars have the luxury of deciding whether we want to include a chapter on Africa or have a female contributor. Often, the decision is made on calculations of capital accumulation. Importantly, our worth is not put into question. Examples of white male gatekeeping in the discipline are abundant, so let me simply offer two brief personal anecdotes that capture the essence of this practice. When I was previewing a friend's edited volume on American foreign policy, I noted that all the contributors were white American males; moreover, there was no chapter on a particular non-white region of the world. When I pointed this out to him, suggesting that including a feminist or non-American critique would help him achieve the broad representation of perspective he was claiming, he dismissively responded that his was 'not that kind of book'. Another anecdote: discussing a colleague's work on armed youth movements, I noted that, since the overwhelming majority of these armed youths are male, a gendered analysis would be useful, if not necessary. He responded by claiming that gender did not matter in this case and he did not do 'that kind of thing'.

In both cases, one might well wonder what 'kind' of work each scholar was trying to avoid. I suspect that both want to do the 'kind' of work that would be taken seriously by the discipline. Given the fact that our discipline is discursively structured to privilege white male subject positions and associated methodologies, work that questions, challenges or even draws attention to this structure may be seen as a threat or dismissed as poor scholarship employing a flawed methodology/theory (see Ackerly et al. 2006). In these anecdotes, both scholars were operating from within a privileged *habitus* of the discipline. The kind of work from non-white and white feminists/females that stepped out of the accepted framework was not the serious kind of IR scholarship with which they wanted to be associated. To put it another way, I suspect neither wanted to be associated with 'that kind of girl' lest their friends made fun of them or rejected them from their social circle.

In both these cases, I think it is significant to recognize that a non-self-reflective practice of inclusion and exclusion was taking place. My anecdotes are meant to illustrate the fact that the power to ignore race and gender, when white is the race and male is the gender, is a privilege, a societal and an academic advantage. On one hand, it needs to be remembered that privilege flows from systemic power structures, not merely from individual acts. In his discussion of gender privilege, Harry Brod notes, 'We need to be clear that there is no such thing as giving up one's privilege to be "outside" the system. One is always *in* the system. The only question is whether one is part of the system in a way which challenges or strengthens the status quo' (1989: 280). On the other hand, it should also be recognized that my two friends chose to actively strengthen the status quo. Both initially failed to see, among other things, how they were an active part of a racist and sexist system. In both cases, the invisibility of privilege had profound ontological, epistemological and methodological implications. Yet, in both cases, their failure to see was challenged by my intervention; and in both cases, my colleagues made an active choice to reinforce the system of discrimination and privilege by underscoring the role of agency in maintaining these structures of power. To return to Bourdieu, the structures of privilege were reinforced not only by structuring structures but also by the structuration of practices.

It should be noted that because white male scholars often enjoy the privilege *and ability* of determining the worthiness of others, past attempts to open up multicultural space have been met with limited and contradictory success. As Richard Dyer warns, 'postmodern multiculturalism may have genuinely opened up a space for the voices of the other, challenging the authority of the white West, but it may also simultaneously function as a side-show for white people who look on with delight at all the differences that surround them' (1997: 3–4). By failing to trouble their own privileged subject positions, white males can appropriate postmodern multiculturalism to reinforce a liberal project that strengthens their positions of privilege. One way to address this, however, is to place white male privilege under a critical gaze. In her discussion of classroom conversations about whiteness, bell hooks notes that white students often react with anger and amazement at being placed under a critical ethnographic gaze. She writes, 'Often their rage erupts because they believe that all ways of looking that highlight difference subvert the liberal belief in a universal subjectivity (we are all just people) that they think will make racism disappear' (1992: 167). Though they regularly see others predominantly through racialized and gendered lenses, white males continually fail to view themselves the same way. Rather, they project themselves as being just people, which, as noted earlier, allows them to define the parameters of normality and speak for all of humanity while also acting as the gatekeepers at the boundaries they have helped construct.

Setting the agenda, while presuming innocence

Because they define the norm and can claim to speak for all people, white male IR scholars are able to set the agenda for what matters in world politics – in terms both of practice and acceptable objects of study. Imperial white males (and some females), in an attempt to govern their fractious empires, invented the field of anthropology. Similarly, political science and IR have been shaped by the needs of the dominant Anglo-American white males for the past century. This should be self-evident to anyone who closely follows the evolution of the discipline.

In a recent International Studies Association presidential address, it was argued that the discipline of IR 'makes very important assumptions about what constitutes violence and what kinds of deaths are relevant to explaining the world of international relations' (Smith 2004: 507). Those assumptions may not be very relevant to the lived experiences of most of the world's population. In order to illustrate this point, the speaker drew upon the UNDP *Human Development Report* for 2002, which 'makes for sober reading for anyone concerned with violence in international politics, except, of course, that the violence discussed there does not really fit within the international relations discipline's definition of international violence' (ibid.: 508). In fact, 'the discipline of International Relations does not "see" these forms of violence as core concerns [...] The problem is that the discipline of international relations has defined its core concerns in such a way as to exclude the most marked forms of violence in world politics, in favor of a relatively small subset which ultimately relies on the prior moves of separating the outside from the inside of a state, separating economics and politics, separating the public from the private, separating the "natural" from the "social" worlds, separating the female from the male, separating the moral from the practical, and separating causes and effects.' The speaker concluded by pointing out that 'the discipline's definition of violence looks very closely linked to the concerns of the white, rich, male world of the power elite' (ibid.: 509–10).

I feel this is a highly accurate description of the discipline; and in many ways, because this speech was by an established white male in the field, it was a surprising and refreshing moment of candour. At the same time, however, feminist and other outsiders have been making the exact same points for ages. It seemed that such critiques gain acceptability when offered by white male insiders, which illustrates yet another example of white male privilege within the discipline.

Of course, in the wake of this speech the needs and interests of a select group of white males continue to frame the agenda within IR, relegating other forms of violence such as disease, environmental degradation, rape, poverty, etc. as peripheral if not completely outside the mainstream. Interestingly, even as they help establish an acceptable agenda, white males benefit from a presumption of innocence. Yet this is a further manifestation of privilege. In larger Western society, when something goes wrong, white males are not immediately assumed to be the probable cause of the problem. With regard to the field of IR, this form of privilege is reflected in the assumption that IR is merely reflecting the world, not constructing it. As IR scholars, many of us ignore the fact that our theories, the content of those theories, or policies drawn from those theories have supported certain social forces and work to aid certain sides on major ethical and political questions.

The claim is made that we merely reflect the world as it is, while denying our often active role in helping to make the world we live in. This claim is continually reasserted even though there have been many voices within the field proclaiming the absurdity of such a position. Within American political science, the connections between theory and practice are often open for all to see. Simply put, IR scholars have been complicit in the constitution of the world of international relations. Or more baldly, white male IR scholars remain complicit in the constitution of the world of international relations; but their position of privilege frequently allows them to presume their own innocence. Even self-proclaimed critical theorists who reject dominant IR discourses tend to simultaneously rearticulate and retrench masculinist and racial discourses and practices; thus, they re-establish a new dominance within the discipline.

Faith in existing authority and power structures

The privileging of white male needs and interests at the head of Western IR's agenda is not surprising, given the power structures that produce such positions of privilege. One important by-product of this privilege is a pronounced faith held by many white males in existing authority and power structures. In some ways, this faith is understandable given that so many privileges flow from existing power structures (see Cohn 1987). As Wildman and Davis note, 'members of the privileged group gain many benefits by their affiliation with the dominant side of the power system. This affiliation with power is not identified as such; often it may be transformed into and presented as individual merit. Legacy admissions at elite colleges and professional schools are perceived to be merit-based, when this process of identification with power and transmutation into qualifications occurs. Achievements by members of the privileged groups are viewed as the result of individual effort, rather than privilege' (1996: 14–15).

At the professional level, white males in Western IR benefit from the structural effects of racism and sexism to gain access to highly valued graduate programmes, foundations and professional associations. How many hiring and tenure decisions have been based on a candidate's academic pedigree or socio-economic class? The connections between opportunities in higher education and race, gender and class are well established and cannot be considered revelatory. Yet I would suggest that most white males in IR remain unreflective of their educational and social privileges, preferring instead to maintain the myth of individual merit. This is not to discount their hard work and accomplishments, but it requires supreme and wilful ignorance to pretend that there is a race-, gender- and class-neutral playing field within academia.

I suspect, however, that many white males will deny such academic privileges. This is often because privilege is not distributed equally and whom we compare ourselves to in social categories often functions to obscure the experience of *being* privileged but not *feeling* privileged. For example, comparing me to white males from higher socio-economic classes makes me feel non-privileged, underprivileged or even mistakenly oppressed. When I compare myself to certain white males, I see how their pedigree has been shaped by their higher social class: attending elite boarding schools and enrolling in competitive undergraduate institutions that greatly increase their chance to get into the top-ranked graduate school programmes that are beyond my reach. Thus, by setting up my comparisons according to whom I am measuring myself against, I do not feel especially privileged at all. But that obscures the very real and significant ways in which I am privileged in this system.

Moving beyond the personal/professional level, white males in IR also exhibit a remarkable degree of faith in existing structures of power within world politics. This is not to suggest that many white males are not critical of existing authorities and institutions. Upon close reading, most white males in the discipline and practice of IR display a degree of faith in the established rules of the game and existing power structures. For example, some may be critical of the Bush administration, but still maintain faith in the righteousness of American power. Others might be critical of the United States in general but are reluctant to cast aspersions on the larger international political and economic order. This largely is the result of all that has preceded in this chapter: as the privileged subject position, white males define what is normal, set the agenda, judge others by their own standards, and believe themselves to be worthy innocents in this world they create. Many white males have been socialized to believe their own myth of whites and males as good, superior, benign and non-threatening.

Towards a conclusion

With an eye on the IR field's continuing obsession with security and terror, I want to offer bell hooks's personal reflection about *whiteness as terror*. Growing up in the United States, hooks recalls that 'black folks associated whiteness with the terrible, the terrifying, the terrorizing. White people were regarded as terrorists, especially those who dared to enter that segregated space of blackness ... They terrorized by economic exploitation ... I learned as a child that to be "safe," it was important to recognize the power of whiteness, even to fear it, and to avoid encounter ... All black people in the United States, irrespective of their class status or politics, live with the possibility that they will be terrorized by whiteness' (1992: 170). I have no doubt that many white males in IR will deny the relevance of hooks's observations for conversations about terror and security, because they sharply and violently cut across the grain of their own narratives. I have no doubt, because I have experienced so much anxiety and resistance from white males in IR when I raise such concerns in an explicit attempt to make them face the ways in which white male privilege works in IR. But I take that heat as the by-product of the energy needed to actively deny and hide what I am trying to illuminate and investigate here.

Having shared earlier drafts of this chapter and presented them at academic conferences, I am aware that I am able to write this chapter because of my position of privilege. Being a white male often allows me to slip in and out of conversations about race, gender and hegemony without being questioned about my loyalty. I can speak up about racism and sexism without being seen as self-serving. Rather, I can position myself as being altruistic and bask in the praise my position generates. On one occasion, a commentator noted that, if I were a woman, this chapter would have come across as a flailing, man-bashing screed. An insightful intervention, to be sure, and one to which I still do not have an adequate response.

I seriously seize the task before me. In a time when we are witnessing the fierce protection of white male privilege from minority encroachments, I believe white males have a sober responsibility to support moves for social justice, not just globally but in our academic backyard. As R. W. Connell notes, 'men (often specific groups of men) control most of the resources required to implement women's claims for justice. Men and boys are thus in significant ways gatekeepers for gender equality' (2005: 1802). The same applies to whites on the issue of race equality. Rather than it being a utopian ideal, there is strong evidence that many men around the world are engaged in gender reforms, for both selfless and selfish reasons (see ibid.: 1817–21). As Connell notes, 'What is needed now is a widespread sense of agency among men, a sense that this transformation is something they can actually share in as a practical proposition' (ibid.: 1818). Reviewing the fifth anniversary of the 1995 Beijing Conference on Women, the United Nations General Assembly stated that 'men must involve themselves and take joint responsibility with women for the promotion of gender equality' (United Nations 2001: para. 6). For white males involved in the study and practice of IR, asking the 'man question' means exposing systems of discrimination and privilege, challenging our own agency in supporting that status quo, and finding ways of changing them.

Notes

* In addition to Jane Parpart and Marysia Zalewski, I would like to thank Donna Albro, Terrell Carver, Cristina Masters, Richard Salter and Jutta Weldes for their valuable feedback on earlier drafts of this work.

1 It is unfortunately outside the realm of this chapter; but given

the emerging Asian powers (China, Japan, India, etc.) and the sustained post-colonial interventions, one should take seriously the implications that a more global perspective on IR would entail, both for the discipline and white male privilege. I would suggest that the anxiety generated by these 'challengers' to North American/western European hegemony (with regards to both policymakers and scholars) is linked in significant ways to race and gender.

2 I recognize at the outset several problematic elements of this polemical intervention. Addressing racism and sexism simultaneously, as I do in this chapter, is highly problematic because it can present the illusion that all patterns of domination are the same and that manifestations of privilege are likewise interchangeable – particularly regarding other forms of domination not explored explicitly here, such as classism or heterosexism. I also fear that the chapter runs the risk of diverting attention from racism, sexism and their effects, making white males the centre of attention once again (see the joke that opened the first volume in Zalewski 1998: 1). I can only ask the reader to be forgiving.

3 Doing so, moreover, would be doubly illuminating since 'white' and 'male' are social constructions and the four examples mentioned would provide very different understandings of how discourses of masculinity and whiteness have been historically constructed and performed. For instance, Marx was Jewish, and so not generally regarded as 'white' by the standards of his own European culture.

4 There are, of course, a few exceptions. An excellent example is Michael Schatzberg's *Political Legitimacy in Middle Africa* (2001).

5 While I find much of value in their work, I am not suggesting that Inayatullah and Blaney are exemplars of a feminist intervention – far from it, given the active marginalization of gender in this work.

References

Ackerly, B., M. Stern and J. True (2006) *Feminist Methodologies for International Relations*, Cambridge: Cambridge University Press.

Adkins, L. and B. Skeggs (eds) (2005) *Feminism after Bourdieu: International Perspectives*, London: Blackwell.

Bourdieu, P. (1984) *Distinction: A Social Critique of the Judgment of Taste* (trans. Richard Nice), Cambridge, MA: Harvard University Press.

— (1990) *The Logic of Practice* (trans. Richard Nice), Stanford, CA: Stanford University Press.

— (1998) *La Domination Masculine*, Paris: Seuil.

Brod, H. (1989) 'Work clothes and leisure suits: the class basis and bias of the men's movement', in M. Kimmel and M. A. Messner (eds), *Men's Lives*, New York: Macmillan.

Cohn, Carol (1987) 'Sex and death in the rational world of defense intellectuals', *Signs*, 12(4): 687–718.

Connell, R. W. (2002) 'Long and winding road: an outsider's view of US masculinity and feminism', in J. Kegan Gardiner (ed.),

Masculinity Studies and Feminist Theory: New Directions, New York: Columbia University Press.

— (2005) 'Change among the gatekeepers: men, masculinities, and gender equality in the global arena', *Signs*, 30(3): 1801–25.

Dalton, H. (1995) *Racial Healing*, New York: Doubleday.

De Beauvoir, S. (1952) *The Second Sex*, New York: Knopf.

Dunn, K. C. (2001) 'MadLib #32: the (blank) African state: rethinking the sovereign state in international relations theory', in K. Dunn and T. Shaw (eds), *Africa's Challenge to International Relations Theory*, London: Macmillan.

Dyer, R. (1997) *White*, London and New York: Routledge.

Elliott, A. (1999) *The Blackwell Reader in Contemporary Social Theory*, Oxford: Blackwell.

Eng, D. L. and D. Kazanjiian (2002) *Loss: The Politics of Mourning*, Berkeley: University of California Press.

Ferguson, K. E. (1993) *The Man Question: Visions of Subjectivity in Feminist Theory*, Berkeley: University of California Press.

Halberstam, J. (2002) 'The good, the bad, and the ugly: man, women, and masculinity,' in J. Kegan Gardiner (ed.), *Masculinity Studies and Feminist Theory: New Directions*, New York: Columbia University Press.

hooks, b. (1989) *Talking Back: Thinking Feminist, Thinking Black*, Boston, MA: South End Press.

— (1992) *Black Looks: Race and Representation*, Boston, MA: South End Press.

Hooper, C. (2000) *Manly States:*

Masculinities, International Relations and Gender Politics, New York: Columbia University Press.

Inayatullah, N. and D. L. Blaney (2004) *International Relations and the Problem of Difference*, London and New York: Routledge.

Jensen, R. (2005) 'White privilege shapes the US', in P. S. Rothenberg (ed.), *White Privilege: Essential Readings on the Other Side of Racism*, 2nd edition, New York: Worth Publishers, pp. 115–18.

Johnson, A. G. (2001) *Privilege, Power and Difference*, Mountain View, CA: Mayfield Publishing.

Lindqvist, S. (1992) *Exterminate All the Brutes*, New York: New Press.

Lovell, T. (2000) 'Thinking feminism with and against Bourdieu', in B. Fowler (ed.), *Reading Bourdieu on Society and Culture*, Oxford: Blackwell.

McClintock, A. (1995) *Imperial Leather: Race, Gender and Sexuality in the Colonial Contest*, London: Routledge.

McIntosh, P. (2005) 'White privilege: unpacking the invisible knapsack', in P. S. Rothenberg (ed) *White Privilege: Essential Readings on the Other Side of Racism*, 2nd edn, New York: Worth Publishers, pp. 109–13.

Morrison, T. (1997) 'The official story: dead man golfing', in T. Morrison and C. Brodsky Lacour (eds), *Birth of a Nation'hood*, New York: Pantheon Books.

Oren, I. (2002) *Our Enemies and US: America's Rivalries and the Making of Political Science*, Ithaca, NY: Cornell University Press.

Rothenberg, P. S. (ed.) (2005) *White Privilege: Essential Readings on the*

Other Side of Racism, 2nd edition, New York: Worth Publishers.

Schatzberg, M. (2001) *Political Legitimacy in Middle Africa: Father, Family, Food*, Bloomington: Indiana University Press.

Smith, S. (2004) 'Singing our world into existence: international relations theory and September 11', *International Studies Quarterly*, 48(3): 499–515.

Tickner, J. A. (1988) 'Hans Morgenthau's principles of political realism: a feminist reformulation', *Millennium*, 17(3): 429–40.

Todorov, T. (1984) *The Conquest of America: The Question of the Other*, New York: Harper and Row.

United Nations (2001) *Beijing Declaration and Platform for Action, with the Beijing +5 Political Declaration and Outcome Document*, New York: Deptartment of Public Information, United Nations.

Wildman, S. M. with A. D. Davis (1996) 'Making systems of privilege visible', in Wildman (ed.), *Privilege Revealed: How Invisible Preferences Undermine America*, New York: New York University Press.

Wise, T. (2005) 'Membership has its privileges: thoughts on acknowledging and challenging whiteness', in P. S. Rothenberg (ed.), *White Privilege: Essential Readings on the Other Side of Racism*, 2nd edition, New York: Worth Publishers.

Zalewski, M. (1998) 'Introduction: from the "woman" question to the "man" question in international relations', in M. Zalewski and J. Parpart (eds), *The 'Man' Question in International Relations*, Boulder, CO: Westview Press.

Zalewski, M. and J. Parpart (eds) (1998) *The 'Man' Question in International Relations*, Boulder, CO: Westview Press.

Mending the Helicopter

I'm too busy mending the helicopter
To wash up yesterday's dishes.

I'm too busy mending the helicopter
To pick up the kids from school.

I'm too busy mending the helicopter
To talk to your doctor about my cigarettes.

I'm too busy mending the helicopter
I'll have to work through the night with arc lights.

Who do you think I'm mending this helicopter *for*?

Reply
I've already mended the helicopter
Leave those rotorblade sprockets alone.

I've already mended the helicopter
While you were watching *Apocalypse Now*

I've already mended the helicopter
It needed mending. Radar was a terrible mess.

I've already mended the helicopter
Why are you out there at night on the lawn

Taking the whole thing to bits?

Robert Crawford (2004)

THREE | The machine in the man

TERRELL CARVER

Metaphors, masculinities, militaries

What are little boys made of? The nursery rhyme metaphor-pastiche ('slugs and snails and puppy dogs' tails') is not that far off the mark. In this chapter I ask 'the man question' in a feminist frame, not so much about individual 'peacetime' experience as about the larger structures of war and peace, and in particular the paradigmatic concepts of 'civilization' and 'barbarism' through which this (often rather tenuous) distinction is asserted and defended in international politics. The feminist frame raises the issue of gender; 'woman' is the marker that usually makes it visible. 'The woman question' was historically a man's question, a response to feminist activism framed by a masculinist point of view (Lopes and Roth 2000). It was in that context that eventually feminists won, in some places, something like woman's right to speak, although there are relatively few men with any interest in listening seriously. In 'a man's world' – i.e. one in which men own and control the vast majority of resources, compared with women – relatively few have incentives to do so (Seager 2005; see also Dunn, this volume). 'The man question' is perhaps gaining ground as a feminist question, asked by women, and sometimes by men, though inevitably with different issues and goals in mind.

'The man question' in this chapter is posed to make men and masculinity problematic. It presupposes an understanding of masculinity as operating in two important ways. The first is through an apparently de-gendered (yet covertly gendered masculine) concept of 'man' as a generic or normal human individual, an abstract person or citizen, prior to an identification as one sex or the other (see Dunn, this volume). Moreover, this abstraction is itself always a marker for exclusions and subordinations within the hu-'man', not least that of women, but also of further abjects denoted by sexuality, race, class, ability, religion, language and other supposed signs of 'difference' and 'less than human' status (Lloyd 2007). The second is through the operation of overtly gendered (yet selected and sanitized) concepts of 'man' as husband, father, brother, son, etc. – i.e. a good man and therefore masculine role model (Carver 1996, 2004a; see also Munn, Conway, and Whitworth, this volume).

While it is likely that masculinities across the globe operate in very similar ways, given the near-universal dominance of men in most societies and most respects, I concentrate here on modern 'Western' forms of masculinity which most readers will recognize – warrior-protector and rational-bureaucratic – themselves predicated on competitive hierarchies of exclusion beyond that of gender, notably 'race'/ethnicity, class and any number of other cultural markers of 'difference' and 'superiority'/'inferiority' (Hooper 2001; Connell 2002; Pease and Pringle 2002; Jones 2006). These 'Western' forms are of course predicated on the very exclusions and constructions (notably that of 'the Oriental' and other colonized and subaltern subjects) through which 'the West' constructed itself, and this point of view in turn is sometimes reflected in the views and subjectivities of 'non-Western' peoples themselves (Said 2003 [1978]; Spivak 1999). But at the same time these 'Western' forms are readily recognizable as the masculinities of contemporary globalization, where this is understood as a neocolonial exercise in economic and cultural transformation (often with attendant violence) through which vast areas and populations of the world are subjected, in an uneven way, to 'Westernization' and 'development', particularly that of capitalism as pursued in the 'neoliberal' project (Hooper 2001; Steger 2003; Barkawi 2006).

It takes more than simply naming a constitutive 'outside' or 'other' in *human* terms, however, to tell us what some categorical subsection of the species is like, namely 'the male', i.e. not female, and to tell us what masculinity is, i.e. not weakness, emotionality, irrationality, softness, inclusiveness, passivity, etc. – qualities typically associated with femininity. In practice masculinities are commonly delineated through what are obviously metaphors, as in the nursery rhyme and its visual equivalents, such as the 'Lion King', rather than entirely through human description and example, e.g. heroes, celebrities, leaders, etc., where descriptive accounts in literal language would seem to be the natural linguistic register. Descriptive categorizations themselves, however, depend on the literal/metaphorical trope, that is a supposed distinction between literal language which *reflects* 'the facts' and 'merely' metaphorical language which does not, or, worse, mystifies and confuses our perceptions. Post-structuralist theories of language use and meaning argue, convincingly, I think, that the supposed literal/metaphorical distinction is itself a trope or metaphor, so in essence all language is metaphorical

(Shapiro 1985/86). Animals and machines are particularly important in helping us do the further discursive work required to tell us 'what a man is', beyond merely pointing to human exemplars of warrior virtues and rational-bureaucratic success, since in practice this is a complicated concept requiring continual construction, all of which is metaphorical (see Masters, this volume). This occurs through any number of discursive claims and suggestions, textual and visual, 'scientific' and otherwise (for this methodology, see Carver 2004b *passim*; on animals and animal metaphors, see Davis 1999).

Both warrior-protector and rational-bureaucratic masculinities are deeply invested with animal metaphors, though not necessarily the same ones in the same way. Animal metaphors invoke 'the natural' as essential, defining, fixed, good and sanctioned by God as Creator or by Darwinian evolution – despite the anthropomorphism that should be glaringly obvious. Foxes are not really foxy, humans are; lions are not lion-like, humans idealize them in that way. For classical writers like Machiavelli (1988: ch. 18; Carver 2004b: 105–29) 'lion or fox' may have been an amusing trope, that is a colourful and memorable way of getting his point across, precisely because it is both metonymical and symbolic – foxes recognize traps, whereas lions cannot; lions can frighten away wolves, whereas foxes cannot; the wise and 'manly' prince should imitate both. For sociobiologists, however, the whole exercise is much more serious, in that the male sexual difference (from females[1] – not from each other's variations) is variously located in animal territoriality, brutal competition for choice of mate or harem (or possibly selection by a 'superior' female), or even on occasion heterosexual monogamy and attentive parenting (i.e. the overtly gendered roles as 'good' husbands and fathers through which normalized masculinities are selectively and symbolically constructed) (Carver 1996). But this is a case of choose your animal, and choose your moment. Rutting stags are always popular; emperor penguins are a current fad; male-birthing seahorses could well be next; and of course there will be considerable cultural variation within what seems a near-universal practice. While there are conventional associations in any culture between masculinity and some animal metaphors, and between femininity (as the supposed opposite) and other animals, the point is the way that metaphors are organized into a pastiche of supposed similarities on the one hand, and supposed opposites on the other, all of which are projected via linguistic ascription on to animals, and then read off them again as metaphor, hence meaning.

Animals, however, are not the only relevant trope. R. W. Connell (1995), in her foundational work *Masculinities*, takes up the metaphor of 'the body as machine' (see Masters, this volume). She does this when she discusses sociobiological accounts of gender that set up supposed facts of male and female difference, and in particular accounts of masculinity that link it with (supposed) hormonal difference and (allegedly) innate aggression: '[T]he power of this perspective lies in its metaphor of the body as machine. The body "functions" and "operates". Researchers discover biological "mechanisms" in behaviour. Brains are "hardwired" to produce masculinity; men are generically "programmed" for dominance; aggression is in our "biogram"' (ibid.: 48). Arguably one of the originating points for the machine metaphor is Hobbes's *Leviathan* (1996 [1651]).[2] The links between Hobbes's metaphors and masculinity on the one hand, and mechanisms on the other, have been noted in some detail by Christine di Stefano (1991) in her pioneering feminist work *Configurations of Masculinity*. Offering a 'reading of Hobbes', she writes:

> ... Hobbes's thought reflects and advances a distinctively modern mas-culinist orientation to the realm of social life. This reading of Hobbes by no means supersedes or replaces all others. Rather, it is offered as another interpretive angle on the work of a theorist who defies canoni-cal packaging along limited and mutually exclusive axes of interpreta-tion. (ibid.: 70)

In much the same spirit I wish to take this kind of reading farther and draw out exactly what this 'masculinist orientation' implies, using the mechanical and mechanistic metaphors that Hobbes employs in his materialistic approach to 'man', society and politics. In the end this will leave us the task of enquiring into the extent that Hobbes is right about modern states and modern masculinity, understood as the dominant forms – warrior-protector and rational-bureaucratic. Here, however, I take Hobbes on trust and pose this question: Does a mechanistic model of hegemonic masculinity produce a political world-machine? A politi-cal world-machine is one (as Masters argues in this volume) in which characteristic masculinities are remapped on to military technologies, creating a post-human subjectivity of destruction and subjugation to which human 'wetware' – i.e. bodies and minds – is a mere adjunct.

Di Stefano gets the discussion going:

> Those who would refute Hobbes by pointing out various features of human behavior or sensibility that are conducive to peaceful social

relations are taking the wrong tack, for these are never enough to
override the fundamental anarchy of social interaction. Hobbes's point
is not that human beings are especially evil or deliberately antisocial.
It is rather that we inevitably get in one another's way. As appetitive
machines that engage incessantly in the pursuit of pleasure and avoidance of pain, we cannot help 'bumping' into and thereby impeding the
'motion' of others. Totally impeded motion is what we commonly refer
to as death. (ibid.: 80)

Her conclusion is not that Hobbes's 'chronicle of the passions' is 'an
ugly portrait of human nature', but rather 'that it presents a view of desire,
motivation, and identity that is strictly *self*-originating and self-driven'
(ibid.: 80–81). I am arguing here that what can be added to this discussion
of modern warrior-protector and rational-bureaucratic masculinities is an
explicit and informative link back to Hobbes's foundational mechanistic
materialism and his extravagantly metaphorical concepts of automata,
particularly watches and clocks (Hobbes 1996 [1651]: Introduction). Di
Stefano rightly says that accounts of masculinity and identity suggest that
this is a masculinized and male-identified concept of selfhood: 'strict differentiation of self from others, identity conceived in exclusionary terms,
and perceived threats to an ego thus conceived which is vulnerable to
displacement or dissolution by an invader'. To which di Stefano opposes
a 'female material presence', one not only less strictly differentiated from
others but also open to the embodied multiple selves of pregnancy (di
Stefano 1991: 82–3). Hobbes's mushroom metaphor (in *De Cive*) suits
di Stefano's analysis well, in terms of drawing the contrast between
the masculinized concept of 'man' and the female/maternal contrast
in 'woman':

[Hobbes's] grand artifice consists of a clever recombination of the
given elements of the state of nature. These elements are 'natural'
males atomistically conceived along egoistic masculine lines. This
masculine tenor may be found initially in Hobbes's conception of
a self-possessed and discrete ego, one that is unassailable except in
combative terms, and is socially approachable only on the terms of
contracted and nominalist exchanges. It is an ego constituted in strict
either-or terms of total integrity unto itself or total disintegration at
the hands of a similarly constructed opposing ego. We can discern
modern masculinity at work in the fantasy pattern that underlies this
account: men magically sprung like mushrooms, unmothered and

unfathered. While such a fantasy deals a blow to parenthood and to the organic notion of generational continuity, it strikes especially hard at the maternal contribution, whose denial is uniquely remarkable and difficult to implement since it is so biologically and socially apparent (even to Hobbes). Hobbes's omniscient and self-sprung ego owes no dues to others except those that are freely and individually contracted. (ibid.: 88–9)

Intriguingly, many of the same concepts, and indeed similar metaphors, help to explicate both the mushroom and the watch, e.g. 'self-sprung' and 'self-generated movement'. It is easier, though, to see the components of a watch in a relationship with each other that is (metaphorically) 'calculating and instrumental', and certainly controlled by an overall regulatory system that stops the 'wheels and springs' from 'bumping' into each other (ibid.: 92). The mushroom cluster does not quite live up to this, however well it illustrates the (apparently) motherless quality of self-generation and (apparently) history-less appearance of individuals as interchangeable and uniform entities. Ultimately, as di Stefano says, we confront today the Hobbesian solution to the inevitable civil war of all against all that masculinized egos generate: 'narrowly calculating leaders' ruling social and political worlds (ibid.: 103). An honest look at (so-called) democratic governments will make us realize that the Locke/Hobbes contest concerning restrained or unlimited power, divided or singular sovereignty and accountable or absolute government has not gone as overwhelmingly in the Lockean direction as most people are led to believe, not least by governments themselves (Hobbes 1996 [1651]: ch. XIX; Locke 1988: ch. XIII). Di Stefano rightly concludes that insofar as we live in a world of 'self-sprung men', it is not surprising to find authorities who follow the Hobbesian model of sovereignty in imposing order on what would (so it seems) be an 'unredeemable anarchy' (di Stefano 1991: 103–4).

What does the Hobbesian exposition of this masculinized self have to tell us about modern warrior-protector and rational-bureaucratic masculinities? My hypothesis is that mechanics, mechanisms, automata and disciplinary uniformities all flow from Hobbes's central trope and his mechanistic metaphorical extravagances. Connell's historical account of a transition in masculinized labour from a working-class association between males and heavy machinery and a more recent re-masculinization (and de-feminization) of certain more skilled and highly remunerated

sedentary jobs, which have become iconically middle class and masculinized, takes off from the Hobbesian trope:

> The class process alters the familiar connection between masculinity
> and machinery. The new information technology requires much sed-
> entary keyboard work, which was initially classified as women's work
> (key-punch operators). The marketing of personal computers, however,
> has redefined some of this work as not working-class. These revised
> meanings are promoted in the text and graphics of computer maga-
> zines, in manufacturers' advertising that emphasises 'power' ... and in
> the booming industry of violent computer games. Middle-class male
> bodies, separated by an old class division from physical force, now
> find their powers spectacularly amplified in the man/machine systems
> (the gendered language is entirely appropriate) of modern cybernetics.
> (Connell 1995: 55–6)

While the metaphor 'road warrior' captures this nexus of technologized
masculinity in the corporate world,[3] the analysis that really puts this
together in the starkest, most Hobbesian terms is James der Derian's
work on the most obvious and most violent nexus between men and
machines, the modern military. The interchangeability between 'natural'
(i.e. masculinized humans) and 'artificial' components of a metaphorically mechanical, and therefore literally mechanistic, system or 'machine'
constitutes one of the main features of his analysis. That is, humans
not only tell machines what to do, but machines acting as super-sense
perceptors tell humans what to do ... and then they do it. Der Derian
discusses a variety of circumstances and incidents in which the 'machine'
view or analysis directs human thinking. He also notes that disaster
occurs (e.g. an Iranian Airbus was shot down from the USS *Vincennes*)
when truth (factual and moral) is defined as that which corresponds with
the machines' sensory apparatus and conceptual programming (i.e. what
is or is not a threat or target) (2001: 14).

Insofar as the military system is acting within itself to preserve the lives
of those who have opted for obedience to its singular internal sovereignty
(as it is in the military's portrayal of itself), then an orderly system of
command acts on the 'society' of obedient 'men' in the way that Hobbes
advised, namely it commands them and they obey. The last thing that a
military organization will tolerate is 'civil war' within, and indeed the first
thing that generates credible threats of martial justice is disobedience
to a sovereign command. Unsurprisingly, metaphors of cogs and wheels,

well-oiled machines and conservation-of-motion efficiencies represent and reinforce the disciplinary norms among the overt categorizations of functional and interchangeable parts that constitute 'the ranks'.[4] In volunteer armies the Hobbesian subjects of the sovereign have even got into that position through, as he says, 'pact or covenant', obliging them to (almost) unconditional obedience.[5]

It is another question how similar to, or different from, so-called civilian life this military-cybernetic model actually is. Armed forces have an investment in both hegemonic masculinities[6] (witness the struggles over women and gays in the military) and a distinction between themselves and 'civvies'. The former – ensuring that the military continues to exemplify an alpha-rated hegemonic masculinity – helps to secure the latter – ensuring that the military is paid and rewarded, resourced and unregulated in a manner commensurate with corporate cultures. Corporate cultures may look less alpha-masculine ... but only just. Hooper's persuasive analysis of the ways that representations of international warrior-protector masculinity help construct current images of rational-bureaucratic corporate masculinity illustrates precisely the point at issue.

> A contribution to the project of exploring the politics of masculinities is the mapping of Anglo-American hegemonic masculinity. The ideal types of citizen-warrior and bourgeois-rational man ... have proved useful guides to the various constructions of Anglo-American masculinities ... Indeed, they have matched so well the various representations of masculinity that have been discussed here that it seems clear that Anglo-American hegemonic masculinity is indeed largely made up of shifting combinations of elements from these particular ideal types. While the bourgeois-rational model may be in the ascendant, it is important not to underplay the influence of the others, which continue to provide an elitist element of contemporary constructions, even as the twenty-first century opens. (Hooper 2001: 221)

The Hobbesian world of automata, singular and material, neither 'natural' nor 'artificial' in any important sense, requiring regulations, barriers, apparatuses of rigid control, simply *is* the dominant metaphor of modern, 'rational', calculating hegemonic masculinity. As Carol Cohn (1987: 717) concludes, 'The dominant voice of militarized masculinity and decontextualized rationality speaks ... loudly in our culture.'

In practical terms machines are of course human creations and therefore invested with anthropomorphism. Rather than an anthropomorphism of faces, bodies and behaviours, though, the human qualities are rather more abstract ones: rationality, logic, economy, functionality, specialization, infallibility, consistency, value, reliability, interchangeability and, most importantly, freedom from emotion, personality and will. Aristotle cast human slaves in exactly this mode, and then fantasized self-moving automatons to do their work *in their way* (Aristotle 1996: 1253b; Carver 2004b: 46–7). For all its invocations of the 'human spirit' and paeans to romantic concepts of self-fulfilment (suitably filtered through marketized societies), liberal humanism is deeply invested with concepts that are exactly the opposite. If it were not so, then 'liberal' economics, which invokes interchangeable and coldly calculating individuals as the constituents of its founding concept – the 'consumer' – would never work. In this way rational-bureaucratic modern man is not so distant from the warrior-protector man of tradition, in that organized warfare and organized trade are not as conceptually, constitutively and practically distant as one is led to think. Indeed, in terms of the revolving doors between government officials (elected and non-elected) and the arms trade and so-called defence industries, combined with the technologized nature of contemporary 'civilized' warfare (as opposed to supposed 'terrorism'), it would seem that the two masculinities are effectively merged (Hooper 2001; Barkawi 2006: 18–24).

The terms of trade are not set magically by mutual advantage; they are set through the brutalities of military threat and armed intervention. Armies that we would recognize are machines, *and* they are economic systems, in that both instantiate logics, rationalities and interchangeabilities that give sense to the concepts of organization, system, achievement and power. The Roman army was a machine (it was not 'like a machine'); it just had human cogs and wheels alongside wooden ones. Modern militaries are not intrinsically different, nor are modern economic warriors behaving in any radically different way in their economic battlegrounds. The boys have somewhat different toys, but the idea is the same. Unfortunately the boys have not noticed that systematic organization makes them cogs in a machine much larger than their toy ones (or if they do, they only complain that the system makes them 'feel like' they are, and that the experience is 'inhuman'). It is, in truth, human, all too human. What else could it be?[7]

War and peace

Concepts of masculinity have functioned in a patriarchal context and have deeply structured human experience, not just as one half of a gender binary, but as the dominating 'half' in a steeply hierarchical ordering (Butler 1999). Feminists have identified 'woman as other' to this in terms of codes of inferiority, 'otherness' and any number of 'deviations' from the male norm. As well as some feminists, sociologists and others working on masculinities have identified masculinity historically with a sharp pyramid of domination and exclusion among men, usually based in war or warrior-like activity, sexual 'conquests' and in more recent times a commercial transposition of these 'battles' and values into the economic sphere. All these things famously 'sort out the men from the boys', where 'boys' here is a metaphor for those men whose masculinities fall below the 'alpha-male' version of success, whether in overtly military activity or the parallel world of economic activity, or even the world of sexual competition, wherein men rate each other in public ways such as celebrity and commonplace claims and ascriptions of superiority and inferiority (Elshtain 1993; Stiehm 1983; di Stefano 1991; Connell 1995; Hooper 2001).

Thus this masculinized outlook on 'civilization' presumes that human experience divides into peace and war, that the appropriate behaviour in each of the two is not very different, e.g. aggressive pursuit of self-interest, considerable effort in defending what has been obtained, a concomitant measure of paranoia about others, and the exercise of fully 'human' agency in terms of intelligence and physicality. The line between civilization and barbarism (or between lawful peace and criminal acts) thus lies in the creation of 'others', namely lawbreakers/barbarians, and the graded array of lesser (because more vulnerable) human beings, who need protection and are owed duties of care. A variety of animal metaphors are available to characterize the latter group of 'innocents', as they are classically termed, chiefly semi-domesticated herbivores, such as lambs.

It should be no surprise, then, that lambs go to slaughter (albeit 'humanely' in a regulated process). This mirrors the ambiguities that Kinsella has traced towards the weak and vulnerable in the practice of total war; namely, the legal and moral prohibitions on killing (the whole point of their being 'protected persons') are all too easily vanquished by realpolitik, because the doctrines and declarations (such as the 'laws of war' and the 'Geneva Conventions') themselves admit of 'exceptions' on these grounds of state necessity, *as judged by states themselves*. Since the boundary between combatants and non-combatants is so difficult and dangerous to operationalize, so the argument runs, then it is also not surprising that those who appear to be civilians/non-combatants/ innocents are regularly killed in the course of 'action'. Often the dead are defined after the fact as potential threats, or as victims of a kind of militarized accident (Kinsella 2004).

In the (supposedly) more modern context of total war, where mass weaponry is deployed with mass casualties, indiscriminately killing those in militarized roles *and* those in civilian ones (this distinction is the trickiest of all, given irregulars, guerrillas, partisans and the 'support-ing community'), the animating metaphor is still the machine, but no longer one that is capable of making and enforcing the fine distinctions that international lawyers and diplomats have had in mind (Kinsella 2006). The 'banality of evil' from within the bureaucratic/technological 'machine', the distancing effects of technology (pushing a button from high up in the sky) and the de-realization effects of virtual warfare (with computer-driven targeting and weapons systems) are all instances of this (Arendt 1963; Der Derian 2001). They are projections outward of our 'inner machine', which works by a ruthless logic, matching effects (mass destruction, rather than limited self-defence) to causes (mere possession of the weaponry and systems). Mere possession is a cause, because the ruthless logic of total war connects the 'need' to develop mass weaponry of ever greater destructive power with its use. Or to put it the other way round, the international successes in regulating weaponry have very largely come with technologies that are actually of little or limited utility, except in provoking emotional reactions and 'terror' in the 'other side' (e.g. 'biological' warfare).

My point here is that logic, willpower and (what's left of) emotion now merge into behaviour and decisions that are genuinely machine-like, in that they are reductionist, simplified, relentless, unstoppable, 'unconscious', repetitive, etc., albeit provided *ex post facto* with moral justifications and political rationalizations (such as 'collateral damage', or 'correct targeting'). Modern civilized 'warrior man' is thus a curious throwback to the 'frenzied barbarian' who represented the antithesis of civilization. The machine metaphor now licenses this behaviour, formerly attributed to (supposedly) wild animals, and the distinction between civilized warfare and 'barbarian frenzy' has largely collapsed. Or at least it has with respect to the USA (together with its 'coalition' partners in Iraq, now steadily shrinking in numbers and commitment), which is the major power for making war at present, given its disregard for the apparatus of international law and the 'public opinion' of the international community. Curiously the operative metaphor for US interventions is now 'surgery', as in 'surgical strike', although there is a huge gap between what happens (insofar as it is reported, or, perhaps more importantly, pictured) and anything that could count as surgery. What emerges from this discussion is that 'othering' as projection (whether as wild animals or killing machines – the very terms through which the 'fanaticism' of 'others' is typically 'understood') is exactly that ... 'we' in our human 'essential' identity didn't do those things.

This apparently contradictory outcome (why do we have prohibitions that admit to self-defined and self-judged exceptions?) is explicable because the (supposedly) unitary masculinized human individual is himself conflicted in two ways, conceptually and empirically. Empirically it is not the case that warrior males are made by nature; they are socially produced, and produced in infinite gradations and variety. Militarization is notable for its 'uniform' attempts to make warriors uniform, but this is of course a masquerade (literally!).[8] No military is a 'well-oiled machine', and military personnel are not identical cogs in a mechanism. These are productive metaphors, but as with all human production, the results are mixed. In this case there are empirical excesses over and beyond the concept. Conceptually the apparently unitary masculinized individual is even in theory inherently weak and vulnerable; it does not take much to wound a warrior, or to damage his technology (which is just as vulnerable and error prone as he is, metaphorical hype to the contrary) (see Whitworth and Masters, this volume). Even without being wounded, the masculinized human soldier (who could, of course, and in some senses, be a woman) is a complex consciousness with all the concepts of his weak and vulnerable 'others' well within the realm of his imagination, feeling and reality. Much the same applies in the commercial world, where legitimate and fraudulent practices share a realm of negotiation with agencies and institutions whose approach is anything but hard and fast, provided you exemplify the higher reaches of bureaucratic/commercial masculinities, and do not occupy the lower ones. In those, poverty, ascriptions of crime and other negative markers create *gradations* of esteem/disdain, rather than consolidations into unitary subjects whose activities fit self-evidently on one side of the line or the other (Evans 1993). Whether we consider presidential impeachments or pardons, or the victimization, plea-bargaining and 'narrow escapes' that characterize commercial scandals such as Enron, it is apparent that categories, even legalistic ones, are not binaries but rather gradations around a *supposed* binary.

In this way masculinity is a myth that defies examination, since it posits and maintains itself as unitary and powerful, whether this is the humane power of civilization or the inhumane power of the barbarian. Needless to say these are mutually opposed projections, not objective categories, i.e. it depends which side you are on whom you put into which camp. While there is every need to focus on disadvantaged 'others', who are the victims of outrages every moment (more the result these days of behaviour that is metaphorically machine-like than metaphorically animal-like, though the latter can happen, as in guerrilla or other forms of warfare or terrorism), it does not follow that the 'hu*man*' of civilization or barbarism is self-evident and immune to deconstruction. Because so many processes make this apparent unity visible in performance, and make the inner 'others' so impossible to conceptualize, the concept of projection is required to make this deconstruction work. It is very difficult and indeed almost oxymoronic to conceptualize the vulnerable warrior, the male (rape) victim, the female killer, the mother-murderer, etc. because these oxymorons defy the 'logic' of the binary and hierarchical concepts of gender through which human life is most commonly made intelligible (Zarkov 2001).

While the overall framing distinctions through which this discourse operates – civilization/barbarism, peacetime/wartime – can be read through gendered discourse to a certain extent (with the feminine on the side of civilization and peace, and the masculine on the side of barbarism and war), gendered discourse itself arises in much the same way as the (second) Creation story in Genesis posits 'man' and then derives 'woman' from him as a 'helpmeet' and (obvious) inferior and 'other'. This happens even before the Garden/Temptation/Fall parable of female weakness of will (allied to a curiously unexamined male weakness, only visible once female intrusion has disrupted the original projection of the Creator's image on to his male creation). Or to put the matter somewhat differently, and somewhat the other way round, a concept of unitary masculinity, unsullied by a significant gendered other, animates the civilization/barbarism distinction through which various gradations of 'otherness' and (supposed) inferiority become visible. The 'internal' projections from which these 'others' arise are in that way banished metaphorically from the being that contains the unitary masculine myth, which then does not invite examination. Rather the 'others' do, because they have been made problematic. This leads to a certain self-subverting emphasis on the weak and vulnerable in both the discourses of international politics and those of liberal democracy, because centring the weak (and feminized) leaves the strong (and masculinized) at the margins ... where they (the strong) lack visibility, look unproblematic and gain power over their 'others', including subordinated masculinities ascribed to men. As feminists have observed, women did not gain much power from becoming 'a problem' studied by men, and subjected to their therapies and interventions (Elshtain 1993).

These (supposed) distinctions of civilization/barbarism, vulnerable/invulnerable are not themselves produced by a gender distinction, and the gender distinction maps on to them rather uneasily, rather more because men are less consistently warriors than women are less consistently peaceful. Instead they are the foundation stones of a process of 'othering' via metaphorical projections, with which the metaphors that produce gender importantly intersect. The gender distinction, and in particular the 'natural' sex of woman (which marks her off from the unitary 'human' as a masculinized mythical figure), works to stabilize both the domestic and international orders (because they are interlinked via political doctrines of order in the heterosexual household projected outwards on to nation-states). That discursive strategy operates only within prior distinctions that determine the 'human', however, and these are derived from a myth of a unitary masculinized being, the 'man' in the human, the humane and the humanitarian.

Only after asking 'the man question' can all this be traced out, making the double-edged character of the institutional processes involved in 'protecting the innocent' visible: power grants you an exception to the rules that prohibit and enjoin. While this is somewhat clearer in the world of international realpolitik and the law of war than in the world of domestic justice and supposed equality before the law, it is true there as well (e.g. Richard M. Nixon was pardoned of any offence before he was ever charged). This does not mean that there is no point in the prohibitions and injunctions; there is. Rather than give up, we should be more awake to the power politics involved in institutionalizing those lines as vectors of enforcement, and be less mystified by ritual repetitions of 'equality before the law' and invocations of supposed conventions on 'civilized' war and declarations of human rights. Note the ease with which the USA made a mockery of all these during the recent Asian and Middle Eastern wars and Guantánamo Bay and other incarcerations. The supposed line between civilization and barbarism is but one of the mobile army of metaphors, through which 'civilized' humans do what they love best – fighting each other, whether with weapons or money, and then excusing the misery that results from this with moralized rationalizations that favour the rich and powerful (Nietzsche 1971: 46–7).

Conclusions

This framework of civilization/barbarism incorporates a myth of a unitary, unproblematic masculinized being – 'warrior man'/'economic man' – whose world is not in fact bifurcated by a war/peace distinction, but is rather *one* world of competitive, aggressive, self-interested and somewhat paranoid strategic interaction. While this masculinized being has an obvious relation to sex, gender and sexuality, it is curiously prior to the gender binary. Indeed, a projection from 'within' itself (of woman as an 'other') is the foundation of the gender binary as such, and of the heterosexualized understanding of sex and sexuality. As the foundational 'man' in the hu*man*, the hu*man*e and the hu*man*itarian, this figure is the source of the animal and machine projections through which human characteristics are given metaphorical reality in language, both as 'outward' projections through which 'othering' takes place (from which real 'others' are identified in graded categories) and as recursive re-projections through which the myth of the unified masculine being is itself animated.

There will be very little real protection for those who are really vulnerable in society (not always the same as those who have vulnerability ascribed to them), however they are defined and represented, unless and until this quintessential human subject is no longer mythologized as unitary and unproblematic. It is in fact constructed in the very ways that give the lie – through the peacetime/wartime and civilization/barbarism dichotomies – to the values of care and protection to which (some) humans aspire. The 'man' in the human, the humane and the humanitarian is the locus through which power-flows negate the moral categories (in declarations and conventions of rights and protections) that – far from being genuinely respected – are subverted by the destructive peace/war and civilization/barbarism dichotomization of human experience.

Notes

1. For an exemplary and thorough treatment of the quest for sexual difference, see Fausto-Sterling (2000).

2. The discussion of Hobbes below is adapted from Carver (2004b: 144–50).

3. See <www.globalroadwarrior. com> accessed 29 April 2007. See also Hutchings, this volume.

4. Carol Cohn draws attention to the connection between militarized masculinity and 'imagery that reverses sentient and nonsentient matter' (Cohn 1987).

5. The exception is a sovereign command to kill oneself or another (hence putting oneself in mortal danger).

6. The role of the military in constructing and reinforcing 'sexual citizenship' is detailed in Snyder (1999); see also Munn, Dunn, and Conway, this volume.

7. These lines of thinking are more fully developed in Carver (2006).

8. See the cover and content of Goldstein (2001).

References

Arendt, H. (1963) *Eichmann in Jerusalem: A Report on the Banality of Evil*, London: Faber & Faber.

Aristotle (1996) *The Politics and The Constitution of Athens*, trans. J. Barnes, ed. S. Everson, Cambridge: Cambridge University Press.

Barkawi, T. (2006) *Globalization and War*, Lanham, MD: Rowman & Littlefield.

Butler, J. (1999) *Gender Trouble: Feminism and the Subversion of Identity*, 2nd edn, New York: Routledge.

Carver, T. (1996) '"Public" man and the critique of masculinities', *Political Theory*, 24: 673–86.

— (2004a) 'War of the Worlds/ Invasion of the Body Snatchers', *International Affairs*, 80: 92–4.

— (2004b) *Men in Political Theory*, Manchester: Manchester University Press.

— (2006) 'Being a man', *Government and Opposition*, 41: 477–95.

Cohn, C. (1987) 'Sex and death in the rational world of defense intellectuals', *Signs*, 12: 687–718.

Connell, R. W. (1995) *Masculinities*, Cambridge: Polity Press.

— (2002) *Gender*, Cambridge: Polity Press.

Davis, M. (1999) *The Ecology of Fear: Los Angeles and the Imagination of Disaster*, London: Picador.

Der Derian, J. (2001) *Virtuous War: Mapping the Military-Industrial-Media-Entertainment Network*, Boulder, CO: Westview Press.

Di Stefano, C. (1991) *Configurations of Masculinity*, Ithaca, NY: Cornell University Press.

Elshtain, J. B. (1993) *Public Man/ Private Woman: Women in Social and Political Thought*, 2nd edn, Princeton, NJ: Princeton University Press.

Evans, D. T. (1993) *Sexual Citizenship: The Material Construction of Sexualities*, London: Routledge.

Fausto-Sterling, A. (2000) *Sexing the Body: Gender Politics and the Construction of Sexuality*, New York: Basic Books.

Goldstein, J. (2001) *War and Gender: How Gender Shapes the War System and Vice Versa*, New York: Cambridge University Press.

Hobbes, T. (1996) *Leviathan*, ed.

R. Tuck, rev. edn, Cambridge: Cambridge University Press.

Hooper, C. (2001) *Manly States: Masculinities, International Relations, and Gender Politics*, New York: Columbia University Press.

Kinsella, H. (2004) 'Securing the civilian: sex and gender in the laws of war', in M. Barnett and B. Duvall (eds), *Power and Global Governance*, Cambridge: Cambridge University Press.

— (2006) 'Gendering Grotius: sex and sex difference in the laws of war', *Political Theory*, 34(4): 161–91.

Jones, A. (ed.) (2006) *Men of the Global South: A Reader*, London: Zed Books.

Lloyd, M. (2007) 'Women's Human Rights', *Review of International Studies*, 33: 91–103.

Locke, J. (1988) *Two Treatises of Government*, ed. P. Laslett, Cambridge: Cambridge University Press.

Lopes, A. and G. Roth (2000) *Men's Feminism: August Bebel and the German Socialist Movement*, Amherst, NY: Humanity.

Machiavelli, N. (1988) *The Prince*, ed. Q. Skinner and R. Price, Cambridge: Cambridge University Press.

Nietzsche, F. (1971) *The Portable Nietzsche*, rev. edn, ed. and trans.

W. Kaufmann, London: Chatto & Windus.

Pease, B. and K. Pringle (eds) (2002) *A Man's World?: Changing Men's Practices in a Globalized World*, London: Zed Books.

Said, E. (2003 [1978]) *Orientalism: Western Conceptions of the Orient*, London: Penguin.

Seager, J. (2005) *The Atlas of Women in the World*, London: Earthscan.

Shapiro, M. (1985/86) 'Metaphor in the philosophy of the social sciences', *Culture & Critique*, 2: 191–214.

Snyder, R. C. (1999) *Citizen Soldiers and Manly Warriors*, Lanham, MD: Rowman & Littlefield.

Spivak, G. C. (1999) *A Critique of Postcolonial Reason: Toward a History of the Vanishing Present*, Cambridge, MA: Harvard University Press.

Steger, M. (2003) *Globalization: A Very Short Introduction*, Oxford: Oxford University Press.

Stiehm, J. (1983) *Women and War*, Dobbs Ferry, NY: Transnational.

Zarkov, D. (2001) 'The body of the other man: sexual violence and the construction of masculinity, sexuality, and ethnicity in Croatian media', in C. O. N. Moser and F. C. C. Clark (eds) *Victims, Perpetrators, or Actors? Gender, Armed Conflict, and Political Violence*, London: Zed Books.

FOUR | Bodies of technology and the politics of the flesh¹

CRISTINA MASTERS

The absence of bodies in the discourse of a discipline [IR] that was born of a concern with war, and hence violence against bodies, raises curiosity as to the conditions of possibility that enabled this absence. (Jabri 2006: 825)

Desiring cyborgs

In *Fact and Fantasy: The Body of Desire in the Age of Posthumanism*, Renée C. Hoogland argues that '[i]n the increasingly technologized age of posthumanism, bodily matters are, quite simply, too substantial to be left to the empirically inclined minds of natural scientists' (2002: 214); and therefore calls on cultural theorists to take up the weighty issue of bodily matters. Recent developments indicate, however, that bodily matters are coming more and more under the ambit of the 'strategic' and 'security'-inclined minds that populate military institutions and government administrative offices, which is perhaps far more troubling and disturbing in all of its potential and real implications. Indeed, in the post-9/11 context of the war on terror, one can scarcely overemphasize the dangerous possibilities signalled in this shift. Dangerous, in that bodily matters are being taken up by institutions primarily concerned with defence and security of the nation-state in an increasingly bio-political architecture of power.

For many this development is as it should be, with such matters taken up by the entity that we have authorized to act in our name and in our defence – the state.² Others, however, in particular critical theorists of international politics, have expressed grave concern over the deadly security practices at work in the US-led war on terror, including, to name a few, the war on Afghanistan and Iraq; and significantly, the new security measures concerning immigration and asylum; individual freedoms and liberties; search and seizure; and the power to indefinitely detain (see Dillon and Reid 2001; Edkins et al. 2004; Butler 2004; Dauphinee and Masters 2007). This concern, in part, has been critically motivated by

Michel Foucault's lectures at the Collège de France in 1975/76 (further developed by Agamben 1998), where he began the process of tracing the changing nature of sovereign power, specifically the shift to a form of power increasingly concerned with the living body/ies of the populace. For Foucault, sovereign power as bio-political signalled a significant rearticulation of the nature of the state's relation to those under its protection, namely an emergent focus on all the potential threats to the health of the population. Thus, he gestures towards the shift from the sovereign right over death – the nightwatchman – to the right over life – the bio-politician. In the words of Foucault, 'power is decreasingly the power of the right to take life, and increasingly the right to intervene to make live ... power begins to intervene mainly at this level in order to improve life by eliminating accidents, the random event, and deficiencies ...' (1997: 248). While this has translated into outwardly positive developments in the last fifty years in areas such as the welfare state, it has simultaneously rendered more worrying changes in the practices of state. The troubling effect of such changes is perhaps best captured in Foucault's (ibid.: ch. 1) contention that bio-political power signifies the inversion of Clausewitz's famous dictum from 'war as the continuation of politics by other means' to *politics as the continuation of war by other means*. Even though Foucault's inversion appears a subtle shift, the implications are significant, giving new meaning to our understanding(s) of politics and the practices of state outside the more obvious instances of war. Indeed, politics as war evokes a profoundly different set and sense of relationships of power; and these new configurations of power are what we, as critical scholars, need to heed closely.

The changes that are of consequence to this chapter are tied up in the current bio-political fetishization of technology evident in contemporary practices of war. Without a doubt, there are a number of critical issues at stake in thinking through advanced technology and war, such as legitimacy and indiscriminacy (see Beier 2006; Zehfuss 2007), but there are two issues of central concern that this chapter discusses. These concerns are driven by a feminist curiosity about questions of subjectivity and the attendant material effects of such articulations in the context of increasing militarism and war – specifically, a feminist curiosity about debates pertaining to the ethico-political possibilities of technology and the attendant claims that advanced technology is both liberatory and transgressive. To be sure, feminists, as much as militarists, have pointed to the virtues of advanced technology in addressing some of the pressing issues of our day, whether explicitly those of identity politics or of war. With regard to the latter, nowhere is this more apparent than in the US military, wherein technology has been lauded as the answer to the question of security, namely that of terrorism. As one proponent of technology's liberatory potential has argued:

> Today we are once again seeing renewed optimism that technology might yet provide relief from the nightmare of war. Recent scientific developments raise hopes that 21st century warfare – if not avoided altogether – might nevertheless be waged in a more humane manner. Much of this optimism is traceable to the Gulf War where the application of high technology seemed to minimize allied and Iraqi casualties alike. (Dunlop 1999: 24)

Feminists, such as Jean Bethke Elshtain (2003), have also linked advanced military technology to just war practices. Also, a number of feminists have advanced arguments in favour of technology's transgressive potential, both in terms of challenging the strictures of gendered regimes of power and with regard to women's participation in institutions such as the military (see, for example, Stiehm 1996; D'Amico and Weinstein 1999; D'Amico 1998; and Solario 2006).

Perhaps one of the most well-known feminist advocates of the transgressive potential of technology, Donna Haraway (1991, 1996), has critically engaged the possibilities of technology in enabling the subversion of binary structures of gendered knowledge. Haraway contends that advanced technology, captured in the figure of the cyborg, can fundamentally challenge traditional Western discourses grounded in dualisms as it effectively blurs distinctions between mind/body, self/other and man/woman by making apparent the social construction of unitary identity and ultimately revealing the multiplicity, contextuality and contingency of subjectivity (see also Halberstam 1998). At the same time, however, she has recognized '[t]he main trouble with cyborgs, of course, is that they are the illegitimate offspring of militarism and patriarchal capitalism ... But illegitimate offspring are often exceedingly unfaithful to their origins. Their fathers, after all, are inessential' (Haraway 1991: 151–2). Yet in this so-called technologized age of post-humanism it appears the problem persists, i.e. the figure of the cyborg remains rather *faithful* to its origins. So while the figure of the cyborg may provide new grounds upon which to reveal gender representations as contingent and historically grounded social constructs, at the same time we need to attend to the ways in which the figure of the cyborg continues to represent a desire for total control and domination.

While technology may hold emancipatory potential, this chapter begins with a feminist scepticism about the role of technology as constituted within the architecture of the US military. As such, it seeks to explore a dual question: *Is technology liberating us from the strictures of gendered regimes of knowledge and thus from the deadly politics of war?* In considering this question, it is necessary to explore the representative practices at work in the interface between man and machine in the military and the ethico-political implications therein. It does so by tracing the constitution of the cyborg solider in the US military through both techno-scientific and masculinist discourses of power. It will also think through the role 'dominant forms of masculinity play in legitimating violence' and 'what part ... gender play[s] in cultures of violence and institutions that use force' (Connell 2003: 257). The chapter thus explicitly works with the 'man' question as it seeks to explore how masculinity, and gender writ large, is being rearticulated within this particular context. Considering that feminists are fundamentally asking after power, critically engaging the constitution of the cyborg is essential.

To do so, however, requires technology to be read as a productive site of power/knowledge. This demands critical enquiry into how cyborg soldiers are constituted through military techno-scientific and masculinist discourses within bio-political architectures of power. Consequently, the chapter will explore the dangerous possibilities represented in the interface, wherein one such notable danger is the heightened and hyper-disembodiment and disembeddedness from the materiality of war. Thus, violently inscribed alien bodies appear as little more than blips on radar screens, infrared heat-sensor images, precision-guided targets, numbers and codes on computer screens, and enemy targets in virtual reality military training simulations. Certainly, the discursive dehumanization of the enemy-other is not a new phenomenon; but, as this chapter will argue, the cyborg further embeds these processes by leaving very little evidence of the enemy or, for that matter, any evidence of the other in the desired subject self. Significantly, this desire to transcend the organic body and construct the perfect subject is animated by bio-power's desire to attend to all the potential threats to the populace as a whole. This is especially troubling when such power claims that 'the death of the other, the death of the bad race, of the inferior race (or the degenerate, or the abnormal) is something that will make life in general healthier: healthier and purer' (Foucault 1997: 255).

This also calls for critical enquiry into the militarization of masculinity and into the discursive inscription of masculinity on to advanced military technologies by provoking a critical feminist enquiry into questions of subjectivity. The grafting of subjectivity on/into military technologies within the American military, as this chapter will argue, violently delimits the terrain of alternative possibilities, not least because these processes enable and constitute representations of an American self without the burden of responsibility. In the words of Judith Butler: 'it will be as important to think about how and to what end bodies are constructed as it will be to think about how and to what end bodies are *not* constructed and, further, to ask after how bodies which fail to materialize provide the necessary "outside," if not the necessary support, for the bodies which, in materializing the norm, qualify as bodies that matter' (1993: 16). Therefore, the driving concern of this chapter is that the more bodily matters are taken up by military and government institutions, the more bodies are disappeared and made absent. Navigating the ethical possibilities and implications of inscribing military technology with masculine subjectivity requires thinking through the processes by which the cyborg has been constituted as a legitimate political subject to the detriment of the living, laughing, loving body. It seeks to ask after the conditions that enable, and indeed demand, the absence of fleshy bodies in contemporary configurations of techno-war.

The interface: militarized masculinity and cyborg soldiers

> A cyborg is ... a hybrid of machine and organism, a creature of social reality as well as a creature of fiction. (Haraway 1991: 149)

At present, advanced technologies constitute an integral component of the American military apparatus and necessarily shape, inform and (re)produce military techno-scientific discourses.[3] As such, American soldiers have had to be (re)made to fit into, operate and function in this ostensibly new technological age; new times seem to require new soldiers for the job of defending the nation. Conversely, military discourses have given birth to what we have 'virtually' witnessed only in sci-fi novels, Hollywood productions and *Star Trek* episodes – the cyborg soldier. Neither old nor new, neither worldly nor out of this world, neither entirely man nor machine, the cyborg soldier represents the 'juncture of ideals, metals, chemicals, and people that makes weapons of computers and computers of weapons and soldiers' (Gray 1997: 8).

The making of humans into machines, however, is scarcely a new phenomenon. For instance, Michel Foucault argued in *Discipline and Punish* that by the eighteenth century the human body was already becoming a primary site of technological inscription. In his words:

> The human body was entering a machinery of power that explores it, breaks it down and rearranges it. A 'political anatomy', which was also a 'mechanics of power', was being born, it defined how one may have a hold over others' bodies, not only so that they may do what one wishes, but so they may operate as one wishes, with the techniques, the speed and the efficiency that one determines. (1977: 138)

This machinery of power signalled a profound shift from the coercive power of old to a new form of power as a productive force; a power that was not negative but rather positive in its constitutive strength. As disciplinary, power no longer operated as a simple external force on the body; rather, it was taken up by the body to produce a particular subject: in the prison, the model prisoner; and in the asylum, the insane, abnormal and deviant patient. As Foucault detailed, the military has been exemplar in this constitutive process where, through its disciplinary techniques, it came to produce the subject desired – the soldier. In approaching the human body as machine, boot-camp training exercises, drill sergeants and the barracks became the processes, figures and architecture by which the mechanical could be inserted into the biological to construct the practised and performative killing machine.

Without a doubt the human body continues to be a key site of technological grafting in the American military wherein '[t]oday the basic currency of war, the human body is the site of these modifications, whether it is of the wetware (the mind and hormones), the software (habits, skills, disciplines), or the hardware (the physical body)' (Gray 1997: 195–6). These arguments, however, do not fully capture the reconfiguration of the twenty-first-century cyborg soldier; and a few modifications are necessary to follow, complicate and contextualize contemporary reconfigurations of subjectivity within the American military. While historically humans could be and have been disciplined into fine-tuned fighting machines, they no longer seem able to meet the demands of sovereign power and its advanced bio-political technologies.[4] Instead, humans have implicitly been constituted through contemporary military techno-scientific discourses, as evident in the Revolution in Military Affairs (RMA), as having hit a developmental wall that seemingly cannot be surpassed.[5] The 'be all that you can be', the well-known motto of the US Army, is insufficient; no matter how much the mechanical is inserted into the biological, humans still need to respond to the mundane tasks and needs of the flesh.

This is evident in the ways human soldiers are cast more and more as vulnerable and sometimes troublesome problems in need of solutions. For instance, the growing number of soldiers living with post-traumatic stress disorder, which the military works hard to hide and deny, is narrated as part of the problem (see Whitworth, this volume); and implicitly, technology appears as the perfect solution since computers rarely get stressed out. In the context of cyborg desires, what is most significant is the reality that human soldiers meet death on the battlefield; and deaths are no longer acceptable in the eyes of the public. One can trace this to the post-Vietnam identity crisis of the American military and the US body politic. At large, this arose from the supposed failure of American soldiers to live up to representations of post-Second World War American hegemony – the dead, wounded and maimed American soldiers, images of whom were broadcast for all Americans to see, returned from the war in Vietnam belying the ubiquitous warrior myth. All the training and discipline of American soldiers, it appeared, could not conquer the Vietnamese enemy-other, and 'the fear of Vietnam functioned very much as castration anxiety for an emasculated American manhood that could only be soothed by an open and overwhelming display of prowess in the Gulf ... the war took place not with Iraq but with the self, with America itself' (Farmanfarmaian 1992: 112–13).

Thus, the Vietnam War, one could argue, exposed the vulnerability of the human body and, most importantly, the vulnerability of the human body as representative of American hegemony (see Boose 1993 for a more detailed discussion of America's identity crisis post-Vietnam). One thing seemed clear during the Gulf War: the American body politic would now only support wars that kept US soldiers out of harm's way. This 'making live' of American soldiers has been one of the critical driving forces behind the RMA and ultimately has served as a rationale for increasing technological superiority. It is not that high-tech weapons necessarily win more wars than low-tech weapons, but they *virtually* keep *our* soldiers safe. The contemporary technophilia (Stabile 1994) manifest in American military techno-scientific discourses represents the desire to win wars and, more importantly, the desire for absolute dominance. Integral to this is keeping soldiers safe. By constituting human soldiers within the remit of protection, the cyborg represents the changing nature of sovereign power, where power is increasingly centred on the right to 'make live' rather than on the right to 'make die'. In other words, it is to read the techno-scientific knowledge at work in creating the cyborg soldier as *simultaneously* the attempt to protect particular bodies – bodies that are now included within the realm of political protection – and the attempt to regulate against the very deficiencies made apparent in human soldiers with disciplinary technologies of power insufficient for creating the subject desired. As such, the constitution of the cyborg soldier signifies bio-politics in the very attempt to control mortality; indeed, power is emanating from the very capacity to 'make live' wherein death is no longer indicative of power. The reconstituted American prowess exemplified in the Gulf did not make the same mistake of constructing American identity embodied and represented in the white male *human body*. In its place, American military techno-scientific discourses have constructed a much more resilient subject, effectively circumventing the imperfections of the human body while simultaneously maintaining a close identification with masculine subjectivity.

Cast as unreliable and unruly, the human body in the age of technology is less and less, I would argue, the primary site of representational inscription in the military, with the triad more appropriately understood as such: the *hardware* has come to represent a whole range of advanced high-tech weapons; the *software* represents information and communication technologies; and the *wetware* represents the embodied human soldier and, significantly, the weakest link in the triad. Thus, what constituted the cyborg in its earlier manifestations, as explored and detailed by Foucault, namely the insertion of the mechanical into/on to the biological to enhance the biological through disciplinary *technes* (technologies/techniques) of power, no longer fully captures the shifts motivated by the current fetishization of advanced technology in the military. Alternatively, what we are witnessing and indeed participating in with the constitution of the cyborg soldier is, I would argue, a radical rearticulation of subjectivity. In this way contemporary military techno-scientific discourses have profoundly altered the subject of discursive power productions, with the fleshy body of the soldier no longer standing in as the agent of politics by other means or, in this case, war by other means. With the discursive positioning of military technologies as superior to the human soldier, machines are now the subject of the text (see also Beier 2006).

In response to this failure of human soldiers, twenty-first-century military techno-scientific discourses have reconstituted the soldier in such a way as to allay the susceptibility of the human body through the discursive construction of technology, not the male body, as the subject capable of the discursive transcendence of embodiment. High-tech weapon systems, state-of-the-art computer systems and information technology, artificial intelligence, complex virtual reality simulated training exercises, digitized battlefields, and so on, animate the current debate surrounding the RMA and form integral components of existing US military war doctrine. Command, control, communications, computers, intelligence, information and interoperability, certainly a stretch from the cold war days of C3I, inform, shape and constitute contemporary techno-scientific military discourses (Gray 1997). And advanced military technologies have now been constituted as superior in almost every way to the human male body. They are superior at information and intelligence gathering and remote sensing; and they are stronger, faster, more agile and have much more staying power. Indeed, the apparent effect has been the circumvention of the emotional and biological limitations of bio-bodies through the interface, wherein the insertion of the biological into the mechanical has ensured that techno-scientific discourses can discriminately pick and choose what does and does not get inserted into the mechanical by discursively breaking down the biological. Indeed, the cyborg soldier signifies the desire to acquire maximum, if not total, control precisely by escaping the imperfections of the human body. As Sara Cohen Shabot argues (2006: 226): 'Such a figure represents no less than the omnipotence of the *more-than-human*. It is a body which overcomes the *failures* and the *problems* of the *old* and the *obsolete* organic body.'

At the same time, the constitution and production of the cyborg soldier is rearticulating the ever-present relationship between techno-scientific discourses and masculinist discourses. Hierarchical dualisms, which have traditionally distinguished between masculinity and femininity, culture and nature, mind and body, superior and inferior, subject and object, objectivity and subjectivity, disembodied and embodied, strength and weakness, active and passive, and rational and irrational, have come to represent the distinction between cyborg and humanoid. As such, the characteristics traditionally inscribed on male bodies have been re-articulated by military techno-scientific discourses and remapped on to military technologies. So, while the cyborg soldier has blurred particular distinctions between machine and man, where *technology* embodies *masculinity*, the distinctions between the cyborg soldier and the traditional soldier have become discursively formalized along the lines of masculinity and femininity. The effect is that military technologies have been *techno-masculinized* while human soldiers, apart from technology, have been feminized and reconstituted within the realm of those needing protection.

Indeed, techno-militarized masculinity has come to symbolize the *model* American soldier represented in the machine–man interface through the reciprocal processes of technologies constituting soldiers and militarized masculinity constituting technology. In the American military, the normalization of the machine–man interface is evident in everyday interaction with advanced technology from weapons to computers, surveillance, reconnaissance, delivery systems, and from training simulations to real battle (see note 4). The interface is also significantly metaphorical, in the sense that it is clearly much more than *male* soldiers interfacing with technology. Rather, the interface represents the discursive *unhinging* of male subjectivity from the physical male body and the reinscription of male subjectivity on/into military technologies. Put differently, masculinity no longer need coincide with the bio-male body. 'It is not that the soldier is influenced by the weapons used; now he or she is (re)constructed and (re)programmed to fit integrally into the weapon *systems*' (Gray 1997: 195). The significant effect is that advanced technologies are now the subjects of discursive constructions, and as such they have become the key signifiers performing and representing American identity.

In many ways, the inscription of technology with masculine subjectivity is easily recognized in military techno-scientific discourses. Phallic-shaped missiles, precision-guided missiles that easily find the target (unlike their immature counterparts which needed to try again and again to find the target) and aerial bombings that leave one with the impression of an orgasmic ejaculation impregnating their target with death and destruction are only a few of the more obvious representations of the discursive inscription of masculine subjectivity on/into military technology. What is less obvious, but fundamentally crucial, is the discursive inscription of masculine intelligence (knowledge) on/into military technologies, particularly military technologies that are gendered in capabilities (computer and information technologies) instead of being overtly gendered in shape, size and overall appearance. 'At the heart of most dreams for absolute information, there is the ideal of pure intelligence.

It is a peculiar version of rationality that is masculine, mathematical, emotionless and instrumentalist' (ibid.: 70). While masculine subjectivity has historically represented the mastery of mind over body, rationality over irrationality, and intellect over emotion, inscribed on the white, heterosexual male body, the human male body has proven to be a serious liability to achieving superior or even absolute intelligence.

As such, the cyborg can be read as fundamentally post-human (see, for instance, Springer 1996; Hoogland 2002; and Shabot 2006), significantly representing a profound rearticulation of the political; in other words, the constitution of the cyborg soldier as a radical rearticulation of human subjectivity. This post-human subjectivity is represented through the cyborg in the very processes of transferring human reasoning and thinking from human subjects on to technology. The infusion of technology with the ability to reason and think, without being interrupted by emotions such as guilt or bodily limitations such as fatigue, is indicative of the constitution of the fleshy body as no longer capable of producing and projecting desired representations of the American self. This post-human subjectivity needs, however, to be read through Enlightenment humanist discourses, wherein the constitution of the cyborg soldier represents a nostalgia that coincides with the teleological trajectories of Cartesian and Kantian discourses – the separation of reason from emotion and mind from body – in other words, a libertarian technophilia (Gabilondo 1995: 431). As Shabot argues, the cyborg picks up on the Western epistemological desire to 'lose' the body (2006: 226).

Significantly, the constitution of the soldier as cyborg has also altered *who* is constituted as a soldier. Traditionally, the signifier *soldier* was confined to combatants; in other words, *soldiers* were men who actually engaged in physical battle. The fusion of technology and masculinity has significantly blurred this traditional distinction such that civilians can now be considered soldiers, and more specifically *cyborg* soldiers (see Armitage 2003). Military personnel who will likely never be in physical battle and who sit in front of computer screens have now been constituted as soldiers through the interface, effectively enlarging and reconfiguring the representations of soldiers. In the words of US colonel Ehrhard: 'It is the software engineer who kills now' (Beal 2000: 26). Cyborg soldiers, almost by definition, may never have to lay *human eyes* on their enemy again; the gaze will be that of the gunsight, the computer screen and global positioning satellite targeting systems. On the continuum of traditional discursive depersonalization and dehumanization, the cyborg soldier represents the extreme of abstract disembodiment in that the discipline traditionally required to remove oneself from the reality of war, if even possible, is no longer necessary. Indeed, the high-tech weapons of the cyborg, whether computers or stealth bombers, deepen and remystify the discursive processes of disembodiment. A mental image of an air fighter's bomb's-eye view during NATO's humanitarian intervention in Kosovo frighteningly captures this: 'Killing people does not go through your mind ... From the air, the human factor doesn't mean what it would in an army guy. When you're a fighter pilot, you don't see eyes. You see things – a building, a truck, a bridge, a dam. It's all so technological. I had no Serbian in mind ... I was shooting at a radar pulse' (Wallace 2000).

Considering this, what then are the ethico-political implications of this masculine desire to transcend the organic body by constructing the perfect technological subject? In the words of Claudia Springer (1998: 494):

> by escaping from its close identification with the male body, masculine subjectivity has been rearticulated, suggesting that there is an essential masculinity that transcends bodily presence ... What this reconfiguration of masculinity indicates is that patriarchy is more willing to dispense with human life than with [masculine] superiority.

To put it bluntly, it is life which is at stake when abstract disembodiment, made possible through masculine desires to transcend the body, has all but erased the very material realities inscribed in the interface. The first Gulf War, for instance, became 'the ultimate voyeurism: to see the target hit from the vantage point of the weapon. An inhuman perspective ... Seeing was split off from feeling; the visible was separated from the sense of pain and death. Through the long lens the enemy remained a faceless alien, his/her bodily existence derealized ... Perversely, war appeared as it really was' (Robins and Levidow 1995: 121). Far from minimizing the deadly effects of war, technology instead 'produces "a kind of isolation" from the violence of war that allows for its unrestrained prosecution ... removed from the bloody results of their decisions' (Gray 1997: 200). The effect is the rationalization of the disappearance of the body from war through the fundamental denial of the 'sentient physicality of human embodiment' (Gusterson 1998: 124).

The denial and suppression of embodiment is indicative of the inscription of military technology as the subject of techno-scientific masculinity and of human bodies, both soldier and civilian, as objects of power and knowledge. In other words, technology has become the surface upon which power has been inscribed, namely the power to write the world through violence and domination (Haraway 1991: 175). The transference of subjectivity on to technology has fundamentally grafted military technology with agency and power through the discursive reinscription of hegemonic techno-militarized masculinity as representative of machine. The cyborg soldier now plays a central role in constructing meaning with its primary language, violence, which has the power to generate meaning and knowledge about the bodies upon which it acts. The *other*, gendered, racialized and sexualized, is constituted as less human, as object, as different, as a code problem, and a danger in need of techno-scientific solutions. The language of the cyborg necessitates the denial of the body of the self so it can act upon the body of the other, effecting a distance and disassociation from the other in order to engage in practices of domination. The profound effect is the depoliticization and naturalization of the machine–man interface in order to legitimize practices of violence and dominance.

The affinity between machine and masculinity within the American military apparatus has been made to appear as a natural process deepening and reinforcing the split between mind and body, 'which effectively disembodies ethical deliberation' (Shildrick 1997: 116). Indeed, high-tech weapons are rationalized through bio-political discourses of protection and defence, which effectively deny the subjectivity of the other. In so doing, questions of responsibility to the other – the constitutive outside to the cyborg – are all but ignored and denied. As Chris Gray (1997: 103) argues: 'Technology not only becomes a shield for humans but in many ways it seems headed toward literally replacing human responsibility.' This is the essential, and deadly, paradox of the bio-power at work in the desire for the cyborg: the right to make live 'is actually the right to kill' (Foucault 1997: 240). It is, however, a right to kill without committing murder, because to constitute killing as murder would necessitate the recognition of life. Blips on radar screens, infrared images, precision-guided targets and numbers and codes on computer screens make certain that no *life*, that is politically qualified life, is present. The cyborg soldier, one could argue, represents the power to kill without committing murder by constituting the bodies upon which it acts as bare life: life neither worth saving nor worth sacrificing. In other words, it is life with no political value – *Homo sacer* (Agamben 1998: 139–40). It is to kill without the attendant responsibilities associated with such an act.

As such, the fleshy body is more and more cast as outside the realm of sovereign protection. Thereby, I would argue, bio-power is fundamentally a masculinist project in that it represents a masculine desire to overcome death by making obsolete a body that must die. Indeed, the cyborg represents the ultimate masculine fantasy: the cyborg as the colonization of the last vestige of feminine power, or *the power of giving life*, wherein the fetishization of technology signifies this very possibility. Constituted through the omnipotent masculine gaze of dominance, the cyborg can seemingly live for ever. The question that lingers is what exactly is the cyborg giving life to? What politics, if any, does it signify?

With the help of Hollywood, 70-inch plasma screens and 'crystal-clear video images of war-zone action' (Gill 2003: A14), we *watched* all the weaponry, gear and technology of the cyborg being set up in and around the borders, boundaries and bodies of Iraq for Operation Iraqi Freedom. Through our equally high-tech TVs in our living rooms, we *heard* that this war was about saving the Iraqi people from the weapons of mass destruction in Saddam Hussein's possession. We were *told* that this war was about peace, freedom, liberty and democracy; thus, it was a war for all humanity. This time it seemingly was not specifically about saving some people from other people; it was about saving us from all that Saddam Hussein was said to represent, especially his weapons of mass destruction. In the words of Foucault: 'killing takes place "in the name of life necessity"' (cited in Shapiro 2002). To this end 23,000 cyborg-guided bombs were dropped on Iraq, in comparison to the 9,500 dropped the first time around in Operation Desert Storm; and this time, they 'hit the buildings they were aimed at nearly 100 percent of the time' (Houlahan 2003). (One probably does not want to know how many targets were missed in Operation Desert Storm.) As well, with the help of global positioning system satellite signals instead of the topographic maps stored in the electronic brains of the Tomahawks in 1991, more than eight hundred cruise missiles were launched, in comparison to 333 launched in Gulf War I (ibid.). All in all, the number of smart, cyborg weapons used was twice that used in Kosovo and six times that used in the Gulf War of 1991 (Forbes 2003). Consider the following two images from the opening nights of the war:

> The surgical removal of a one-party police state while trying to leave the civilians and the infrastructure as untouched as possible is an operation of unusual difficulty. Yet the pictures from the opening nights of the war told the story: plumes of smoke from precision strikes on

Saddam's instruments of power while the city lights remained on and cars casually traversed the streets. (Krauthammer 2003)

The smoke rose above Baghdad in plumes of thick, black soot, carrying with it the ashes of a dying regime. The nights were full of fire and noise, as thousands of Tomahawk missiles and smart bombs crashed into their targets, sending up balloons of searing orange flame into the night sky. In the light of day, calm descended on the city's streets, and the silence was pierced only by the crackle of burning buildings and the wail of emergency vehicles. (Ratnesar 2003)

The cyborg soldier, it appears, has been constituted as the perfect witness, the perfect testimony, the perfect evidence, and the perfect alibi to war waged humanely.

To be sure, the story of the cyborg transmitted to us on our television screens, as evidenced in the passages above, is one of clean surgical precision, excising the metaphorical cancerous mass while leaving vital organs intact. From the vantage point of the cyborg, one is left with the impression that only a few buildings were destroyed; death has all but been silenced. While the techno-fetishism engendered by the cyborg narrative is certainly seductive and powerful, some critical but simple questions need to be raised – for instance: where are the people of Baghdad – indeed, the people of Iraq – in this narrative? Whom is the emergency vehicle, with its sirens wailing in the light of dawn, trying to reach? Who is in the car casually traversing the street? For whom were the city lights glowing in the dark of night? Whose ashes were mixed into the dark plumes of smoke that filled the night sky? Whose screams pierced the silence that followed precision-guided smart bombs? And significantly, are we not the least bit interested?

As J. Marshall Beier (2006: 268) argues: 'What we do not see, of course, is the perspective of the targets and of those who reside within.' In the American security desire to once again wage war on the bodies and terrain of Iraq, it appeared to be through the violent gaze of the cyborg that the bodies that mattered materialized, the body of the cyborg soldier and the cyborgs sitting on their sofas in front of their television screens; while the bodies that failed to materialize, or which disintegrated before our cyborg eyes, are bodies that apparently do not matter. As Michael Dillion (2003: 145) argues, 'power over life becomes allied with power over death in a complex convergence of sovereign geopolitics with global politics gone digital'. Technologized war has paradoxically rendered human bodies more vulnerable than ever before; and at the same time, war has become almost entirely devoid of human presence.

While some may argue this is changing, with growing dissent against the war in Iraq and disillusionment with an administration that has wilfully misled its people, this has not worked to diminish the effects of war and increasing militarism, in particular for the people of Iraq and Afghanistan, and also for many around the world subject to increasingly militarized security measures. We could argue that the cyborg soldier has not been effective in this more recent war on terror; but as Bonnie Mann (2006: 148) suggests: 'Maybe there is an aesthetics of war that displaces the need for good reasons altogether.'

Fleshy politics

Our machines are disturbingly lively, and we ourselves frighteningly inert. (Haraway 1991: 152)

Charles Sheperdson argues that the body is 'the impasse of our knowledge' (cited in Hoogland 2002: 214). In our contemporary context of the war on terror, where in the desire to overcome the fleshy body, signified in the constitution of the cyborg, the fleshy body has become the very bloody target of sovereign power, these words resonate. To answer the question of whether or not the cyborg represents a transgressive political subjectivity in an increasingly bio-political architecture of power, the answer is no, it cannot. And to answer the question of whether or not we have overcome the deadly politics of war in the age of technologized post-humanism, the answer must also be a resounding no. Current architectures of power have served to constitute subjectivity in such a way as to render the death of fleshy bodies as simultaneously necessary to, and absent from, politics. Put differently, fleshy bodies are central yet incidental to this new configuration of power.

Not only has the constitution of the cyborg soldier discursively flattened difference, multiplicity, contextuality and contingency, it has also rearticulated a masculine aesthetic of war that is even more violent (Mann 2006). The enduring problem, however, is that we cannot even see this; violence has been rendered invisible in the interface. We are not witness to complex realities and experiences; instead we are witness to a *virtual* reality that, more often than not, has very little association with lived fleshy realities. Did we see, for instance, the complex, multidimensional realities of the people of Iraq in the Gulf Wars? More specifically did we see anything at all through the masculine gaze of American military technology which indicated any life, any *other* bodies? In the techno-logized age of bio-political war, bodies are absent.

While the construction of the cyborg soldier has blurred some dis-tinctions, those distinctions have been extremely particular, primarily between masculinity and machine but not between masculine/feminine, self/other and mind/body. More importantly, the constitution of the cyborg has reconstituted and resolidified distinctions between masculin-ity and femininity, mind and body, and self and other. The cyborg soldier has not blurred the hierarchical binaries of dominance and control that inform American sovereign power; rather, it has served to reinforce them. So while the cyborg has been read as a possibility for resolving and/or dissolving gender and difference, this chapter has argued that the cyborg in fact is reworking, replaying and rewriting gender in significant and dangerous ways. In the words of Sara Shabot (2006: 226):

> By now, the danger that the hyper-sexualized cyborgs present to post-modern-feminist conceptualizations of subjectivity might be seen as obvious: reinforced stereotypes of masculinity and femininity leave the essentialist myths of *manhood* and *womanhood* untouched, and with them, they also leave unquestioned the roles that men and women *are due* to play in society (mostly technological domination and military control versus reproduction, respectively).

There is little transgressive potential to be found in the figure of the cyborg as it leaves intact and further embeds gender as a regime of power.

Without a doubt, cyborg desires are dominated by anxieties about threatened masculinity, indicating a deep crisis in the American rep-resentation of self in its attempt to construct an invulnerable subject position by ridding itself of the fleshy body. This desperate, anxious, fearful and violent attempt to make possible what can never be, the mastery of an American Self, has had profoundly violent effects on the fleshy bodies upon which American identity has been articulated and inscribed. In signalling a desire for total control, the cyborg soldier is eviscerating and erasing the messiness and excess that makes embodied experience potentially subversive. This chapter is an attempt to bring forth experience and embodiment through a challenge to the very figure that has all but replaced the fleshy body as the subject of politics. As Vivienne Jabri (2006: 823) argues: 'When war is spectacle, experience and its materiality in the body are somehow occluded for discourses that merely see the aesthetic in its technological rendition. Any discourse that brings forth experience and its embodiment comes to constitute a moment of resistance.' Thus, this chapter calls for a re-engagement with the fleshy body and is a call to take up the body as a critical site of 'embodiment in all its complexity and irreducibility' (Hoogland 2002: 214). It is to refuse a politics that denies the richness of difference by desiring a figure that attempts to overcome this through a form of power that fundamentally denies embodiment; as such, the cyborg can never be the figure of transgression. The challenge, then, is to radically *restyle* the subjects of ethics and responsibility (Jabri 1998). To do so demands a critical rethinking of the relationship between the fleshy body and politics and a call for a different politics, one that revels in embodied difference rather than a violent refusal of it.

Notes

1 For an earlier version of this chapter see Cristina Masters (2005), 'Bodies of technology: cyborg soldiers and militarized masculinities', *International Feminist Journal of Politics*, 7(1): 112–32.

2 See, for instance, the letter in support of the war on terror penned and signed shortly after 9/11 by many leading scholars in the field of international politics, 'What we are fighting for: a letter from America.' The letter can be found at <http://www.americanvalues.org/html/wwff.html>.

3 See Haraway (1991, 1996) for further discussion of techno-scientific discourses.

4 While this does suggest that at some point in the past soldiers have in fact been the desired subject, this isn't in fact the case. It is necessary to remember that representations are just that – representations – they are not mere reflections of reality. The significant difference is that representations matter in that they construct our claims to knowledge and it is these claims which need to be critically explored.

5 See, for instance, the US Department of Defense document *Military Transformation: A Strategic Approach* (Fall 2003); David S. Alberts and Richard E. Hayes, *Power to the Edge: Command and Control in the Information Age* (Department of Defense Command and Control Research Program, June 2003); and *A Network-centric Operations Case Study: US/UK Coalition Combat Operations during Operation Iraqi Freedom* (Department of Defense, Office of Force Transformation, 2 March 2005).

References

Agamben, G. (1998) *Homo Sacer: Sovereign Power and Bare Life*, trans. Daniel Heller-Roazen, Stanford, CA: Stanford University Press.

Alberts, D. S. and R. E. Hayes (2003)
*Power to the Edge: Command
and Control in the Information
Age*, US Department of Defense,
Command and Control Research
Program.

Armitage, J. (2003) 'Militarized
bodies: an introduction', *Body &
Society*, 9(4): 1–12.

Beal, C. (2000) 'Brave new world',
Jane's Defense Weekly, 9 February,
pp. 22–6.

Beier, J. M. (2006) 'Outsmarting
technologies: rhetoric, revolutions
in military affairs, and the social
depth of warfare', *International
Politics*, 43: 266–80.

Boose, L. E. (1993) 'Techno-
muscularity and the "boy eternal":
From quagmire to the Gulf', in
M. Cooke and A. Woollacott (eds),
Gendering War Talk, Princeton,
NJ: Princeton University Press,
pp. 67–106.

Butler, J. (1993) *Bodies that Matter:
On the Discursive Limits of 'Sex'*,
New York: Routledge.

— (2004) *Precarious Life: The Powers
of Mourning and Violence*, New
York: Verso.

Connell, R. W. (2003) 'Masculinities,
change, and conflict in global
society: thinking about the future
of men's studies', *Journal of Men's
Studies*, 11(3): 249–67.

D'Amico, F. (1998) 'Feminist perspec-
tives on women warriors', in L. A.
Lorentzen and J. Turpin (eds),
The Women and War Reader, New
York: New York University Press,
pp. 119–25.

D'Amico, F. and L. Weinstein (eds)
(1999) *Gender Camouflage: Women
and the US Military*, New York:
New York University Press.

Dauphinee, E. and C. Masters (eds)
(2007) *The Logics of Biopower and
the War on Terror: Living, Dying,
Surviving*, New York: Palgrave.

Dillon, M. (2003) 'Intelligence
incarnate: martial corporeality in
the digital age', *Body and Society*,
9(4): 123–43.

Dillon, M. and J. Reid (2001) 'Global
liberal governance: biopolitics,
security and war', *Millennium:
Journal of International Studies*,
30(1): 41–66.

Dunlop, C., Jr (1999) 'Technology: replacing moral life for the
nation's defenders', *Parameters:
US Army War College Quarterly*,
24(3): 24–53.

Edkins, J., V. Pin-Fat and M. Shapiro
(eds) (2004) *Sovereign Lives:
Power in Global Politics*, New York:
Routledge.

Elshtain, J. B. (2003) *Just War against
Terror: The Burden of American
Power in a Violent World*, New
York: Basic Books.

Farmanfarmaian, A. (1992) 'Did you
measure up? The role of race
and sexuality in the Gulf War', in
C. Peters (ed.), *Collateral Damage:
The New World Order at Home and
Abroad*, Boston, MA: South End
Press, pp. 111–38.

Forbes, M. (2003) '"Dumb" bombs
used to topple Saddam', *The
Age*, 3 June <http://theage.
com.au/cgibin/common/
popupPrintArticle.pl?path¼ /
articles/200306/03.shtml>,
accessed 5 August 2007.

Foucault, M. (1977) *Discipline and
Punish: The Birth of the Prison*,
trans. A. Sheridan, New York:
Vintage Books.

— (1997) *Society Must be Defended:*

Lectures at the Collège de France 1975–1976, trans. David Macey, New York: Picador.

Gabilondo, J. (1995) 'Postcolonial cyborgs: subjectivity in the age of cybernetic reproduction', in C. H. Gray (ed.), *The Cyborg Handbook*, New York: Routledge, pp. 423–32.

Gill, A. (2003) 'U.S. forces enlist Hollywood to build set for war briefings', *Globe & Mail*, 15 March, p. A14.

Gray, C. H. (1997) *Postmodern War: The New Politics of Conflict*, New York: Guilford Press.

Gusterson, H. (1998) *Nuclear Rites: A Weapons Laboratory at the End of the Cold War*, Berkeley: University of California Press.

Halberstam, J. (1998) 'Automating gender: postmodern feminism in the age of intelligent machine', in P. D. Hopkins (ed.), *Sex/Machine: Reading in Culture, Gender, and Technology*, Bloomington: Indiana University Press, pp. 468–83.

Hall, G. (2002) 'Para-site', in J. Zylinska (ed.), *The Cyborg Experiments: The Extensions of the Body in the Media Age*, New York: Continuum, pp. 131–46.

Haraway, D. (1991) *Simians, Cyborgs, and Women*, New York: Routledge.

— (1996) *Modest_Witness@Second_ Millennium. FemaleMan_Meets_ OncoMouseTM: Feminism and Technoscience*, New York: Routledge.

Hoogland, R. C. (2002) 'Fact and fantasy: the body of desire in the age of posthumanism', *Journal of Gender Studies*, 11(3): 213–31.

Houlahan, T. (2003) 'Analysis: strategic bombing in Iraq war', United Press International, 23 April, <www.agitprop.org.au/ nowar/ 20030423_houlahan_ bombing_analysis.html>, accessed, 5 August 2007.

Jabri, V. (1998) 'Restyling the subject of responsibility in International Relations', *Millennium: Journal of International Studies*, 27(3): 591–611.

— (2006) 'Shock and awe: power and the resistance of art', *Millennium: Journal of International Studies*, 34(3): 819–39.

Krauthammer, C. (2003) 'Gulf War II is first of its kind', *Townhall*, 15 March, <www.townhall.com/ columnists/charlesKrauthammer/ printck20030410.shml>, accessed 5 August 2007.

Mann, B. (2006) 'How America justifies its war: a modern/postmodern aesthetics of masculinity and sovereignty', *Hypatia*, 21(4): 147–63.

Ratnesar, R. (2003) 'Awestruck', *Time Magazine*, 31 March, <www. time.com/time/archive/preview/ from_cover>, accessed 5 August 2007.

Robins, K. and L. Levidow (1995) 'Socializing the cyborg self: the Gulf War and beyond', in C. H. Gray (ed.), *The Cyborg Handbook*, New York: Routledge, pp. 119–25.

Shabot, S. C. (2006) 'Grotesque bodies: a response to disembodied cyborgs', *Journal of Gender Studies*, 15(3): 223–35.

Shapiro, M. (2002) 'Wanted, dead or alive', *Theory & Event*, 5(4), <muse.jhu.edu/journals/theory_ and_event/v005/5.4shapiro.html>, accessed 5 August 2007.

Shildrick, M. (1997) *Leaky Bodies and Boundaries: Feminism, Postmod-*

ernism, and (Bio)Ethics, New York:
Routledge.

Solario, E. (2006) *Women in the Line of
Fire: What You Should Know about
Women in the Military*, Emeryville,
CA: Seal Press.

Springer, C. (1996) *Electronic Eros:
Bodies and Desire in the Post-
industrial Age*, Austin: University
of Texas Press.

— (1998) 'The pleasure of the
interface', in P. D. Hopkins (ed.),
*Sex/Machine: Reading in Culture,
Gender, and Technology*, Bloomington: Indiana University Press,
pp. 484–99.

Stabile, Carole A. (1994) *Feminism
and the Technological Fix*, Manchester: Manchester University
Press.

Steihm, J. H. (ed.) (1996) *It's Our
Military Too! Women and the
US Military*, Philadelphia, PA:
Temple University Press.

US Department of Defense (2003),
*Military Transformation: A Strate-
gic Approach*.

US Department of Defense, Office of
Force Transformation (2005), *A
Network-Centric Operations Case
Study: US/UK Coalition Combat
Operations during Operation Iraqi
Freedom*.

Wallace, B. (2000) 'Canadian aces of
Kosovo', *Maclean's*, 113(13), 22
March.

Zehfuss, M. (2007) 'Subjectivity and
vulnerability: on the war with
Iraq', *International Politics*, 44:
58–71.

How the Children were Born

Doctors and midwives were aghast.
There, embedded in each infant palm
was the barrel of a tiny gun.

Babies had always raged – but
could any child be born knowing,
and prepared for war?

Enmity was handed down
like an heirloom.
The guns grew with the babies,
poking like bone through the soft skin.

Moniza Alvi (2005)

FIVE | Militarized masculinity and Post-Traumatic Stress Disorder

SANDRA WHITWORTH

The prevalence of Post-Traumatic Stress Disorder (PTSD) among soldiers deployed in combat and peacekeeping missions has attracted increased attention in recent years. In Canada, retired major-general Romeo Dallaire drew public attention to the condition after his service with the UN as commander of the failed peacekeeping mission to Rwanda during the 1994 genocide (Dallaire 2003). In the United Kingdom, an estimated 10 per cent of troops airlifted out of Iraq between January and October 2003 primarily suffered from psychological trauma (Turner et al. 2005). In the United States, disability claims due to PTSD have skyrocketed, with some 34,000 veterans from Iraq and Afghanistan treated at Veteran Affairs facilities diagnosed with PTSD (Corbett 2007: 46). This has prompted some discussion in the Department of Veteran Affairs about revisiting the diagnostic criteria for assessing PTSD, with critics claiming the government is trying to find ways to limit the benefits that go to US veterans who have suffered emotional trauma (Vedantam 2005). One psychiatrist has recently claimed, by contrast, that the US Department of Veteran Affairs has allowed a 'culture of trauma' to blossom within its bureaucracy (Satel 2006).

These debates signal some of the questions that have been raised since psychiatric distress in combat was first haltingly recognized in the First World War: is it real and should soldiers who suffer from it be compensated, as they would be for physical injuries sustained during training or combat (Lerner 2003)? Many militaries have resisted, and continue to resist, claims of PTSD among soldiers; and many soldiers insist that acknowledging they are suffering from PTSD can result in shame, ostracization and demotion (Greene 2005). The argument of this chapter is that militaries resist PTSD for reasons more complex than simply avoiding compensation claims. PTSD tells us a series of stories about militarized masculinity; stories that those who support militaries and militarism would prefer we not think about too deeply.

Importantly, the stories that PTSD tells us about militarized masculinity are themselves complex. Feminist analyses of PTSD have already pointed to the way in which some of the first medical accounts of PTSD – reports of 'shell shock' in British soldiers after the First World War – treated it as a male form of female 'hysteria'. Both the condition itself and soldiers who became victims of it were dismissed and denigrated through being feminized. As Sandra Gilbert (1983: 447) writes, 'paradoxically ... the war to which so many men had gone in hope of becoming heroes, ended up emasculating them' (see also Showalter 1985; Whitworth 2004). Part of the argument of this chapter is that PTSD in men lays bare the fragile ground on which militarized masculinity is built; it provides a stark illustration of the illusion of stable gender identities and confirms the malleability of gender. Consequently, it is a story that most militaries are not keen to acknowledge.

But PTSD also signals another set of stories militaries are equally concerned to keep quiet. These stories emerge when we examine the incidence of PTSD among both female soldiers and soldiers of colour. Like their white male counterparts, female soldiers and marginalized men are sometimes reluctant to report PTSD; and all experience the same kinds of symptoms. This, however, is where the similarity seems to end. Research indicates that the majority of cases of PTSD in female soldiers result not from witnessing or participating in horrific events in a combat setting and the fear, pain and anxiety that result, but from sexual harassment and abuse experienced within a military setting (Fontana and Rosencheck 1998). Similarly, soldiers of colour report that their emotional pain is often directly related to their discovery that, once deployed on missions, they were tasked with the most dangerous duties and more often put at risk more than their white comrades.

Thus, differential rates of PTSD tell us a related set of stories about militarized masculinity. One concerns the sense of entitlement inculcated through military indoctrination and the other points to some of the effects associated with entitlement for specific groups.[1] These are the stories that usually remain invisible within official accounts of soldiering. Male soldiers who experience pain, fear or anxiety in the face of combat learn they have failed to live up to the military ethos of appropriate masculinity; soldiers of colour and female soldiers learn that their presence within the military has violated an unstated military ethos, one that does not fully recognize their presence in the first place. Whereas white soldiers discover through their emotions that they have not lived up to the norms of the warrior brotherhood, women and marginalized men discover they were never equal partners in the 'brotherhood' in the first place.

Making soldiers[2]

While some essentialist accounts of masculinity, violence and warfare suggest that young men have a natural affinity for the violence required in armed conflict, critics of essentialism point out that whatever natural instinct some men may have for violence is not nearly as widespread as believed. It is not the trustworthy instinct that most military decision-makers have felt they could count on to produce the type and quantity of warriors they require. The qualities demanded by militaries, such as the requisite lust for violence when needed and a corresponding willingness to subordinate oneself to hierarchy and authority when needed, must be self-consciously cultivated. Few new male recruits arrive as ready-made soldiers; and as Ehrenreich (1997: 10) notes, 'The difference between an ordinary man or boy and a reliable killer, as any drill sergeant could attest, is profound. A transformation is required.'

Historically, this transformation has been accomplished in different ways, sometimes through drinking wine or liquor or taking drugs and in other instances through social pressure or ceremonies designed to urge young men to fight. By the seventeenth century in Europe, as Ehrenreich (ibid.: 11–12) describes it, the process had become more organized:

> New recruits and even seasoned veterans were endlessly drilled, hour after hour, until each man began to feel himself part of a single, giant fighting machine. The drill was only partially inspired by the technology of firearms. It's easy enough to teach a man to shoot a gun: the problem is to make him willing to get into situations where guns are being shot and to remain there long enough to do some shooting of his own ... In the fanatical routines of boot camp, a man leaves behind his former identity and is reborn as a creature of the military – an automaton and also, ideally, a willing killer of other men.

The contemporary practices of boot camp are remarkably similar across most modern state militaries, and they involve the same sets of practices, whether focused on male or female recruits. It is a tightly choreographed process aimed at breaking down the individuality of the recruits, and replacing it with a commitment to and dependence upon the total institution of which they are now a part.[3]

As Christian Appy (1993: 88) describes 1970s-era US basic training:

'Every detail of life was prescribed, regulated, and enforced. Every moment was accounted for. There was a method and time for every action. Even using the bathroom was limited to short, specified times or required special permission ... Some men went for a full week before they were able to defecate in the time allotted.' By its end, recruits should conform to the official attitudes of military conduct, be able to follow orders instantly and without question, and commit themselves to the larger group (whether that is co-recruits, barrack, regiment, battalion, military or state) over any personal or individual commitments they previously held (Arkin and Dobrofsky 1978: 158).

New recruits are separated from families; undergo tests of physical endurance and sleep deprivation; and are forced to participate in numerous arbitrary, often mundane and apparently irrelevant tasks. All have similar shaved heads, wear identical uniforms, eat the same food, sleep in the same uncomfortable beds, must conform to the same expectations, and follow the same rules (Gill 1997: 15). They learn how to march in unison with one another, a task aimed entirely at teaching them that they are no longer individuals but members of a group.[4] As one male US Marine described it, 'They tore you down. They tore everything civilian out of your entire existence – your speech, your thoughts, your sights, your memory – anything that was civilian they tore out and then they re-built you and made you over' (Appy 1993: 86). The new soldier also faces the humiliation strategies common to most national militaries. Upon arrival, the new recruit might face a drill instructor who screams in his/her ear, 'You no good civilian maggot ... You're worthless, do you understand? And I'm gonna kill you' (ibid.).

The tactics used to humiliate and degrade the recruit will vary depending on the military. In some, physically brutalizing new recruits remains an acceptable strategy, whether by officers or more senior recruits. In other militaries where physical punishment in principle is prohibited, drill sergeants often have at their official disposal only the threat of violence and verbal assaults. Here, the new recruit is not only constantly reminded of his or her incompetence but faces a variety of gendered and raced insults crafted to play upon her or his specific feminine or masculine anxieties, including labels such as whore, faggot, sissy, cunt, ladies, abortion, pussy, nigger, Indian, and sometimes simply you woman (Gill 1997: 15; Davis 1997: 14; Appy 1993: 101). Linda Bird Francke (1997: 155-6) notes that the same techniques are also often used to train women. At Fort Jackson in the United States, a 1991 strategy was to shout at female recruits: 'You wuss, you baby, you goddamn female.' Reverse psychology, Francke notes, does not seem to work as a female instructor who yelled 'You boy!' at a straggler discovered, in the context of basic training, that it sounded more like a compliment than an insult.

It is not by coincidence that the insults most new recruits face are gendered, raced and homophobic; young soldiers are learning to deny, indeed to obliterate, the 'other' within the psyche. Difference can include race or ethnic differences. While it can include being a woman, it can also include simply having attended university or college (Appy 1993: 100). Soldiers must, in particular, deny all that is deemed to be feminine; and this is accomplished throughout the training process. The practice of shaving heads, for example, not only exposes the new recruit to the discipline and uniformity of military life but is aimed at 'removing the extra frills of longer hair often associated with individual vanity (vanity believed to be the prerogative of women)' (Arkin and Dobrofsky 1978: 159). The chants to which soldiers march, either denigrating women or linking their militarized masculinity to an aggressive and violent hetero-sexuality, are widely documented, including the call while holding one hand to rifle and the other to crotch: 'This is my rifle. This is my gun. This is for pleasure. This is for fun' (ibid.: 160).

The militaries' organization in highly explicit and aggressively gendered terms should come as no surprise. Militaries are involved, after all, in the making of a solidaristic group of soldiers; militaries have also long promised to 'make a man out of you' (ibid.: 154). Theorists of both militarism and of masculinity have pointed to the intimate connection between military organizations and hegemonic representations of masculinity. As David Morgan (1994: 165) writes:

> Of all the sites where masculinities are constructed, reproduced, and deployed, those associated with war and the military are some of the most direct. Despite far-reaching political, social, and technological changes, the warrior still seems to be a key symbol of masculinity. In statues, heroic paintings, comic books, and popular films the gendered connotations are inescapable. The stance, the facial expressions, and the weapons clearly connote aggression, courage, a capacity for vio-lence, and, sometimes, a willingness for sacrifice. The uniform absorbs individualities into a generalized and timeless masculinity while also connoting a control of emotion and a subordination to a larger ration-ality.

Thus, the myths of manhood into which the new soldier is inculcated throughout basic training are highly specific and privilege courage and endurance; physical and psychological strength; rationality; toughness; obedience; discipline; patriotism; lack of squeamishness; avoidance of certain emotions such as fear, sadness, uncertainty, guilt, remorse and grief; and heterosexual competency (Masters 2005: 115; Arkin and Dobrofsky 1978: 156). The information conveyed through the rituals of military initiation encodes a fundamental connection between masculinity, physical strength and violence, captured well by a 1990s US military recruiting poster which declared, 'Pain is Weakness Leaving the Body.' The hardened body of the soldier warrior is now a real or potential weapon (Hatty 2000: ch. 4). The new soldier is both physically and emotionally tough, portraying little emotion, with the possible exceptions of anger and aggression (Karner 1998: 215). The soldier learns to 'deny all that is feminine and soft in himself' (Goldstein 2001: 266). As American conservative George Gilder writes: 'When you want to create a solidaristic group of male killers that is what you do: you kill the woman in them' (cited in Francke 1997: 155). Anyone who departs from the ideal is neither man nor soldier.

At the same time, however, Charlotte Hooper (2001: 47–8) notes the way in which soldiering also involves many traditional feminine traits such as 'total obedience and submission to authority, the attention to dress detail, and the endless repetition of mundane tasks that enlisted men as opposed to officers are expected to perform'. But these activities are not emphasized in representations of soldiering, illustrating the way in which, for Hooper, 'it is not the actions themselves but the gendered interpretations placed on them that are crucial in determining which activities count as masculine and valued and which count as feminine and devalued'.

After working to break down new recruits, basic training continues and aims to slowly rebuild. While new recruits have been repeatedly told they are worthless alone, they soon learn that through the military, in concert with drill instructors and fellow soldiers, they can achieve almost any goal. The early litany of insults and complaints from superior officers is gradually replaced with occasional words of praise or encouragement for tasks well done, especially if done in concert with others. As Donna Winslow (1998: 353) writes of the Canadian military's current strategies, 'The military does things quite deliberately to intensify the power of group pressure within its ranks as recruits are taught the need for teamwork.' Individuals who fail will bring down their entire squad, platoon, company or regiment; but those who succeed do it together as a team (Arkin and Dobrofsky 1978: 163).

Sanctioned and non-sanctioned initiation rituals break the new recruits' sense of individuality and accomplish the broader goals of militarized transformation: to enforce obedience, underline the importance of the chain of command, and to promote an intense bonding among soldiers who may need to depend upon one another in battle (Harrison and Laliberté 1994: 22–34). Many recruits report that the emotional bond with fellow soldiers and the military itself is stronger than any relationship they had previously experienced (ibid.: 27–8), including familial and intimate relations. Most have come to see themselves as members of a new common family, a warrior brotherhood, which is very distinct from the larger world around them. That new family has its own set of values, prizes stoicism and solidarity, and engages in force when necessary; and it usually supports its members with medical and dental care, housing and educational services as well as a complex social network. As Harrison and Laliberté (ibid.: 29–33) note, the 'caring military community [is] often cherished by members and their families'.

Through these various means, military indoctrination promotes loyalty and conformity to a set of militarized and highly masculinized values and behavioural expectations. Post-Traumatic Stress Disorder reveals what happens when soldiers depart in any way from these expectations; or when they, in turn, learn how truly empty the promises into which they have been inculcated are.

Post-Traumatic Stress Disorder

Until recently, militaries have largely ignored the psychological impact of combat and combat-like situations on soldiers. Yet what is now known as Post-Traumatic Stress Disorder is something that has long affected soldiers. One recent study discovered that almost half the Canadian soldiers who survived the battle of Dieppe during the Second World War still suffer post-traumatic stress (Canadian Broadcasting Corporation n.d.). In the United States, some 30 per cent of male Vietnam war veterans experienced PTSD, while 26 per cent of female Vietnam veterans did so at some point during their lives (Price 2007). As one soldier recalls: 'Bodies without heads; bodies without arms and the smell, the horrible, horrible smell of death ... That's the kind of thing that stays with you' (Canadian Broadcasting Corporation n.d.). A related form of psychiatric distress in battle, Combat Stress Reaction (CSR), constituted

23 per cent of all Israeli casualties in the 1982 Lebanon War (Solomon et al. 1996: 104).

The manifestation of a soldier's breakdown usually involves a wide variety of symptoms, including acute anxiety, fear of death, anger, depression, nightmares, vivid intrusive reliving of their most horrible experiences, intense distress, hyper-vigilance, exaggerated startle responses, and crying. It is described as a debilitating condition, often leading to breakdowns in personal relationships, unemployment, alcoholism and even suicide (Novaco and Chemtob 2002: 123; Calhoun et al. 2002: 133; Solomon et al. 1996: 105; Gibson 1991: 84; Kulka et al. 1990: 33).

Militaries can accommodate physical injuries, most especially those sustained in battle; but the traumatic reactions resulting from battle or the risks associated with participating in militaries are injuries most militaries find difficult, if not impossible, to reconcile. During the First World War, for example, the response was relatively straightforward: 'A man was shot for cowardice' and any officers who failed to carry out such executions were themselves arrested (Solomon et al. 1996: 111). When soldiers were not executed for having human emotions, for betraying, and acting upon their fear and dread, they were usually simply ignored.

Most male soldiers, having been trained in the ideals of hyper-masculinity, learn there is little place in the military family for them to express emotions or reactions that do not accord with those ideals. Even soldiers who suffer PTSD have claimed 'sometimes I wish I had lost a leg instead of having all those brain cells screwed up' (Canadian Broadcasting Corporation n.d.). Many male soldiers report that although they share a closeness with fellow soldiers that is unmatched, the closeness does not extend to discussions of emotional topics, such as relationship difficulties with wives or girlfriends. It certainly does not extend to discussions of fear and emotional pain. As one US Vietnam veteran commented:

> When you was over there you was a macho figure, that was all you was taught to be, a macho figure, you know, nothing can hurt you, you're scared of nothing, no feelings, no pain, you know, just kill, okay? And everybody has got that feeling so you don't relate to the next guy, 'Hey man, you know I'm really scared that this is happening' ... You don't say that to the next guy because in return he would probably laugh at you, you know, or call you a wimp or puss or whatever and then it gets around and everybody points a finger at this guy, you know, well he's a wimp or he's a puss or queer or whatever. (Cited in Karner 1998: 217–18)

Soldiers who do experience debilitating fear or anguish during battle or as witness to situations of armed conflict risk ostracization from their brotherhood for betraying the ideals of manhood and allowing 'the feminine' within to be expressed. Emotional pain and fear fundamentally contradict the ideals of hyper-masculinity so carefully inculcated into the soldier recruit.

A recent Canadian study into PTSD confirms that members of the Canadian forces with PTSD find little support within their units, and they often face widespread resentment from colleagues. Soldiers who experienced PTSD said they long resisted coming forward to avoid the humiliation and stigma associated with mental illness. Many will not admit to post-traumatic stress out of fear of their brethren's reaction. As one soldier described it: 'To be quite honest, I would rather tell my peer group that I got the dose at a whore house than PTSD' (Marin 2002: 60). Getting 'the dose at a whore house' would not contradict the norms of militarized masculinity; whereas acknowledging feelings of fear, pain and trauma would.

Many in the military also refuse to acknowledge that they might be ill because, as one psychologist reported, to do so would be to admit you are weak. One soldier commented: 'Nobody fucked with me, and here I was having a mental health problem. Soldiers aren't supposed to have that' (ibid.: 62, 91). Concerned about the possibility of PTSD, many soldiers treated colleagues who had come forward and acknowledged their illness as though they might be contagious; in the Canadian military, it is 'a latter-day leprosy' (ibid.: 71). Another said it was as though 'I was the person with the bubonic plague' (ibid.: 70). One senior non-commissioned member described his colleagues' reactions:

> I was completely ostracized by the battalion ... because most of them were afraid to have anything to do with us ... I remember a guy came up to me going, You know ... I don't want to say this, but I can't be caught talking to you ... [If I went into the sergeants' mess] I would probably be asked to leave ... When I was coming back [from treatment for PTSD], there was a Sergeant Major sitting right there, right across from me. I looked at him. He looked away ... These were all people I used to work with. (ibid.: 71–2)

Indeed, by unsettling the norm that militarized masculinity is a fixed identity, the risks of PTSD, if not PTSD itself, might well be contagious; once hyper-masculine men begin to experience and share feelings of fear and horror, the myth of the heroic soldier-warrior is seen as groundless. This may be a more terrifying idea than PTSD.

PTSD is such a profound betrayal of the norms of hyper-masculinity in which militarized men have been indoctrinated that the stigma associated with it extends to family members. Several spouses of Canadian soldiers told investigators they too were ostracized once their spouse's condition became known. As one military wife described it: 'It's just ugly ... We're not treated as human beings. We lost all our friends, military and civilian' (ibid.: 62). What many members of the military and their families discovered was that the idea of a military family 'that would look after its own through thick and thin' did not exist for members with PTSD (ibid.: 92).

Male soldiers who experience PTSD discover they have not successfully obliterated the feminine other and indeed risk becoming 'women'. As Lisa Vetten (2002) writes, the masculinity affirmed by the process of most contemporary military training 'is a fragile one, entirely unable to tolerate traces of femininity'. When the stoic, tough, emotionless soldier begins to feel and react, when he feels pain, fear, anxiety, guilt, shame and despair as a result of the activities in which he participated as a soldier, he violates the precepts of his military identity and can no longer fulfil the myths of militarized manhood that have shaped him.

Importantly, studies in the United States of soldiers with PTSD also signal important differences in rates of PTSD between women and men and between white male soldiers and soldiers of colour. Studies of Vietnam-era veterans showed a higher incidence of PTSD among Hispanic, African American and Native American veterans (Loo n.d.). While in the recent Iraq war, PTSD rates seem to be markedly higher in female soldiers than in male soldiers (Goldzweig et al. 2006: S85; Scharnberg 2005; Brant 2005). What would account for this difference? Are women and marginalized men even more invested than white soldiers in the norms of militarized masculinity that have been privileged through indoctrination techniques and basic training? Or are they ill suited to the rigours of military life? Certainly this latter explanation is circulated widely in the United States today by conservative thinkers who see female rates of PTSD as confirmation of the claims that women simply do not belong in militaries.

Research on female soldiers and soldiers of colour who report PTSD signals another story, however; and this story is that women and marginalized men discover very quickly that the myth of the warrior brotherhood is not one in which they were ever intended to be included. If the racialized and gendered taunts of basic training aimed at exorcizing 'the other' did not already convey this message, female soldiers and soldiers of colour learn the lesson very quickly in combat settings, where women are subject to high rates of sexual assaults and marginalized men are often invited to take on the most dangerous of duties, disrupting for ever the idea of a caring military family.

In studies of Vietnam-era veterans, soldiers reported that their ethnicity and race directly increased their exposure to combat, with Native Americans, African Americans or Latinos often chosen over white soldiers for the most difficult, dangerous and life-threatening tasks (Beals et al. 2002). Racialized soldiers were sometimes shot at because they were mistaken as 'the enemy' or were harassed and assaulted because they were thought to resemble or symbolize 'the enemy' (Loo n.d.). As a Canadian soldier comments, 'The best is having the same colour, the same haircut, the same religion, the same colour of eyes, the same height, the same weight. Because everybody outside of that – we don't like difference' (Harrison and Laliberté 1994: 36–7). When it came to actual combat, in other words, the tight-knit military family broke down along racialized lines; and those faced with the contradiction and betrayal were less able to remain the tough heroic warrior they had been trained to be. Soldiers experienced greater emotional pain when the myths they had been trained to believe began to break down in the face of alternative experiences or readings of the war in which they were engaged.

Female soldiers also quickly discover that they are not part of the myths of the warrior 'brotherhood', and their presence in national militaries already disrupts at least one of the promises of military indoctrination: the myth of an exclusively male-dominated world (see also Kovitz 2003: 9). Female soldiers pay a steep price for violating that promise. Recent studies in the USA indicate that between 43 and 60 per cent of female enlisted personnel experience some form of physical or sexual harassment or violence. Some 90 per cent of female patients at US Veterans Administration facilities after the first Gulf War reported experiencing frequent harassment during tours of duty and some 37 per cent reported being raped multiple times (David et al. 2006: 555–6; see also Goldzweig et al. 2006: S85; Skinner et al. 2000; Corbett 2006: 45). As one twenty-one-year-old female soldier in Iraq describes her reasons for carrying a knife: 'The knife wasn't for the Iraqis ... It was for the guys on my own side' (Benedict 2007: B3).

Complaints of rising instances of sexual harassment and assault in the recent Iraq war prompted the US Secretary of Defense to create a task force to investigate these cases in 2004; and in 2005 the Department of Defense adopted a confidential reporting structure for victims of sexual assault. In its most recent report, the Department reported that it had received 2,374 reports of sexual assault cases involving its members in 2005 (US Department of Defense 2006). These numbers are likely very conservative; at least one Department of Veteran Affairs study showed that 75 per cent of assaulted military women never report the crime to their commanding officer (Lyke 2005). Many women will not report their assaults because to do so would mean 'they won't be "one of the guys"' (ibid.). Others will not report their assailants because those assailants are their superior officers. Indeed, the difficulty associated with reporting assaults, which can be daunting in any setting, is exacerbated in military environments, because of the strict hierarchy imposed in military settings, the cohesion and solidarity expected among military personnel, and because targets of assault and harassment must usually continue to 'live and work with their perpetrators' (Street and Stafford n.d.: 1; Benedict 2007: B3).

Studies on female soldiers and PTSD indicate that male and female soldiers respond to both combat-related stress and military sexual trauma in very similar ways. Military sexual harassment and assault are highly correlated with PTSD in both women and men. In fact, they seem to be far stronger predictors of PTSD than the kinds of stresses otherwise associated with military duty, including risk of death (Kang et al. 2005: 193; see also Wolfe et al. 1998). The significant difference, of course, is that far more female soldiers report experiencing sexual harassment, assault or violence than their male soldier counterparts. With rising numbers of women participating in many Western militaries and a corresponding rising rate of sexual assaults perpetrated against those women, 'PTSD stemming from military sexual trauma', Wendy David et al. (2006: 556) point out, 'is perhaps one of the most pressing mental health concerns facing female veterans today.'

In short, the most important story that PTSD tells is that the promises and myths associated with military training, the promise of turning boys into particular kinds of men, the myth of a male-dominated and exclusively heterosexual world, and the promise of a military family that stands in solidaristic support of its members through all hardship, are precisely that, myths. One way in which the power of militarism is made manifest has been through the effective circulation of these myths.[5] Yet the modern military is neither exclusively heterosexual nor male; its ranks are filled with the often contested presence of women, gay men, lesbians and persons of colour. Finally, the solidaristic military family is shown to quickly collapse under the weight of the myths upon which it was built.

Conclusions

There is a basic resistance exhibited by most militaries to the inclusion of the 'other' within their ranks, whether members of 'other' ethnic or racial groups, gay men and lesbians, or women. And all soldiers are expected to exorcize 'the other' from within, most particularly the feminine other. The presence of the 'other' makes the strategies of recruitment, basic training and inculcation of an appropriate militarized masculinity all the more difficult to accomplish; and those involved in recruiting and training have long understood this. Militaries have long resisted racial heterogeneity; and today it is the prospect of including women or openly gay men and lesbians which provokes those same forms of resistance (Shilts 1994; D'Amico and Weinstein 1999). For some observers, the presence of women within militaries is both a symptom and a cause of the decline of the advanced military.[6] By this view, it will be difficult to attract young men to join militaries that include women, gay men and lesbians and more difficult still to train them to bond with their fellow soldiers. One author notes that by including more women, the American military 'is now paying a heavy penalty for the folly of the responsible politicians and voters as cohesion suffers, training becomes almost impossible, and some of its best personnel are forced out by sexual harassment claims which may or may not be well founded' (van Creveld 2000: 442).

By contrast, the focus of this chapter has been to examine men whose emotional reactions to war and combat lead them to revile who they are, female soldiers who are constantly harassed and subjected to sexual violence, and soldiers of colour who discover they are not comrades but targets. These are all elements of a complex and interrelated story about militarized masculinity. As Judith Stiehm (1989: 226) has written, 'all militaries have ... regularly been rooted in the psychological coercion of young men through appeals to their (uncertain) manliness'. Militaries replace uncertainty with a hegemonic representation of idealized norms of masculinity which privilege the tough, stoic warrior who is capable of and willing to employ violence to achieve whatever ends into which he may be ordered. Militaries work hard to fix the identities of young men in these terms, and have worked equally hard to deny the fragility of this construction or critical analysis of the consequences. Some of the consequences of that construction are revealed through the sexual violence perpetrated by militarized men against fellow soldiers and the targeting of racialized comrades, those who do not belong. Some of the consequences also erupt through the treatment of and reaction to soldiers who express feelings of fear, terror and emotional pain in situations of armed conflict; who do not live up to the ideals of militarized masculinity; and who permit traces of the feminine to re-emerge. Caring, emotive, feeling human beings who experience a connection with other human beings are not, it seems, what most militaries want. All these consequences remind us of the complex ways in which militarism operates, and the myriad of reasons why it must continue to be resisted.

Notes

1 Equally important but not examined in this chapter are acts of violence committed outside military communities, directed at the peoples of countries in which soldiers have been deployed (see Razack 2004; Whitworth 2004).

2 Large portions of the following sections are drawn from Whitworth (2004: ch. 6).

3 For an excellent summary of the goals and procedures of basic training, see Harrison and Laliberté (1994: ch. 1); see also Davis (1997: ch. 2); Goldstein (2001: ch. 5); Arkin and Dobrofsky 1978; Karner (1998: 214–16); Gibson (1991: 72–87); Mc-Coy 1995 and McCoy 1997; Gill 1997; Enloe (1993b: ch. 3).

4 As Gwynn Dwyer (1983) notes, it has been over one hundred years since mass formations were any use on the battlefield, but all militaries still make soldiers march in unison, especially in basic training.

5 It is important to underscore the extent to which drawing attention

to PTSD is not by itself a necessarily critical intervention. Indeed, as Alison Howell has argued, many current discussions of PTSD are aimed not at a critique of militarism but instead at its reassertion in a more effective and apparently more benign form. As Howell notes, through PTSD, 'trauma is medicalized, thus focusing attention on the psyches of soldiers rather than the sources of trauma ... Ultimately, soldiers are supposed to reconcile their experiences through psychological help, instead of politicizing traumatic events' (Howell n.d.: 51). See also Edkins 2003.

6 See van Creveld 2000 and responses to this article by Elshtain (2000) and Croker (2000).

References

Appy, C. G. (1993) *Working-Class War: American Combat Soldiers and Vietnam*, Chapel Hill: University of North Carolina Press.

Arkin, W. and L. R. Dobrofsky (1978) 'Military socialization and masculinity', *Journal of Social Issues*, 34(1): 151–68.

Beals, J., S. M. Manson, J. H. Shore, M. Friedman, M. Ashcraft, J. A. Fairbank and W. E. Schlenger (2002) 'The prevalence of post-traumatic stress disorder among American Indian Vietnam veterans: disparities and context', *Journal of Traumatic Stress*, 15(2): 89–97.

Benedict, H. (2007) 'The private war of women soldiers,' *Ottawa Citizen*, 18 March, p. B3.

Brant, M. (2005) 'Women soldiers more at risk for stress disorder', Newsweek Online, 5 July, <www.msnbc.msn.com/id/8471505/site/newsweek>, accessed 2 February 2007.

Calhoun, P. S., J. C. Beckham, M. E. Feldman, J. C. Barefoot, T. Haney and H. B. Bosworth (2002) 'Partners' ratings of combat veterans' anger', *Journal of Traumatic Stress*, 15(2): 133–36.

Canadian Broadcasting Corporation (n.d.) 'The unseen scars: post traumatic stress disorder', *The National Features*, <www.tv.cbc.ca/national/gpminfo/ptsd/wounds.html>, accessed 16 May 2002.

Corbett, S. (2007) 'The women's war', *New York Times Magazine* (18 March), pp. 41–55.

Croker, C. (2000) 'Humanising warfare, or why Van Creveld may be missing the "big picture"', *Millennium: Journal of International Studies*, 29(2): 449–60.

Dallaire, R. (2003) *Shake Hands with the Devil: The Failure of Humanity in Rwanda*, Toronto: Random House.

D'Amico, F. and L. Weinstein (eds) (1999) *Gender Camouflage: Women and the US Military*, New York: New York University Press.

David, W. S., T. L. Simpson, A. J. Cotton (2006) 'Taking charge: a pilot curriculum of self-defense and personal safety training for female veterans with PTSD because of military sexual trauma', *Journal of Interpersonal Violence*, 21(4): 555–65.

Davis, J. (1997) *The Sharp End: A Canadian Soldier's Story*, Vancouver: Douglas and McIntyre.

Doty, R. L. (1996) *Imperial Encounters: The Politics of Representation in North–South Relations*, Minneapolis: University of Minnesota Press.

Dwyer, G. (1983) *Anybody's Son Will Do*, National Film Board of Canada.

Edkins, J. (2003) *Trauma and the Memory of Politics*, Cambridge: Cambridge University Press.

Ehrenreich, B. (1997) *Blood Rites: Origins and History of the Passions of War*, New York: Metropolitan Books.

Elshtain, J. B. (2000) 'Shooting at the wrong target: a response to Van Creveld', *Millennium: Journal of International Studies*, 29(2): 443–8.

Enloe, C. (1993a) 'The right to fight: a feminist catch-22', *Ms.*, July/August, pp. 84–7.

— (1993b) *The Morning After: Sexual Politics at the End of the Cold War*, Berkeley: University of California Press.

— (2000) *Maneuvers: The International Politics of Militarizing Women's Lives*, Berkeley: University of California Press.

Fontana, A. and R. Rosenaheck

(1998) 'Duty-related and sexual stress in the etiology of PTSD among women veterans who seek treatment', *Psychiatric Services*, 49, May, pp. 658–62.

Francke, L. B. (1997) *Ground Zero: The Gender Wars in the Military*, New York: Simon and Schuster.

Gibson, J. T. (1991) 'Teaching people to inflict pain: state terror and social learning', *Journal of Humanistic Psychology*, 31(2): 72–87.

Gilbert, S. (1983) 'Soldier's heart: literary men, literary women, and the Great War', *Signs*, 8.

Gill, L. (1997) 'Creating citizens, making men: the military and masculinity in Bolivia', *Cultural Anthropolgy*, 12(4): 527–50.

Goldstein, J. S. (2001) *War and Gender*, Cambridge: Cambridge University Press.

Goldzweig, C. L., T. M. Balekian, C. Rolón, E. Yano and P. Shekelle (2006) 'The state of women veterans' health research: results of a systematic literature review', *Journal of General Internal Medicine*, 21: S82–92.

Greene, R. A. (2005) 'UK troops face trauma after Iraq', BBC News website, 8 December 2005, <http//:news.bbc.co.uk/go/pr/fr/-/hi/uk/4632263>, accessed 15 February 2006.

Harrison, D. (2002) *The First Casualty: Violence against Women in Canadian Military Communities*, Toronto: James Lorimer.

Harrison D. and L. Laliberté (1994) *No Life Like It: Military Wives in Canada*, Toronto: James Lorimer.

Hatty, S. E. (2000) *Masculinities, Violence and Culture*, Thousand Oaks, CA: Sage Publications.

Hooper, C. (2001) *Manly States: Masculinities, International Relations, and Gender Politics*, New York: Columbia University Press.

Howell, A. (n.d.) 'Madness in IR: therapeutic interventions and the international management of disorder(s)', PhD dissertation, York University, Graduate Program in Political Science, manuscript copy.

Kang, H., N. Dalager, C. Mahan and E. Ishii (2005) 'The role of sexual assault on the risk of PTSD among Gulf War Veterans', *Annals of Epidemiology*, 15(3): 191–5.

Karner, T. X. (1998) 'Engendering violent men: oral histories of military masculinity', in L. H. Bowker (ed.), *Masculinities and Violence*, Thousand Oaks, CA: Sage Publications, pp. 197–232.

Kovitz, M. (2003) 'The roots of military masculinity', in P. R. Higate (ed.), *Military Masculinities: Identity and the State*, Westport, CT: Praeger Publishers, pp. 1–14.

Kulka, R. A., W. E. Schlenger, J. A. Fairbank, R. L. Hough, B. K. Jordan, C. R. Marmar and D. S. Weiss (1990) *Trauma and the Vietnam War Generation: Report of Findings from the National Vietnam Veterans Readjustment Study*, New York: Brunner/Mazel Publishers.

Lerner, P. (2003) *Hysterical Men: War, Psychiatry, and the Politics of Trauma in Germany, 1890–1930*, Ithaca, NY: Cornell University Press.

Loo, C. M. 'PTSD among ethnic minority veterans', Department of Veterans Affairs, National Centre

for PTSD fact sheet, <www.ncptsd.
va.gov/ncmain/ncdocs/fact_shts/
fs_ethnic_vet.html?opm=1&rr=rr4
2&srt=d&echorr=true>.

Lyke, M. L. (2005) 'Vet becomes
crusader for victims of soldier
rape', Seattle Post-Intelligencer, 11
April, <http://seattlepi.nwsource.
com/local/219613_crusader11.
html>, accessed 24 February 2007.

McCoy, A. W. (1995) '"Same banana":
hazing and honor at the Philippine Military Academy', Journal of
Asian Studies, 54(3): 689–726.

— (1997) 'Ram boys: changing
images of the masculine in
the Philippine military', Paper
presented at the International
Studies Association annual meetings, Toronto, Canada, 18–22
March.

Marin, A. (2002) Canada's Military
Ombudsman. Special Report:
Systemic Treatment of CF Members
with PTSD, Ottawa: Government
of Canada, 5 February.

Masters, C. (2005) 'Cyborg soldiers
and militarized masculinities',
International Feminist Journal of
Politics, 7(1): 112–32.

Morgan, D. H. J. (1994) 'Theater of
war: combat, the military, and
masculinities' in H. Brod and
M. Kaufman (eds), Theorizing
Masculinities, Thousand Oaks,
CA: Sage Publications.

Novaco, R. W. and C. M. Chemtob
(2002) 'Anger and combat-related
posttraumatic stress disorder',
Journal of Traumatic Stress, 15(2):
123–32.

Price, L. (2007) 'Findings from the
National Vietnam Veterans' Readjustment Study', National Centre
for PTSD fact sheet, <www.ncptsd.

va.gov/ncmain/ncdocs/fact_shts/
fs_nvvrs.html?opm=1&rr=rr45&s
rt=d&echorr=true>, accessed 18
March 2007.

Razack, S. (2004) Dark Threats and
White Knights: The Somalia
Affair, Peacekeeping and the New
Imperialism, Toronto: University
of Toronto Press.

Satel, S. (2006) 'For some, the war
won't end', New York Times, 1
March.

Scharnberg, K. (2005) 'Female GIs
hard hit by war syndrome', Chicago Tribune Online, 20 March.

Shilts, R. (1994) Conduct Unbecom-
ing: Gays and Lesbians in the
US Military, New York: Fawcett
Columbine.

Showalter, S. (1985) 'Male hysteria:
W. H. R. Rivers and the lessons
of shell shock,' in The Female
Malady: Women, Madness and
English Culture, 1830–1980, New
York: Penguin, pp. 167–94.

Skinner, K. M., N. Kressin, S. Frayne,
T. J. Tripp, C. S. Hankin, D. R.
Miller and L. M. Sullivan (2000)
'The prevalence of military sexual
assault among female Veterans
Administration outpatients',
Journal of Interpersonal Violence,
15(3): 291–310.

Solomon, Z., N. Laor, and A. C.
McFarlane (1996) 'Acute posttraumatic reactions in soldiers and
civilians', in B. A. van der Kolk,
A. C. McFarlane and L. Weisaeth
(eds), Traumatic Stress: The Effects
of Overwhelming Experience on
Mind, Body, and Society, New York.
Guilford Press.

Stiehm, J. H. (1989) Arms and the
Enlisted Woman, Philadelphia, PA:
Temple University Press.

Five

Street, A. and J. Stafford (n.d.)
'Military sexual trauma: issues in
caring for veterans', Department
of Veterans Affairs, National
Centre for PTSD fact sheet, <www.
ncptsd.va.gov/ncmain/ncdocs/
fact_shts/military_sexual_trauma.
html?printable=true>, accessed
25 February 2007.

Turner, M. A., M. D. Kiernan, A. G.
McKechanie, P. J. C. Finch, F. B.
McManus and L. A. Neal (2005)
'Acute military psychiatric casual-
ties from the war in Iraq', *British
Journal of Psychiatry*, 186: 476–9.

United States Department of
Defense (2006) *Sexual Assault
Report for 2005*, 16 March, <www.
defenselink.mil/news/Mar2006/
d20060316SexualAssaultReport.
pdf>, accessed 24 February 2007.

Van Creveld, M. (2000) 'The great
illusion: women in the military',
*Millennium: Journal of Interna-
tional Studies*, 29(2): 429–44.

Vedantam, S. (2005) 'A political debate on stress disorder: as claims
rise, VA takes stock', *Washington
Post*, 27 December 27, p. A01.

Vetten, L. (2002) 'War and the
making of men and women',
Centre for the Study of Violence
and Reconciliation, South Africa,
<www.csvr.org.za/articles/artwarl.
htm>, accessed 18 May 2002.

Whitworth, S. (2004) *Men, Militarism
and UN Peacekeeping: A Gendered
Analysis*, Boulder, CO: Lynne
Rienner.

Winslow, D. (1998) 'Misplaced loyalties: the role of military culture
in the breakdown of discipline
in peace operations', *Canadian
Review of Sociology and Anthropology*, 35(3): 345–66.

— (1999) 'Rites of passage and group
bonding in the Canadian air-
borne', *Armed Forces and Society*,
25(3): 429–57.

Wolfe, J., E. J. Sharkansky, J. P.
Read, R. Dawson, J. A. Martin
and P. C. Ouimette (1998) 'Sexual
harassment and assault as predictors of PTSD symptomatology
among US female Persian Gulf
War military personnel', *Journal
of Interpersonal Violence*, 13(1):
40–57.

SIX | Contesting the masculine state

DANIEL CONWAY

I have a huge problem that I cannot talk to anyone about. I tried talking to my father and he got so angry with me, I thought he might actually hit me. I do not want to go into the army ... all my friends seem to be looking forward to going into the army. I certainly can't discuss it with them. I feel terribly isolated, like I don't belong anywhere. It's not because I'm a coward.

The [Johannesburg] *Star* replies: Cowardice has nothing to do with conscientious objection to doing military service. Contact the End Conscription Campaign at 011 337 6796. (Letters to the Editor, *The Star*, 12 September 1987)

Asking the man question in a society where compulsory all-male military conscription is standard inevitably requires interrogating how masculinities are militarized and how militaries are masculinized. A militarized state devotes considerable cultural, legal and discursive resources to perpetuating the militarization of masculinities. Men who feel anxious about serving, who consider it a waste of time or see it as an abuse of state power, are likely made to feel they are unreasonable, 'unmanly' and subversive. Exploring the impact of this gender dissidence allows an analysis of Cynthia Enloe's insight that 'if a state's military begins to lose legitimacy, the tension between masculinity and military service can become acute' (1993: 54). In 1980s apartheid South Africa, two years of full-time compulsory conscription existed for all white men and this was followed by a fifteen-year period of alternate-year 'camp duty'.[1] Tensions between masculinity and military service emerged when a small number of white men publicly rejected compulsory conscription. They were then joined by white men and women who established a war resistance and anti-apartheid movement called the End Conscription Campaign (ECC). Objection to military service for expressly political reasons reflected deeper cultural shifts and widening divisions in South Africa's white community (Phillips 2002: 224; Charney 1987) and demonstrated how the contradictory pressures of militarization on a society can provoke profound political change. The analysis of the war resistance movement in South Africa reveals the possibilities and constraints for contesting and destabilizing dominant militarized gender norms and contesting racist and authoritarian rule. The use of sexist and homophobic discourses to stigmatize objectors and their supporters demonstrated the hetero-normativity of the public realm, and the dilemma of how to transgress such stigmatization confronts peace activists across contexts. The case study of war resistance in apartheid South Africa and the cultures of masculinity that underpinned it resonate with social practices in contemporary militarized societies such as in Israel and Turkey. This chapter will begin by theoretically conceptualizing conscription and political objection to it as 'performative' (Butler 1999) acts generative of individual and collective identity. I will move on to analyse the discursive and material means by which the apartheid state militarized masculinity; and finally I will conceptualize and assess resistance to conscription in South Africa.

Militarizing masculinities

Conscription and objection to military service are performative practices generative of individual and collective subjectivities. These subjectivities, however, are 'produced in the complex interplay of discourse, norms, power relations, institutions and practices' (Lloyd 2005: 27). In militarized cultures, such practices intersect with multiple discourses and occur on multiple levels. In South Africa, conscription became a normative practice generative of masculinity and citizenship and was engendered by practices such as cadet duty at school, valorizing sport and the male physique, and by gendered nationalist and cold war discourses in the public realm (Cock and Nathan 1989; Du Pisani 2004). White men engaged with these militarized masculinities and practices at school, on the sports pitch, in the family, in the military, and in the wider public realm (Connell and Messerschmidt 2005). There was, however, a simultaneous resistance to and contestation of these practices and norms. The refusal to serve as a soldier in a conscript army on grounds of conscience, particularly when this relates to political and moral beliefs, is a powerful and transgressive performative practice in the public realm. It is, however, a practice that is ambivalent. Objection to military service, from one perspective, is an alternative 'narrative of citizenship' to that offered by the state (Carver 1998: 15) and one that challenges 'the halo of sanctity surrounding war and military service' (Helman 1999: 46).

Objectors make claims to embody true patriotism, civic duty, heroism, sacrifice and other normative practices of masculinity, norms that the state claims legitimacy to define. In this contestation, there are pressures to assimilate or be subverted by state vilification. Burk notes that many objectors' goal is to at once 'protest *and* to maintain the respect of larger society' (1995: 511). Therefore, they must avoid, in Burk's terms, becoming exiles from the political community (ibid.: 511).The need to be 'taken seriously' and perceived as 'respectable', in order to avoid 'exile', places gendered pressures on objectors and can limit the transformative nature of objection as a performative act. The analysis below demonstrates that objectors and peace activists in apartheid South Africa were acutely subject to these pressures.

A politics of masculinity had always been at the centre of white nation-building in South Africa, and militarization was a critical process in mediating the heterogeneous white community. The experience of military defeat and humiliation by the Afrikaans-speaking population in the Boer War was of profound significance in creating suspicion of English-speaking whites and engendered a need to reclaim honour, heroism and strength (Du Pisani 2004). English-speaking whites (some 40 per cent of the white community) were largely hostile towards National Party (NP) rule during the 1950s; but a combination of rising prosperity, electoral gerrymandering by the NP and disintegration of parliamentary opposition led to increased acceptance of and complicity in apartheid. Nevertheless, the unity of the white *nation* was never assured. The South African Defence Force's (SADF) role in mediating these divisions and symbolizing an ideational white unity and resolve was paramount. The institution of conscription became a primary location where white men from different linguistic, class and national groups mixed (Seegers 1987: 160). The presumed masculine camaraderie of service aimed to forge white national bonds, and the public image of the white male conscript symbolized white South Africa's apparent unity and resolve. Therefore, conscription was a primary means by which the 'imagined community' (Anderson 2006) of the white nation was generated. Nevertheless, opposition to conscription in the 1980s reflected these historical divisions and was centred on English-speaking universities, in the English-speaking churches, through the English-medium press, and in business interests. The linguistic, social and economic divisions in the white community and the iconic, individual and communal practice of all-male military service made the state exceptionally sensitive to individual or collective acts of war resistance. The extent of South Africa's militarization made opposition to conscription a difficult and rare social phenomenon but conversely made the act of objection iconic and destabilizing when it did occur.

The ideological outlook, discourse and personnel of the NP, SADF and South African state had coalesced by the 1980s.[2] It would be incorrect, however, to assume that war resisters faced a rigid monolith of militarized masculinity when opposing the South African state. Indeed, the apartheid state was a conglomerate of shifting, sometimes contradictory and surprising, discourses of masculinity and sexuality. At the centre of this 'uneasy and messy alliance' (MacInnes 1998: 15) of masculinist discourses was the act of conscription. The importance placed on white men serving in the military and being publicly acknowledged as conscripts, however, never wavered. The state's shifts in rhetorical emphasis and articulation, or to borrow Hooper's terms the 'plundering' (2001: 62) of hitherto 'deviant' tropes of masculinity and sexuality as a justification for conscription were aimed at the 'rejuvenation' (ibid.: 62) of the state's norms of masculinity, which were centred on maintaining the legitimacy of conscription. An analysis of the state's evolving and conflicting articulation of militarized masculinities reveals the highly bound and hostile public realm in which objectors had to operate. Also, the cultural impact of war resistance was seen to have threatened (or to potentially threaten) the state. Militarized 'hybrid' (Demetriou 2001: 349) tropes of masculinities emerged as the circumstances of the state changed, the impact of war resistance was gauged, or the different institutions of the state contradicted one another.

At the centre of the cultural production of militarized masculinities was the iconography of the white male conscript. The need for white public complicity with conscription infused NP leaders' rhetoric and South African popular culture. A significant discourse of aspirational militarized masculinity was that of the hyper-masculine *grensvegter* (border fighter). The *grensvegter* was essentially a man who had seen combat against Cuban and Angolan troops in the war on the Namibian/ Angolan border. The *grensvegter* iconography emphasized the adventure and raw masculinity of military service and drew from the Hollywood Rambo imagery of anti-communist guerrilla warfare (Conway 2007). Alongside the hard imagery of the *grensvegter* was that of the *troepie* (or *troopie*). The *troepie* embraced conscripts as the collective sons of white South Africa. One could purchase *troepie* cuddly toys, and the Afrikaans popular song 'Troepie Doepie' defined this trope of masculinity as affectionately regarded rather than revered and hyper-masculine (Drewett 2003). The *troepie* metaphor was particularly emphasized when addressing white women's involvement in militarization. The women of the Southern Cross Fund, a white women's group established to support SADF troops, emphasized men as *troepies*: sons, husbands and brothers deserving the motherly support of South African women (Conway 2007). The need to appeal to *all* white South African men and define service in the SADF as a positive, masculinizing rite of passage, regardless of a man's subjectivities, meant that the tropes of masculinity militarized in state and popular cultural discourse were broad and malleable. The SADF's official magazine, *Paratus*, was on sale to the South African public and served as a key medium by which the state advocated the benefits and importance of military service. *Paratus* featured a 'National Serviceman of the Month' column. The men featured in this column were seldom either Afrikaans-speaking or the idealized *grensvegter* found elsewhere in South African popular culture. Among the 'National Servicemen of the Month' highlighted in *Paratus* were a surfer, a gay novelist, a fashion designer, a singer, an actor and a photographer. They were all portrayed as having developed their skills while in the SADF and as performing a valuable role in the military (March 1987: 62; April 1983: 60; October 1987: 26; January 1986: 69; October 1985: 61; October 1983: 77). The fact that the men were conscripts enabled them to transmute and hone their masculine subjectivities to the needs of the SADF. Had a fashion designer, author and surfer not been conscripts, their masculinity would have been relegated to marginal status, so the practice of military service transformed this. The men could be acknowledged as true men and patriotic citizens. Research in contemporary Israel also supports the notion that individual men experience the benefits of public acknowledgement and esteem by wearing the uniform of a conscript and participating in a collective national endeavour, regardless of their other gendered subjectivities: 'The way people look at you on the bus,' remarked one of Kaplan and Ben-Ari's gay male informants, 'the fact that suddenly you are a soldier, that suddenly you are something' (2000: 408). Munn also documents in this volume how gay men can participate in and valorize conflict and nationalist practices. The idealized masculinity of the South African conscript resonated across popular, legal and political discourses. These discourses were broad and malleable, however, and this was testimony to the vital need for *all* white South African men to participate and *be seen* participating in the SADF.

Iconic objection

It is unsurprising that, given the considerable 'ideological state apparatus' devoted to engendering consent for and participation in the military,
the majority of white men 'complied' with duty (Althusser 1971: 136–45;
Cock 1989: 9). Indeed, even at the height of the ECC's activism, the
organization concluded that 'the bulk of the white community remains
antagonised by a campaign which is seen to threaten their protected
position in society' (Moll 1985: 57). This in itself makes the stand taken
by a small number of individual male objectors to military service and
the larger number of men and women who supported them in the ECC
all the more remarkable. Despite only a handful of public political objectors throughout the 1980s, the self-narratives and performative acts of
individual objection were as iconoclastic as the imagery of the serving
conscript. The English-speaking press, in particular, closely followed
the criminal trials of political objectors in apartheid South Africa. The
personalities and life stories of the individual objectors became the central focus of the war resisters' campaigning message, and the eventual
imprisonment of objectors was portrayed as a form of sacrifice akin to
martyrdom. Martyrdom, as a sacrifice for the common good, invoked and
imitated the sacrifice soldiers supposedly made on behalf of and for the
sake of the nation (Elshtain 1995: 202). The objector David Bruce told
the court during his trial,

> I am prepared to fight in defence of the people of South Africa. Going
> to jail is like reporting for service. By taking this stand I am trying to
> say I am prepared to shoulder the responsibility that falls on young
> men who sacrifice their lives, I have no contempt for the job that
> soldiers do. By being in the army it can mean death, but I am not trying
> to avoid this – I accept that we must defend our people but I cannot do
> this under this present system of government. (*Weekly Mail*, 10 June
> 1988)

Bruce invoked the militarized symbolism of 'manly' self-sacrifice for the
greater good and yet sought to subvert and reconfigure the concept of
sacrifice in anti-apartheid and anti-conscription terms. Ivan Toms, who
was imprisoned some months after David Bruce, remarked upon the
individual resonance of 'martyrdom' as symbolizing a challenge to the
state and the wider citizenry at the time of his objection:

> Some people see me as a traitor, but some white men consider my
> stand a real challenge. I have often been told by young white men that

they support what I have been doing and respect me, but that they
could not do it themselves. At the same time they are thankful that I
am doing it, almost on their behalf. (*South*, 10 March 1988)

The presence of individual white men refusing to serve in the military
and presenting themselves as true symbols of the nation and their duty
were acutely threatening the delicate conglomeration that was white
South Africa. It was for this reason that war resistance in apartheid South
Africa had a far greater power than their physical numbers would imply.
Individual objectors performed a political identity that was iconic, moral
and powerful. Indeed, individual objection continued after the ECC was
banned in 1988 and constituted the primary focus of anti-conscription
campaigns.

At the centre of individual objectors' self-narratives was the concept
of having made a 'break' from white society. ECC activist Janet Cherry
explained, 'we all go through a process, to some extent, of breaking away
from our backgrounds and our parents and from our very sheltered up-
bringing, and we felt it was incredibly important that people made that
break' (cited in Frederickse 1990: 214). This 'break' was most vividly embodied by male objectors as a rejection of the practice of conscription and
an opposition to the conflation of masculinity/patriotism with military
service. As such, objectors could be said to have performed Connell's
advocacy of the 'renunciation' of dominant cultures of masculinity as
a precursor for creating and advocating new selves that effectively challenge the existing content and accepted practices of the status quo (1995:
130). An early ECC campaign, which encapsulated this, involved three
individual objectors fasting in Cape Town cathedral. Articulating the anti-
conscription message using a fast was explained by Richard Steele:

A radical stopping, stepping out and becoming aware of the way we
live our lives. We are socialised to follow certain habits. If you're able
to step out of that habit, even for 24 hours, it gives you a chance to
look at the other habit you are following ... We are focusing on the
SADF, because they are focusing on us, on our lives. (*Weekly Mail*, 27
September 1985)

Making a 'break' from mainstream white society was inevitable if one
were to refuse to serve in the SADF.

The breach white male objectors had made enabled new and transgressive subjectivities to enter the public realm and destabilize militarized
masculinities. Primarily, objectors' self-narratives were premised on the

claim that it was they who were empowered by their act of objection and that conscripts were in fact disempowered and trapped by military service. The 'empowerment' narrative of objection was reflexively developed according to the individual objector's life history, and it formed a critical part of his public narrative of objection. This self-reflexive knowledge was developed by encountering and rejecting militarized masculine norms in school, the army, or from a deeper cultural awareness drawn from Christianity, Judaism or the objector's own masculine or sexual identity. This self-narrative challenged the state's fundamental contention that military service was the only practice that empowered men as individuals and as a group. Many objectors considered their self-reflexivity and attitude towards conscription as a privilege that was denied other white South African men. Indeed, David Bruce, whose Judaism and family experiences in Nazi Germany were decisive to his decision to object, considered that he was 'fortunate that I had that instinct. It was a kind of gift, a kind of blessing almost, that it enabled me to see' (interview with author, 12 September 2002). This was a striking observation to make, given that the state constructed military service, not objection, as a 'privilege' for young men. Charles Bester, who attended Grey College in Bloemfontein, also rejected the hegemonic culture of his school and considered it decisive in his moulding as an objector:

> I didn't have a very happy time at Grey College, I left a year later and as I was leaving the deputy headmaster heard I was leaving and in fact I left mid-week, that's how I felt about the whole thing. I did try to explain why I was leaving this school ... I said, 'Well, I hate having to have hair inspections,' which seemed quite trivial but it was trying to say something about the things that lay behind them and he said, 'Well, what will you do when you go into the army?', because obviously in the army you were going to have your hair cut ... that connection was made and that was the first doubts I had and from there it was a process. (Interview with author, 13 September 2003)

This 'process' of coming to self-awareness and taking the final decision to object was influenced by the resistance to dominant norms in school which were replicated in wider society. Objectors articulated and developed 'hidden transcripts' (Cornwall and Lindisfarne 1994: 24) gained from their life histories and alternative practices of masculinity and citizenship. Just as militarism could become engendered by everyday practices, such as those at school, so could it be resisted.

Bosbefok masculinities

The militarization of South Africa placed extraordinary stresses on white society and upon white men, in particular. As the 1980s progressed, the war on the Namibian/Angolan border escalated and conscripts were sent into South African black townships as rebellion spread across the republic. These developments increased the amount of time conscripts spent in active combat and led to a rising white casualty rate. The international outrage provoked by South Africa's militarily aggressive stance undermined white economic confidence and made the state appear beleaguered and isolated. Mann notes that although militarization may appear all-encompassing and unassailable, 'If the nation is called to real sacrifice, we see that its militarism is not rooted deep; if living standards in a militarised society begin to fall, or should "our boys" be perceived to be "pointlessly sacrificed", militarism is profoundly threatened' (1987: 49). White political unity began to fragment in response to these multiple stresses, and the social and psychological evidence of the damaging effects of sustained military combat began to emerge. The ECC's efficacy was not in mobilizing mass resistance against conscription but in highlighting conscription as a source of growing political, economic and social crisis for white South Africans (Phillips 2002: 224). As the 1980s progressed, disturbing evidence began to emerge about the effects of military service on young white men and wider white South African culture. Indeed, white male suicide rates, instances of interpersonal violence and the phenomenon of 'family murder', whereby white men would inexplicably murder their families and then commit suicide, were among the highest in the world (Marks and Andersson 1990: 61). In 1987, General Malan, the minister of defence, told parliament that 326 national servicemen had attempted suicide during the previous year (18 killed themselves, as opposed to 116 who died in military operations over the same period) (MacLennan, *Saturday Star*, 22 February 1987). The reality of these developments began to influence white popular culture. The slang word *bosbefok* (bush fucked/bush mad) entered common currency as a term of abuse; yet its origins were influenced by the symptoms of Post-Traumatic Stress Disorder exhibited by troops who had served on the Namibian/Angolan border (Thompson and Branford 1994: 100). The metaphor of 'bush fucked' contested the army as a masculinizing experience. It destabilized the tropes of militarized masculinity embodied by the *grensvegter* and *troepie*; men were 'fucked' by military service, demeaned and driven 'mad' as a result.

These cultural shifts were capitalized on by the ECC as an organization. The ECC, as a new social movement, became a subcultural space in white South Africa and developed a particular and transgressive campaigning style from the outset. Using satirical art forms that would be readily identifiable to its youthful target audience and popular music to transmit its message, the ECC developed a significant following on English-speaking university campuses and in the trendy bars of Cape Town, Johannesburg, Durban and Grahamstown. Many activists also recall being part of the movement as a fun and enjoyable experience. ECC leader Laurie Nathan explained to the Truth and Reconciliation Commission that he believed conscripts were 'both victims and perpetrators' and this influenced ECC campaigns (TRC 1997). The ECC frequently used imagery of men being tied up, restricted and restrained in many of its posters; and some images vividly showed men being turned into animals and monsters by being forced into SADF uniforms. In this way, the imagery of the heroic *grensvegter* and affectionately regarded *troepie* was contested; and the white press and even, in 1988, the once ultra-loyal Dutch Reformed Church began to question the continued use of conscripts to fight apartheid's war. The ECC was also a forum where wider critiques of South African society were debated and a multiracial, democratic future was discussed and advocated. The movement's female members, who comprised over 50 per cent of the ECC's membership, conducted considerable feminist debates about the nature of patriarchy in South Africa and about the ECC as an organization. The ECC addressed white women as mothers, wives and girlfriends of conscripts (in similar terms to those of the state) and did so with the aim of further destabilizing militarized masculinity and women's role in sustaining it.[3] The ECC contested militarized masculinities and sought to reformulate them using popular culture and focusing on a practice that was damaging the psychological, physical and economic well-being of increasing numbers of men who were undertaking it.

Response and compromise

The state responded to objectors and the ECC with vitriol and punitive measures. Indeed, the ECC was banned in 1988. The state's attempts to discredit objectors and maintain the legitimacy of conscription were, however, problematic (Conway 2008). The iconic status of individual objectors and the skill with which the ECC used popular culture to develop anti-militarist discourses, already emergent in white society, meant that the state struggled to present objectors and their supporters as danger-ous enemies of the republic. If anything, the trial and imprisonment of individual objectors created ever-greater public concern and sympathy for objectors and caused embarrassment for the legal establishment and the SADF (ibid.). Police harassment and legal restrictions undoubt-edly damaged the ECC's ability to operate. The state also sought to acutely stigmatize objectors and their supporters using homophobic innuendo (ibid.). The branding of objectors as cowardly and sexually 'deviant' sought to neutralize objectors' political message and ensure that the state maintained control of defining and militarizing tropes of gender. Whereas the state sought to incorporate hitherto 'deviant' tropes of masculinity and sexuality in *Paratus* magazine, it did so only in relation to the practice of military service. To not serve in the SADF resulted in the state projecting sexual and gendered 'deviance' on to the resisting subject. What is significant is that this homophobic stigmatiza-tion impacted on the ECC's campaigning style and on the content of its message. Ivan Toms, a gay objector, was dissuaded from incorporating his sexuality into his public act of objection. Toms was presented by the ECC as a 'typical' white man – a good Christian, a former army officer, and a man who had been captain of his school's rugby team (Conway 2004). In 1987, the ECC conducted survey and focus group research among serving conscripts and concluded the following:

> ECC is seen as 'studenty', cliquish and elitist ... A most serious factor undermining ECC is its 'arrogance' in commenting on the army when so many of its publicly identified members have not done military service. This applies as much to men who haven't served as it does to women and older folk who don't face call ups. Those with most cred-ibility in the ECC are the campers [men who had completed the initial period of full-time conscription and were eligible for ongoing 'camp duty'] and the objectors who have been to jail. ECC needs to be repre-sented publicly by a greater number of campers to avoid the perception amongst soldiers that 'it doesn't know what the fuck it is talking about'. Women and older folk who speak on ECC's behalf should talk about how they are affected by militarisation and conscription. Many soldiers believe that the ECC sees them as 'the enemy'. (ECC, Cape Town Conscripts Group, October 1987 [Catteneo Collection])

It is significant that objectors who had been to jail were considered to have legitimacy similar to that of SADF former conscripts. This was indicative of the masculine symbolism shared between soldiering and objection as a performative act. The desire to be 'taken seriously' by serving conscripts, however, and the need to appear 'respectable' in mainstream white society, increasingly dictated the style and content of the ECC's campaigns. There is no doubt that the increased concern for what serving conscripts 'thought' about objectors and the ECC caused controversy within the movement. The ECC also became significantly more conservative than anti-war movements in the Vietnam-era USA and at Greenham Common in the 1980s (Suran 2001). One could argue that this was the inevitable result of the militarized and punitive 'conditions of operation' in white South Africa (Foucault 1969: 117). It does, however, pose the question of whether the ECC sought to assimilate with mainstream norms to the extent of damaging the movement's radicalism.

Conclusion

This chapter has explored the fluidity of masculinism and masculinities and the importance of policing boundaries to maintain the link between masculinism and power. This is not a literal conflation of men and power, but masculinist authority/hegemonic masculinity and power. Donovan argues, 'collective attempts to transform masculinity warrant the attention of pro-feminist men and women' (Donovan 1998: 817). White men who publicly refused to serve in the apartheid army exposed the vulnerability of militarized, masculinist and *raced* state projects. Indeed, the men's whiteness in itself became a transgressive dynamic of their performance of objection. The end of compulsory conscription was concurrent with the liberation of South Africa in 1994. A ceasefire in the Namibian border war had occurred in 1988, followed by Namibian independence from South African rule in 1990. A loss of white public support and the open criticism of South Africa's use of conscripts in the war had been instrumental in provoking the ceasefire (Conway 2007; Wood 1991: 751). This was a dramatic shift in white public opinion from just a few years earlier (Geldenhuys 1982). The activities of the ECC and the public stand taken by white male objectors had helped highlight and exacerbate the stresses that advanced militarization had placed on white South Africans. Indeed, across comparative contexts, the transgressive potential of individual objectors to military service was acknowledged by Helman, who argues that if war is no longer 'considered a collective effort' because objectors have appropriated the state's 'hitherto exclusive prerogative' to define security and national duty, then the individual objector has 'opened the door to challenging the state's demands of the individual' (Helman 1999: 59). The notion of military service as the only acceptable practice of masculinity and citizenship for white South African men was destabilized by individual objectors in iconic terms that mirrored the performative norms, such as embodying publicly acknowledgeable acts of duty, sacrifice and honour, of actual serving troops. This posed significant problems for the state, which was already increasingly mired in a deepening war and a crisis of domestic and international legitimacy.

The state's conflation of hetero-normativity and military masculinities, however, despite the incorporation of 'deviant' tropes of masculinity to engender widespread consent, allowed it to use homophobia and misogyny to stigmatize objectors, and in particular their supporters in the ECC. The ECC found countering this homophobic discourse difficult and sought to assimilate their challenge to the state's militarized gender norms within a hetero-normative framework. This South African case study demonstrates the effect individual acts of resistance can have in destabilizing militarization and the gendered norms that underpin it. Objectors performatively challenged dominant tropes of militarized masculinity by their public refusal to serve in the army and sought to subvert and reformulate normative values such as honour, duty, bravery and sacrifice. The analysis of the ECC, however, also raises the perpetual dilemma peace activists face when seeking to be taken 'seriously' by society at large and to sidestep the state's gendered and sexualized taunts. Phelan contends that if stigmatized social actors do not challenge normative constructions of 'respectability', then 'their attempts at social change will operate only at the more superficial level of discursive consciousness without transforming the more basic structures of identity that shape our reactions to the world' (Phelan 1999: 89). It is in assessing peace activists and objectors' responses to being 'taken seriously' and respected that one can assess war resistance as a performative and transgressive act.

Notes

1 'Camp duty' consisted of a period of three months' military training completed in alternate years for twelve years subsequent to full-time conscript duty. 'Camp duty' could also involve active service on the Namibian border, in Angola and in the South African black townships.

2 The NP had narrowly won office in 1948 and immediately set about entrenching its power base. The NP 'early used legal and extra-legal means to increase their own majority and to hinder the effectiveness of

opposition groups inside and outside parliament, to eliminate dissent, and to emphasise conformity' (Rotberg 1987: 79). The removal of English-speaking senior officers in the SADF and their replacement by Afrikaans-speaking NP sympathizers was also a priority. The SADF's political status and influence increased considerably under the premiership (and later presidency) of P. W. Botha. Botha, a former minister of defence, strongly identified with the armed forces and appointed the former chief of the SADF, General Magnus Malan, as minister of defence.

3 The South African minister of defence threatened to ban any further publication of such interviews. Women in the ECC primarily addressed the South African public as wives and mothers of conscripts, particularly after 1987 (as reflected in the 'give our sons a choice' campaign), and sought to destabilize militarized motherhood and highlight white women's role in fostering militarized masculinities. In Conway (2007) I write of how popular women's magazines in South Africa began to write of mothers' criticisms of the state's use of the military in response to their sons' deaths in the 'Operational Zone' in Namibia and Angola from early 1987 onwards. The women's activism in the ECC clearly highlighted and encouraged white mothers' unease and increasing hostility towards conscription, but also reflected a shift in focus for women in the ECC, who had hitherto resisted being defined as wives and mothers.

References

Althusser, L. (1971) *Lenin and Philosophy and Other Essays*, trans. B. Brewster, London: NLB.

Anderson, B. (2006) *Imagined Communities: Reflections on the Origin and Spread of Nationalism*, London: Verso.

Burk, J. (1995) 'Citizenship status and military service: the question for inclusion by minorities and conscientious objectors', *Armed Forces & Society*, 21(4): 503–29.

Butler, J. (1999) *Gender Trouble: Feminism and the Subversion of Identity*, New York and London: Routledge.

Carver, T. (1998) 'Sexual citizenship: gendered and de-gendered narratives', in T. Carver and V. Mottier (eds), *Politics of Sexuality: Identity, Gender, Citizenship*, London and New York: Routledge.

Charney, C. (1987) 'The National Party, 1982–1985: a class alliance in crisis', in W. James (ed.), *The State of Apartheid*, Boulder, CO: Lynne Rienner.

Cock, J. (1989) 'Conscription in South Africa: a study in the politics of coercion', *South African Sociological Review*, 2(1): 1–22.

Cock, J. and L. Nathan (eds) (1989) *War and Society: The Militarisation of South Africa*, Cape Town: David Philip.

Connell, R. (1995) *Masculinities*, Berkeley and Los Angeles: University of California Press.

Connell, R. and J. Messerschmidt (2005) 'Hegemonic masculinity: rethinking the concept', *Gender and Society*, 19(6): 829–59.

Conway, D. (2004) '"Every Coward's Choice"? Political objection to military service in apartheid South Africa as sexual citizenship', *Citizenship Studies*, 8(1): 25–45.

— (2007) '"Somewhere on the border – of credibility": the cultural construction and contestation of "the border" in white south African Society', in P. Vale and G. Baines (eds), *Bounded States and Border Wars: Southern Africa and the Cold War*, Pretoria: University of South Africa Press.

— (2008) 'The masculine state in crisis: state response to war resistance in apartheid South Africa', *Men and Masculinities*, 10(4).

Cornwall, A. and N. Lindisfarne (eds) (1994) *Dislocating Masculinity: Comparative Ethnographies*, London and New York: Routledge.

Demetriou, D. (2001) 'Connell's concept of hegemonic masculinity: a critique', *Theory and Society*, 30: 337–61.

Donovan, B. (1998) 'Political consequences of private authority: promise keepers and the transformation of hegemonic masculinity', *Theory and Society*, 27: 817–43.

Drewett, M. (2003) 'Battling over borders: narratives of resistance to the South African border war voiced through popular music', *Social Dynamics*, 29(1): 78–98.

Du Pisani, J. (2004) 'Hegemonic Masculinity in Afrikaner Nationalist Mobilisation, 1934–1938', in S. Dudink, K. Hageman and J. Tosh (eds), *Masculinities in Politics and War: Gendering Modern History*, Manchester: Manchester University Press.

Elshtain, J. (1995) *Women and War*, 2nd edn, Chicago, IL: University of Chicago Press.

Enloe, C. (1993) *The Morning After: Sexual Politics at the End of the Cold War*, Berkeley and London: University of California Press.

Foucault, M. (1969) *The Archaeology of Knowledge*, New York: Random House.

Frederickse, J. (1990) *The Unbreakable Thread: Non-Racialism in South Africa*, Bloomington: Indiana University Press.

Geldenhuys, D. (1982) 'What do we think? A survey of white opinion on foreign policy issues', Occasional Paper, Johannesburg: South African Institute of International Affairs.

Helman, S. (1999) 'War and resistance: Israeli civil militarism and its emergent crisis', *Constellations*, 6(3): 391–410.

Hooper, C. (2001) *Manly States: Masculinities, International Relations and Gender Politics*, New York: Columbia University Press.

Kaplan, D. and E. Ben-Ari (2000) 'Brothers and others in arms: managing gay identity in combat units of the Israeli army', *Journal of Contemporary Ethnography*, 29(4): 396–432.

Lloyd, M. (2005) *Beyond Identity Politics: Feminism, Power and Politics*, London: Sage.

MacInnes, J. (1998) *The End of Masculinity: The Confusion of Sexual Genesis and Sexual Difference in Modern Society*, Milton Keynes: Open University Press.

Mann, M. (1987) 'The roots and contradictions of modern militarism', *New Left Review*, 162, March/April, pp. 35–50.

Marks, S. and N. Andersson (1990), 'The epidemiology and culture of violence', in N. Manganyi and A. Du Toit (eds), *Political Violence and the Struggle in South Africa*, London: Macmillan.

Moll, P. (1985) 'The End Conscription Campaign', *South Africa Focus.*

Phelan, S. (1999) *Sexual Strangers: Gays, Lesbians and the Dilemmas of Citizenship*, Philadelphia, PA: Temple University Press.

Phillips, M. (2002) 'The End Conscription Campaign 1983–1988: a study of white extra-parliamentary opposition to apartheid', Unpublished Master of Arts thesis, University of South Africa.

Rotberg, R. (1987) 'The ascendency of Afrikanerdom', in D. Mermelstein (ed.), *The Anti-Apartheid Reader: South Africa and the Struggle Against White Racist Rule*, New York: Grove Weidenfeld.

Seegers, A. (1987) 'Apartheid's military: its origins and development', in W. James (ed.), *The State of Apartheid*, Boulder, CO: Lynne Rienner.

Suran, J. (2001) 'Coming out against war: antimilitarism and homosexuality in the era of Vietnam', *American Quarterly*, 53(2): 452–88.

Thompson, D. and J. Branford (eds) (1994) *South African Oxford English Dictionary*, Cape Town: Oxford University Press.

TRC (Truth and Reconciliation Commission) (1997) 'Special submission on conscription', 23 July, <www.truth.org.za/special/conscrip/conscr01.htm>, accessed 17 July 2001.

Wood, B. (1991) 'Preventing the vacuum: determinants of the Namibian settlement', *Journal of Southern African Studies*, 17(4): 742–69.

SEVEN | National myths and the creation of heroes

JAMIE MUNN

How are national identities (re)constituted in post-conflict societies? How does gender work in this (re)constitution? A number of curiosities inform the writing of this chapter. One involves an interest in the effectiveness of R. W. Connell's thesis on hegemonic masculinity, particularly in light of criticisms that suggest this thesis implies a *natural* inevitable dominance (Demetriou 2001). Other critics claim that, despite its popularity, the implementation of the concept of hegemonic masculinity has not engendered any real social change (Beynon 2002; Dyer 2002; Morton 2001). I began more seriously thinking about Connell's thesis after reading over my interview notes from Kosovo.[1] These conversations led me to ponder the benefit of the concept of hegemonic masculinity in relation to reconstructions of masculine subjectivities in post-conflict Kosovo. The interview material suggested that Connell's framework potentially misses the ways gender works in post-conflict societies, overlooking the complex ways in which masculinity is discursively manipulated so that even those who are perceived to be *less* masculine within the local social hierarchy can maintain or construct a sense of self that is recognizably masculine. In order to make this argument, I use Judith Butler's idea of insurrectionary speech in the context of performativity which can powerfully assist in revealing hegemonic forms of identity (in this case masculinity) as constructed fiction rather than settled norms (Butler 1997: 16, 50, 121).

Thus, the chapter builds on work by Connell's critics, who have identified problems with the concept of hegemony and categorization of masculinities (Whitehead 2002; Beynon 2002: 125; Munn 2006: 291, 296) and explores the relevance of national heroic myths as they have materialized in post-conflict Kosovo. I utilize this work alongside Butler's notion of performativity as my entry points for critically thinking about the relevance of Connell's framework for understanding gender and masculinities in post-conflict non-Western societies. The chapter interrogates the latent insurrectionary power of nationalist myths and practices as narrative performances of hegemonic masculinity. I return to some of these concerns later, but for the moment I will suggest why post-conflict Kosovo is an interesting example in this context. To be clear from the outset, the scaffold for my arguments comes from a position which posits a direct link between the theorization of the reconstructions of nations in post-conflict and the relationship this (re)construction has with masculine identity/ies.

Why Kosovo?

Kosovo is a society (nation) in the midst of creating a self-governed state in a post-conflict environment, which inevitably involves ideas, expressions about and performances of 'national identity'. In order to shed light on the changing narratives of manliness and what is/becomes masculine in Kosovo, I will explore three common trends within the discourse on masculinities: (1) hegemonic masculinity and multiple masculinities; (2) national mythological processes associated with creating and defining 'manliness'; and (3) embodied performances of masculinity as they are represented in Kosovo.

Contemporary writers, across a spectrum of disciplines, have argued for recognition of multiple masculinities (Beynon 2002; Best and Williams 1997; Connell 1995, 2000; Carver 2002; Whitehead 2002; Zalewski 1995). They suggest that multiple masculinities are not disconnected entities without interaction and change, but interact and work in unison as well as in conflict with one another. Connell describes some masculinities as dominant, while others are subordinated or marginalized (2000: 10). Thus, according to Connell, there is one hegemonic masculinity defined as 'the masculinity that occupies the hegemonic position in a given pattern of gender relations, a position that is always contestable' (1995: 76). In the case of Kosovo, multiple masculinities play out in day-to-day civil affairs. Men from different backgrounds engage with what I will suggest is the embodiment of the most hegemonically masculine figure – the foreign soldier. The foreign soldier holds this role owing simply to status of occupier, protector and, to a certain extent, as provider.[2] Yet the interviews analysed below demonstrate that this interaction does not diminish the sense of masculinity felt by 'less masculine' men, particularly gay men.[3] These struggles have often led to violence that is frequently explained and legitimized by commentators on Kosovo in gendered language, particularly by redefining the meanings of gendered identity and group membership. I will work with my interview material to explore the idea that Connell's framework neglects an important way in which gender works in post-conflict societies and consequently has difficulty theorizing the paradoxical ways in which masculinity is discursively manipulated.

Nationalist histories have been identified as a medium through which myths are circulated. Moreover, Tosh has suggested that the narrative structure of the nation itself may be instrumental in setting up the binary story of manliness, womanliness and heterosexual subjectivity as culturally primordial (2004: 38). Others argue that some nations, such as post-communist and twentieth-century new states, are more preoccupied with narrating masculinity than others; and these nations are not dissimilar to Kosovo (Drulak 2001; Enloe 1993; Sokolewicz 1999). As such, a discussion of any nationalist struggle necessarily includes a discussion of the connection between masculinities and the mythical narratives circulating in national religious, secular or popular cultures. Whitehead suggests that national identity and formations of hegemonic masculinity are reinvigorated through 'mythical narratives that turn on recounting as hero-myth, the actions, trials and triumphs of certain (possibly fictional) men' (2002: 98, 127,176). The ritual of storytelling around dominant men is at the foreground of Kosovo's ongoing nation- and state-building project. In the case of Kosovo, it must be noted that it is not so much the nation which is under construction but external recognition of Kosovo as a state.[4] Kosovar stories of heroic men have become a means through which the community has constructed a sense of manliness and masculinity (see Parpart, this volume).[5] At the same time as exalting manly warriors, the narratives also marginalize less masculine men as outsiders, non-Albanian men, homosexuals and women.[6] It is worth noting, however, that these narrative myths of feats and courage are not limited to a particular type of man and are in fact utilized to redefine masculinities or manliness across subcultures; the dominant masculinity, at times, can be the poet, the warrior, the despot or the benevolent prince.

Connell attempts to address the power of narratives by claiming that it is a concept of gender drawing bodies into history, since bodies are arenas for the making of gender patterns (2000: 12). Gender is materialized through 'a range of "body practices", which address, sort and modify bodies' (ibid.: 58). With regard to masculinity, the warrior becomes a key site through which masculine hero-myths meet ritualized structuring of men's relationships to their bodies. When analysing the role of masculinity in provoking or perpetuating violence in Kosovo, it is necessary to make a distinction between men's embodied performances of their own masculinities, which are necessarily multiple, and their expectations of masculinity, which are limited to normative models. This modelling includes what men are taught they should aspire to be and how they judge who they are. With this reading of the narrative, men are judged and assessed by the nation as validated, demeaned or rebuked.

During my various visits to Kosovo to speak to men and women, it became apparent that a powerful mixture of pre-Yugoslavian, anti-Serbian and now post-conflict messages has led to a position where stereotypes and narratives of what men and women are like have become polarized by what they should be like and should do, and what their position in Kosovo should be.[7] Not unlike their Balkan neighbours, men are expected to be heterosexual husbands and fathers; and their status depends on having a wife and children and their ability to control them. An unmarried man, for example, is called a 'boy/kid' ('*çunak*') and is not taken seriously – he is not *yet* a *man*. Some interviewees reported that unmarried men are thought of as unable to participate in political life. Given that some of my informants were young unmarried men who fought in the national struggle as Kosova Liberation Army soldiers, this assumption about adult masculinity raises interesting questions about the subject of heroes. They were, at that time, represented as the dominant man and the powerful myth/hero; yet in post-conflict Prishtina, the public sees them once again as a *çunak*, a less manly entity. Whereas any married man is responsible, the *çunak* is stereotyped as selfish, impatient and a fun-lover. As a result, these supposed heroes are seen as being in an indeterminate state of manliness.

It should be noted that the current narrative of Kosovar masculinity is often portrayed, both within the nation and to non-members, as a pure *Albanian* ethnic identity, with a long history of a military, violent culture. It is problematic that this narrative is so deeply entrenched in the national psyche, just as it is embedded in an internationally negative image of Albanians (Mertus 1999). The negative image of Albanians as drug smugglers, pimps and human traffickers has become an international myth in its own right (Mostov 2000; <http://news.bbc.co.uk/1/hi/uk/4287432.stm>). Throughout various episodes of Balkan history, the Albanian Kosovar has been seen as a fierce warrior to his neighbours in Serbia, Macedonia, Albania and Greece. This legacy has created a *national* narrative reinforcing and applauding dominant masculine men as fighters and perpetrators of violence, which has been played upon by

Serbs to justify the authoritarian control imposed on the province in the past. It is also part of the international portrayal of Kosovar Albanians as undesirables. This stereotyped reputation is juxtaposed with a Kosovar self-perception of a nation capable of calmness and rationality that has been led during critical national histories by great intellectual *men*. It can be said, of course, that these positive internal perceptions are as much subject to manipulation as the negative external ones.

It is important to stress that Kosovar men, in some way, have to integrate this masculine narrative of what they 'ought to be' into the underlying truth of their situation, namely that they are dominated by foreign warriors. The foreigner is the OSCE administrator, UNMIK and NATO soldier. Many interviewees note that protection and occupation under either the international foreigner or Belgrade still represent weakness and non-recognition as a valid nation to most Kosavars.

In August 1991, Milošević gave an interview to BSkyB reporter Arnot Van Liden, denying involvement in the Croatian conflict. When he was asked about a call for independence from 'the people of Kosovo', his response was, 'What part of the people? The Albanians? The Albanians are a national minority in Yugoslavia. You know very well that there are no international obligations, UN or CSCE obligations or the like which determine the right of national minorities to establish their own state' (Sky Television/Belgrade TV, 7 August 1991). Van Liden's subsequent question illustrates Milošević's views on Albanians. My assertion is that these views are part of the national narrative, thus a part of the masculine narrative:

Van Liden: But the Serbs in Croatia are a minority?
Milošević: No, they are not. No Yugoslav people are a minority anywhere in Yugoslavia. We are living in Yugoslavia and we cannot be a
national minority depending on the place we are living in. Croats are
not a national minority in Bosnia, despite the fact that they are only
15 per cent. They are a people. All Yugoslav peoples in Yugoslavia are
equal and not one of them can be a national minority. Albanians are
not a people; they are not really Yugoslav because they are not Slavs.
Albanians are not even Europeans. (ibid.)

Thus, the ongoing debate on Kosovo's autonomy coincides with a discourse that devalues Kosovar manliness to the status of *çunak* in a nation on an indeterminate path to state(man)hood.

Just as the mythical hero forms part of the hegemonic narrative, so do bodies and sexualities. Connell has expressed the embodiment of masculinity partially through discussions of sexuality, stating that 'the most symbolically important distinction between masculinities is in terms of sexuality. Hegemonic masculinity is emphatically hetero-sexual, homosexual masculinities are subordinated ...' (2000: 102; see also Anand's chapter, this volume). Contrasting versions of masculinity are, however, highlighted in the Kosovar narrative. Contrary to the gender stereotypes about men and relationships, there are variations. Florin, aged twenty-three, tells a story about breaking out of the old Kosovo frame, suggesting that life in 2003 was structurally more fluid after the arrival of international forces and support agencies.

> I would like to tell people that I am a gay but I am also afraid ... I fear from other Albanian guys because of my sexuality and because of the present [situation], there is no effective police or justice system to protect me from homophobic attacks. So, I have a girlfriend. But when Kosovo is a real country and in [the] EU I can be gay. I will get a boyfriend and people can't touch us then. I am still very nervous and shy [when] meeting guys so I only go with internationals, they like my sex. They see gays as normal ... supernormal. We can meet and they know I am a gay even though no friends [of mine] can tell. I hide as a real man; they are so stupid.

We might read this as Florin seeing his own body and sexuality as part of the shifting from outsider (unaccepted gay man) to insider (Kosovar/EU citizen). He believes his sexuality may free him from the constraints of the past and give him the ability to forge a new life on different principles as he matches the change he sees in the status of Kosovo to his self-development and pleasure. As he says himself, he constructs a supernormal self. Florin, it could be said, is not performing the old Kosovar masculine narrative, but the narrative that is becoming a new masculinity in the new Kosovo.

Florin's interview makes it clear that masculinities are also bound up with constructions of ethnicities; for him, the international, *hegemonic*, masculine man accepts his sexuality without questioning his manliness. The key point to draw here is that understandings of the performance narratives of sexuality are highly relevant to an analysis of a society freshly emerging from conflict. For this reason, the images of warfare and the soldier, both the nationalist fighter and the international warrior, are implicated in the overlapping construction of masculinities.

Following on from this, if Connell can be read as providing a descriptive analysis of how masculinities are negotiated as a 'snapshot' of a particular culture, then the account of hegemonic masculinity is identified as having a distinctively deterministic outcome (Kaufmann and Williams 2004; Connell and Messerschmidt 2005). In the case of Kosovo, the hegemonic masculinity in its narrative and embodied forms alters from Serb to KLA fighter to UNMIK or NATO soldier within a period of months. It could be understood from reading Connell that social change is entirely left out of the equation.

Bringing in Butler

It is now time to suggest a provocative pairing of Connell's hegemonic masculinities thesis and Butler's insurrectionary speech. By pulling the two together, I hope to present a new way of challenging how performance and narratives of national struggles, taking the guise of social change, can be conceived as influencing masculine identities and encouraging multiple versions of hegemonic masculinities (Butler 1997).

As is now familiar to those studying the feminist canon, Butler posits gender and other social convention patterns as protected and affirmed using various symbols and social actions. In Kosovo, one could argue that these symbols and social actions are in the form of iconography. Iconographies are seen in stories of the Racak massacre of 1999, the potent manliness in Mehmet Kajtazi's novels, the ultimate self-sacrificing woman embodied by Mother Teresa and the renaming of Prishtina's main streets to memorialize Albanian heroes, as in Bill Clinton Street. Together, these national emblems and performances give Kosovars a story of their recent past, one that defines the 'gendered subject-patterns' of masculinity and femininity (Butler 1993; Zalewski 1995). These configurations of gendered histories are, however, neither solid nor permanent. Each social rule or act provides only a particular snapshot and how that snapshot is framed can alter the status quo. Therefore, the way in which each snapshot is placed and ultimately becomes a part of the national narrative develops Kosovo's potential for social change. It is from this perspective that Butler's view of gender, as open to insurrection by the use of symbols and performances, is most useful when analysing Kosovo masculinities today.

I want to use Butler's work on 'insurrectionary speech' to explore the possibility that various gendered performances and depictions in Kosovo are 'instrument[s] of resistance in [a] redeployment that destroys the prior territory of [their] operation' (Butler 1997: 163). In unveiling particular cultural readings of gender from various interviews, 'insurrectionary speech' represents the status quo out of context; and in this way, it unsettles the status quo (ibid.). One outcome of this is social and cultural performances appearing solid in that they create counter-hegemonic ways, such as Florin's reading of the hegemonic foreign soldier accepting his homosexuality as supernormal. When applied to hegemonic masculinity, Butler's insurrectionary speech can provide a strategy for destabilizing the hierarchy hegemony imposes (see Schauer 2004: 31). By means of interrupting the narrative performance of hegemonic masculinity, it may be possible to disturb Kosovars' hierarchy of masculinities.

This becomes tantamount to deconstructing the national gendered narrative; Butler allows us to see the norm/narrative as malleable. Thus, my project does not aim to simply deconstruct one ontological vision of gender in order to replace it with another; that would be counterproductive. Although Connell has challenged Butler by arguing that she is only responding to the question of social change by focusing on the individual and not the larger picture, I think this statement neglects the point that social change is influenced by which performances circulate and what myths achieve national authority (2000: 20). Thus, my point in making this argument is that social change revolves around the symbolic mechanisms through which hegemonic masculinity is performed and potentially unseated through some representations of post-conflict Kosovar society.

A new start for state and heroes

As touched upon earlier, some existing research on post-conflict societies suggests how hegemonic masculinities are reinforced through fictional representations of the emerging nation/state (Ayres 2000; Buchenau 2005; Ibeanu 2001; Munn 2006). The general narratives are laid out in three parts. First, the antagonist and hero tend to be mutually constitutive. For Kosovo, this takes the form of oppressive Serbia as the antagonist and the Kosovar resistance or militiaman as hero. The narratives constructed for each neatly reinforce a sense of national identity and hegemonic concepts of masculinity. Second, these national narratives reify the binary division of male heterosexuality and homosexuality, subordinating the latter. Third, nationalists' myths that focus on the figurative male support the *expected* embodiment of what is to emerge as masculine.

Kosovo is important to both Serbian and Albanian nationalist narratives; the province is seen by Serbs as the heartland of the medieval kingdom where many cultural and national monuments are located. For the Albanians, it is the centre of national revivalism and the founding of the League of Prizren in 1878.[8] During the 1970s, Kosovo was granted considerable autonomy and representation in all federal Yugoslav institutions, but not republic status. The longevity of the Kosovo issue and the raising of expectations among Albanians for increased autonomy polarized the two groups. In 1981, nationalist unrest among Albanians, exacerbated by economic problems and the failures of economic and political policies, led to mass demonstrations in support of secession from Serbia and full republic status within the Yugoslav federation. The demonstrations and their violent suppression were particularly important in the current national narratives of both sides.

Nationalist fighting heroes are seen as resolutely individualistic, moral, rebellious and tough. Within the nationalist myths, we see the state as the oppressor, inhumane and mechanical. The hero's quest becomes escape from slavery, rebellion against the system, or a struggle to maintain his humanity under difficult circumstances. Thus, triumph over the status quo requires a certain kind of hero. In fact, the narrative answer to the problem posed by the state is a hegemonic masculine protagonist. Nationalist myths tend to be constructed/remembered in such a way as to validate particular qualities that are attributed to the hegemonic masculine subject. The traditional qualities of a national identity are also reflected in those that might be said to include independence, insubordination and toughness.[9]

Male bodies in the fight for the nation

In 1993, Serbia attempted to alter the demographic make-up of Kosovo by actively removing Albanians from their employment, evicting them from their homes and encouraging Serbian migration into Kosovo. Ibrahim Rugova, president of Kosovo's parallel parliament established in 1998 in defiance of the continued removal of political autonomy, was seen as the embodiment of the hegemonic narrative. Rugova was a member of Kosovo's intelligentsia and an acclaimed poet and writer. He attempted to lead a peaceful resistance against Serbian control. Even as the Yugoslav wars of secession were taking place across the federation, Rugova advocated: 'The slaughterhouse is not the only form of struggle. There is no mass humiliation in Kosovo. We are organised and are operating as a state. It is easy to take to the streets and to head towards suicide, but wisdom lies in eluding a catastrophe' (*Guardian*, 4 June 1993). Rugova embodied one form of the masculinities narrative and represented the internal national narrative of Kosovars as intelligent, peaceful and Western. He held the widespread support of his nation for a period. It may be said that Kosovars saw their peaceful resistance to Serbian authoritarianism as something that the West would reward since the rest of the federation fell into war. It was not until 1995, when Kosovo was ignored in the Dayton Accords, that Rugova's role began to weaken.[10] The counter-narrative of the warrior and the old stories of national heroes from Kosovo Polje began to take hold of the nation once again; and the emergence of the Kosovo Liberation Army (KLA) in 1997 altered the national narrative, which also altered the representation and embodiment of hegemonic masculinity. This turn to the mythical rebel and a reinvigorated manliness surged in Kosovar history. It was this form of masculinity which the nation relied on to secure its autonomy. Thus, not only had the hero-myth become an essential part of national identity and hegemonic masculinity but it also gained credibility through the narrative structure of many stories and cultural imagery. Furthermore, thematic and symbolic parallels exist between the political enemies of the hero and the oppressive state. As the province of Kosovo lends itself to the mythical narratives of both Kosovars and Serbs, their own national stories have mixed and evolved one from the other, each relying on imagery that shows the other as the national and natural enemy.

The KLA utilized these symbolic parallels as socializing influences for gaining the popular support and weakening Rugova's message of passive resistance. For instance, Zani, a former KLA fighter, spoke of a need for Kosovars to display toughness, courage and willingness to fight as important means of presenting a positive identity to both Serbs and the rest of the Europe.

> If [the] KLA did not exist and we allowed people like Rugova and the rest of parliament to make our decisions for us ... still we would never have survived and nobody would ever take us seriously. Look at the Muslims in Bosnia, they are still controlled by the dogs, Kosova has proven it has a backbone – push us and we push back harder ... and we will prove it again and again. We are not Muslims alone, we are Albanians. Europe now listens when Kosovo speaks.

The construction of a nationalist myth, wherein the militiaman-hero challenges the oppressive regime, has certain consequences. Questions about statehood become questions about the survival of the hero and are performed as the hero's triumph for the nation. The hero's battle is won through patriotism, ingenuity, hardiness and so forth. Thus, hegemonic masculinity is reaffirmed; and questions about violence and abuse are neatly avoided. Caprioli claims 'motivation for collective action coupled with group identification is not a sufficient cause of conflict', but they are necessary (2005: 163). When questioned further on the internal violence and bullying of boys and men to join the KLA against their will, Zani does not want to speak about it much; his only comment being that if 'they do not want to join us then they were cowards and not worth our time ... I would [have] happily given them to the Serbs'. Another interviewee, Jetmir, aged twenty-seven, was much more willing to talk about intimidation and bullying of Kosovars and their families who refused to join him in the KLA. He stated,

Of course there are cowards in Kosova ... like anywhere ... some are too weak anyway, who would want them, they could never fight. Some guys were under pressure from families not to fight or were scared, but after you squeeze them most came around to the idea. Other 'boys' were like the girls ... [laughing] running out of Kosovo and stepping on the grannies to get to a border, any border ... faggot queers, we don't want them anyway.

I asked Zani about the rumours of rape by KLA soldiers, and although the translator made a mistake in my question, Zani's answer was more telling than I thought it would be. The translator asked, 'Tell me about cases of KLA soldiers raping each other,' at which Zani become very upset and shouted, 'We never raped each other, if that ever happened you would be killed ... [We] did have sex with some women, yes ... but that is normal. [We] did torture some guys too and maybe they [were] forced into sucking cocks, but that is all. It was never about sex.' Real stories of conflict and war can then become a fantasy that reaffirms national identity along with an idealized version of masculinity. This happened on both sides of the Kosovo conflict. Serb forces used masculine imagery of rape, penetration and sexual conquest during the war. A commonly reported phrase written by Serbian forces on Albanian burned-out homes during the conflict was 'Shiptar, watch your ass'. The process of defining masculinity continues through a treatment of homosexuality.

Homosexuality as insurrection

According to Connell, hegemonic masculinity is controlled by way of an imposed binary between homosexuality and heterosexuality; dominant masculinity is heterosexual. This may go some way to explain why homosexuality receives such negative attention in masculine activities such as fighting for one's nation. Yet when homosexuality becomes an overt/explicit issue, as in the context of gays in the military, its treatment by mainstream discourse confirms the cultural legislation of hegemonic masculinity as resolutely heterosexual. Furthermore, within this frame, sexual domination of one over another is implied if not explicit. Serbs and Albanians have used similar depictions of sexuality in their rhetoric, both seeing the other as the sexual aggressor or the sexual victim to be conquered. One thing that remains clear is that such sexualized discourse is from a heterosexual standpoint. This is clear when considering language context, such as the rape of Serbian monasteries. Attacks, which need defence, are seen as heterosexual rapes on women; and attacks that are offensive, such as against the enemy, are phrased by both sides as homosexual rapes of men. A Serbian religious layman in late 2001, while discussing the state of the Serbian monasteries in Kosovo, reported to me, 'Under the new leadership in Belgrade, Serbia is spreading its legs for NATO when it talks of Kosovo. She will let anyone enter her these days. For me it is the same disgrace as being personally sodomized.'

As a result, while a somewhat hysterical fear of homosexual assault characterizes aggressive nationalist discourse, more positive, consensual homosexual relationships are absent. Violence and aggression may be displayed as a way to meet the gender expectations of the nation as well as to more broadly meet the hegemonic notions of masculinity. Fatmir, aged twenty-eight and a former KLA fighter, says, 'Everything I did was in service to Kosovo. Sometimes that included things I am not proud of … but I had to do these things to prove I was a good Kosovar.' I asked whether he would tell me what things he meant and he replied, 'You know, beating on old people, girls were used and stuff like that. It was harder for me maybe as a gay [man] but I had to do [them] anyway … just because I am gay does not mean I [am] not a good Kosovar or a good fighter.'

During a second interview with Zani (approximately three months after the first time we spoke), it was clear he wanted to address the question of rape and attempt to 'clear up things'. He said, 'It is common knowledge that Serb girls are all whores, they have no respect for their sex and give it to people … we didn't rape them really. When it happened and not much, it was when they were ready only.' It was obvious that Zani was attempting to justify the actions, be it his or those of his friends. But he did return to the question of male rape. He asked whether it was true that I was speaking to Fatmir. I told him I was not permitted to say as all interviews were confidential. He then said,

> I bet you, man, that Fatmir gave sex to some Serb guys. [Laughing nervously] He was in my troop for most of the war and we all saw how he looked at the guys, even me! It was not nice, but he is strong. If you want to write about punishing someone ... it is Fatmir that you should say was evil. Even Serb guys [should not] get fucked. I would kill anyone trying that on me.

This further implies that homosexual relationships are always violent, non-consensual ones. Accordingly, during my interviews, when the topic of KLA *brotherhood* or emotional connections between soldiers was discussed, the majority responded quickly with a line similar to 'we were like brothers or cousins – not like gays'. There tends to be a focus on violent homosexual acts, which were presented sometimes as power struggles and most often as abuse or assault. Consensual, emotional depictions of homosexuality were often excluded. As a result, the interviewees' narratives of their experiences in the Kosovo conflict reinforced the binary division that Connell identifies as key to defining and policing hegemonic masculinity, the dominance of heterosexuality and its radical separation from homosexuality (Schauer 2004).

The narrative of dominant masculinity is, in part, that of a bodily practice (Connell 2000). Certain types of male bodies are represented in Connell's *The Men and the Boys* as ideal; and, through narrative representation of the nationalist hero, hegemonic masculinity acquires an embodied image. Mertus, in *Kosovo: How Myths and Truths Started a War*, gives an excellent account of how Kosovo's nationalist myths allow for the militiaman-hero to take a male heterosexual dominant form. She shows how myth and experience inform the political ideologies of Kosovo and explores how these competing beliefs have been created and perpetuated from the thirteenth century to the present KLA fighter. Hegemonic masculinity in nationalist myths has been performed in a number of ways: through the depiction of bodies, through narrative and visual treatment of sexuality and via the myth of the hero's quest. Setting up the state as political oppressor structures a nationalist narrative in which the main obstacle becomes the institution and its agents, as in the case of Kosovo versus the Serbian oppressor. The answer to this problematic situation is an embodiment of the mythical hero whose triumph hinges on maintaining his nationalistic and masculine identity. His weapons of defence are the characteristics of male strength, courage and resourcefulness. The militiaman-hero is incarnated in hyper-masculine physical form. Friendly homosexuality is not an option for the hero; in fact, this type of relationship is not part of the nationalist narrative and is completely ignored by both sides during the conflict.

Conclusion: insurrectionary potential

This chapter contemplates the latent insurrectionary power of nationalist myths and practices as narrative performances of hegemonic masculinity. There is no one correct reading of the myths and legends that have constructed Kosovars' hegemonic masculinities; and such myths and narratives take the form of constructing embodied metaphors that assist the nation in a given time and space. By placing the state of Serbia and its people in the role of an oppressive regime, one that has dehumanized and devalued the Albanian population, the Kosovo mythic narrative forces the state to become the primary obstacle for a nationalist militiaman-hero to overcome. The state is set up in contrast with the nationalists' own superior type of masculinity. The narrative structure pays tribute to the heroes' hegemonic masculine qualities and feats in war. Hegemonic masculinity is further reinforced by the performance of the militiaman-hero's body; it becomes the emblem of the nation at war. For Kosovo, this depiction has been through men attempting to emulate the heroes of Kosovo Polje in deed and manner. This process continues through depictions of homosexual contact between men as violent and threatening, unlike the heterosexual contact between man and woman, even when it is violent.

Some nationalist movements, such as the positioning of Rugova, complicate this picture, making porous the binary categorization of male relationships into heterosexual and homosexual. These relationships might be formed along the lines of complicit masculinity, gentry or exemplary masculinities (Connell 1995: 79). In truth, it is in understanding the renderings of homosexuality in narrative performances that I see the most likely insurrectionary potential. Homosexuality has long been a theme in counter-nationalism, just as hegemonic masculinity has been a key to nationalism.[11] I hope this investigation will convince other researchers that exploring narratives like those of Zani, Fatmir and

Florin will highlight individual experiences and truths and raise questions about the infallible connection between the nation and masculinity. Hence, research focused on investigating the insurrectionary potential of the binary of heterosexuality and homosexuality, not forgetting the multiple masculinities that narrate both, may be the difference needed to deconstruct the 'man' in international politics.

Notes

1 During a number of field visits to Kosovo I interviewed men, women and boys (between the ages of thirteen and sixteen); for the purpose of this chapter the time frame is 2000 through to 2005.

2 This point will be explored in greater detail later in the chapter.

3 Over a period of four years, I have interviewed many men who struggle with 'acting out' their masculinity in a society that they see as 'occupied' and in a state of flux.

4 Kosovar Albanians have always maintained that the objective of the civil war was to be an independent state, whereas the minority Kosovan Serbs are supported by Serbia in the argument that Kosovo is a core of the Serbian national identity.

5 For the purposes of the chapter I will refer to Kosovar Albanians as Kosovar.

6 I have explored this point at length in 'Gendered realities of life in post-conflict Kosovo: addressing the hegemonic man', *Nationalities Papers*, 34(3): 289–304.

7 Fieldwork was conducted over various visits between late 1999 and 2004. The examples given in this chapter are drawn largely from my personal observations and interviews over that period. I interviewed forty women and sixty-five men. All names

have been changed as requested by the majority of those interviewed.

8 The League of Prizren, a military and political organization, was created to re-establish the autonomy of a unified Albanian state. There was a second League of Prizren, also founded for the unification of ethnic Albanians, in 1943. Neither of the leagues actually saw success in their lobbying to create a greater Albania.

9 I have discussed the connection of Kosovo's national narrative and the rise of a hegemonic masculinity in detail in Munn (2008).

10 The Dayton Accords ended the war in Bosnia. The Accords recognized that conflicts (national and ethnically driven) have a short-term and a longer-term feature, the short-term being the end of hostilities and the longer-term the longevity of international involvement and investment. See Swomley (1999).

11 Counter-nationalism contains definitions of masculinities which can influence the hegemonic narratives and complicate definitions of men and masculinity.

References

Ayres, R. W. (2000) 'A world flying apart? Violent nationalist conflict and the end of the cold war', *Journal of Peace Research*, 37(4).

Best, D. and J. Williams (1997) 'Sex, gender and culture', in J. Berry, M. Segall and C. Kagitcibasi (eds), *Handbook of Cross-Cultural Psychology*, volume 3: *Social Behaviour and Applications*, 2nd edn, Boston, MA: Allyn and Bacon.

Beynon, J. (2002) *Masculinities and Culture*, Maidenhead: Open University Press.

Buchenau, K. (2005) 'What went wrong? Church–state relations in socialist Yugoslavia', *Nationalities Papers*, 33(4).

Butler, J. (1993) *Bodies that Matter: On the Discursive Limits of 'Sex'*, London: Routledge.

— (1997) *Excitable Speech*, London: Routledge.

Byrne, B. et al. (eds) (1996) *Gender, Conflict and Development*, Vol. II: *Case Studies: Cambodia; Rwanda; Kosovo; Algeria; Somalia; Guatemala and Eritrea,* BRIDGE: Institute of Development Studies, Report 35.

Caprioli, M. (2000) 'Gendered conflict', *Journal of Peace Research*, 37(1).

— (2005) 'Primed for violence: the role of gender inequality in predicting internal conflict', *International Studies Quarterly*, 49(2).

Caprioli, M. and M. Boyer (2001) 'Gender, violence and international crisis', *Journal of Conflict Resolution*, 45(4).

Carver, T. (2002) 'Gender', in Bellamy, R. and A. Mason (eds), *Political Theory and the Concept of Politics*, London: Sage.

Connell, R. W. (1995) *Masculinities*, Cambridge: Polity Press.

— (2000) *The Men and the Boys*, Los Angeles: University of California Press.

Connell, R. W. and J. Messerschmidt (2005) 'Hegemonic masculinity: rethinking the concept', *Gender and Society*, 19(6).

Demetriou, D. (2001) 'Connell's concept of hegemonic masculinity: a critique', *Theory and Society*, 30(3).

DfID (2004) *Regional Assistance Plan for the Western Balkans 2004/05–2008/09*, September.

Drulak, P. (2001) 'The return of identity to European politics', in P. Drulak (ed.), *National and European Identities in EU Enlargement: Views from Central and Eastern Europe*, Prague: Institute of International Relations.

Dyer, R. (2002) 'The white man's muscles', in R. Adams and D. Savran (eds), *The Masculinity Studies Reader*, Oxford: Blackwell.

Enloe, C. (1993) *The Morning After: Sexual Politics at the End of the Cold War*, Los Angeles: University of California Press.

— 'All the men are in the militias, all the women are victims: the politics of masculinity and femininity in nationalist wars', in L. A. Lorentzen and J. Turpin (eds), *The Women and War Reader*, New York: NYU Press.

Ferguson, K. (1993) *The Man Question: Visions of Subjectivity in Feminist Theory*, Los Angeles: University of California Press.

Foucault, M. (1978) *The History of Sexuality*, New York: Vintage Books.

Gamson, J. (1997) 'Messages of exclusion: gender, movement and symbolic boundaries', *Gender and Society*, 11(2).

Geis, M. (1987) *The Language of Politics*, New York: Springer.

Gibson-Graham, J. K. (1997) 'Queering Globalization', *Rethinking Marxism*, 9(1).

Goldberg-Hiller, J. (2002) 'Rights as excess: understanding the politics of special rights', Unpublished paper.

Goldstein, J. (2001) *War and Gender*, Cambridge: Cambridge University Press.

Gurr, T. R. (1970) *Why Men Rebel*, Princeton, NJ: Princeton University Press.

— (1994) 'Peoples against states: ethnopolitical conflict and the changing world system: 1994 presidential address', *International Studies Quarterly*, 38(3).

— (2000) *Peoples Versus States: Minorities at Risk in the New Century*, Washington, DC: US Institute of Peace.

Hageman, K., S. Dudink and J. Tosh (eds) (2004) *Masculinities in Politics and War. Gendering Modern History*, Manchester: Manchester University Press/St Martin's Press.

Hobden, S. and J. Hobson (eds) (2002) *Historical Sociology of International Relations*, Cambridge: Cambridge University Press.

Human Rights Watch/Helsinki (1993) *Open Wounds: Human Rights Abuses in Kosovo*, London: HRW.

Ibeanu, O. (2001) 'Healing and changing', in S. Meintjes, A. Pillay and M. Turshen (eds), *The Aftermath: Women in Post-Conflict Transformation*, London: Zed Books.

Jones, A. (ed.) (2004) *Gendercide and Genocide*, Nashville, TN: Vanderbilt University Press.

Kaufmann, J. and K. Williams (2004) 'Who belongs? Women, marriage and citizenship: gendered nationalism and the Balkan wars', *International Feminist Journal of Politics*, 6(3).

Lister, R. (2004) 'Citizenship and gender', in K. Nash and A. Scott (eds), *Blackwell Companion to Political Sociology*, Oxford: Blackwell.

McClintock, A. (1993) 'Family feuds: gender, nationalism and family', *Feminist Review*, 3(17).

Mertus, J. (1994) 'Women in the service of national identity', *Hasting Women's Law Journal*, 5(1).

— (1996) 'Gender in service of nation: female citizenship in Kosovar society', *Social Politics*, 3(1).

— (1999) *Kosovo: How Myths and Truths Started a War*, Berkeley: University of California Press.

Ministry of Defence UK (2002) *Women in the Armed Forces: A Report by the Employment of Women in the Armed Forces Steering Group*, 22 May.

Morton, D. (2001) 'Global (sexual) politics, class struggle and the queer left', in J. Hawley (ed.), *Post-Colonial, Queer: Theoretical Intersections*, Albany, NY: SUNY Press.

Mostov, J. (2000) 'Sexing the nation/desexing the body: politics of national identity in the former Yugoslavia', in T. Mayer (ed.), *Gender Ironies of Nationalism: Sexing the Nation*, London: Routledge.

Munn, J. (2001) 'Culture as process: challenges to International Relations theory through conceptualising culture and humanitarianism', Unpublished PhD thesis, University of Exeter.

— (2006) 'Gendered realities of life in post-conflict Kosovo: addressing the hegemonic man', *Nationalities Papers*, 34(3).

— (2008) 'The hegemonic male and Kosovar nationalism from 2000–2005', *Men and Masculinities*, 10(4).

Murshed, S. M. (2002) 'Civil war, conflict and underdevelopment', *Journal of Peace Research*, 39(4).

Nagel, J. (1998) 'Masculinity and nationalism: gender and sexuality in the making of nations', *Ethnic and Racial Studies*, 21(2).

Parekh, B. (1986) 'The "new right" and the politics of nationhood', in *The New Right*, London: Runnymede Trust.

Pax Christi International (1995) *Stop the Climate of Hatred and Retaliation*, Brussels.

Pipa, A. (1989) 'The political situation of the Albanians in Yugoslavia with particular attention to the Kosovo problem: a critical approach', *East European Quarterly*, 23(2).

Pitts, V. (2000) 'Visibly queer: body technologies and sexual politics', *Sociological Quarterly*, 41(3).

Pugh, M. (2001) 'Civil–military relations in peace support operations: hegemony or emancipation?', Paper presented to the Seminar on Aid and Politics, ODI, London, 1 February.

Riessman, C. K. (2003) 'Performing identities in illness narrative: masculinity and multiple sclerosis', *Qualitative Research*, 3(1).

Ross, M. H. (2000) 'The relevance of culture for the study of political

psychology', in S. Renshon and J. Duckitt (eds), *Political Psychology: Cultural and Crosscultural Foundations*, New York: NYU Press.

Russett, B. (1993) *Grasping the Democratic Peace: Principles for a Post-Cold War World*, Princeton, NJ: Princeton University Press.

Sasson-Levy, O. (2003) 'Body, gender and knowledge in protest movements: the Israeli case', *Gender and Society*, 17(3).

Schauer, T. (2004) 'Masculinity incarcerated: insurrectionary speech and masculinities in prison fiction', *Journal for Crime, Conflict and the Media*, 1(3).

Skeggs, B. (1991) 'Challenging masculinity and using sexuality', *British Journal of Sociology of Education*, 12(2).

Sky Television/Belgrade TV (1991) 'Serbian president interviewed denies involvement in Croatian conflict', 7 August, <www.slobodan-milosevic.org/news/milosevic080791.htm>.

Sokolewicz, Z. (1999) 'Poles "banter about heroes"', in A. Daun and S. Jansson (eds), *Europeans. Essays on Culture and Identity*, Lund: Nordic Academic Press.

Swomley, J. (1999) 'Kosovo: could it have been avoided?, *The Humanist*, 59(4).

Sylvester, C. (1987) 'Some dangers in merging feminist and peace perspectives', *Alternatives*, 12(4).

— (2002) *Feminist International Relations: An Unfinished Journey*, Cambridge: Cambridge University Press.

Tessler, M. and I. Warriner (1997) 'Gender, feminism and attitudes toward international conflict', *World Politics*, 49(1).

Tickner, J. A. (2001) *Gendering World Politics*, New York: Columbia University Press.

— (2005) 'What is your research program? Some feminist answers to International Relations methodological questions', *International Studies Quarterly*, 49(1).

Tosh, J. (2004) 'Hegemonic masculinity and the history of gender', in S. Dudink, K. Hagemann and J. Tosh (eds), *Masculinities in Politics and War: Gendering Modern History*, Manchester: Manchester University Press.

UNIFEM (United Nations Development Fund for Women) (2002) *Progress of the World's Women 2002*, vol. 1, New York: UNIFEM.

UNMIK (United Nations Interim Administration Mission in Kosovo) (2004) *On Gender Equality in Kosovo*, 19 February.

UNPFA (United Nations Population Fund) (2003) 'Ending widespread violence against women', in *Promoting Gender Equality*, <www.unpfa.org/gender/violence.htm>.

Waetjen, T. (2001) 'The limits of gender rhetoric for nationalism', *Theory and Society*, 31(1).

White, J. W. (1988) 'Influence tactics as a function of gender, insult and goal', *Sex Roles*, 18(7).

Whitehead, S. (2002) *Men and Masculinities: Key Themes and New Directions*, Cambridge: Polity Press.

Whitworth, S. (2001) 'The practice, and praxis, of feminist research in International Relations', in R. W. Jones (ed.), *Critical Theory and World Politics*, Boulder, CO: Lynne Rienner.

World Bank (2003) *World Development Indicators*, Washington, DC: World Bank.

Yuval-Davis, N. (1997) *Gender and Nation*, London: Sage.

Zalewski, M. (1995) 'Well, what is the feminist perspective on Bosnia?', *International Affairs*, 71(2).

Zalewski, M. and J. Parpart (eds) (1998) *The 'Man' Question in International Relations*, Boulder, CO: Westview Press.

War's Imperial Museum

Auschwitz is shrunk to an icy cake,
pristine and architectural.
I have seen this blueprint before:
the who, how, what, where of
stuffing everybody in.
This is what scares me.
Not the emaciated corpses tipped
into mass graves like landfill.
Nor the reality of shoes.
Or the fact that Roman Halter,
who buried hope with his father,
still goes to synagogue but cannot pray.

Mercy is a muzzled dog as I meander
from Genocide – 1st Floor to Genocide –
Lower Ground, before arriving at
Crimes Against Humanity: Level 4.
Pol Pot, Kurdistan Rwanda: touch-screen
technology enables the death counts
to scroll like football scores.
Now it is the 21st century, I wonder
if soon we will be required to dismiss
that which has happened the century before.
Who remembers Armenia now?

The name has changed but
inside the old asylum it is still Bedlam.
Departure is harder than I think,
it takes time to exit this predatory basement.
Out past jaunty fighter planes that dangle
in the atrium. Out past the thrusting
guns, two of them, long as a street.
Out into the air, grateful for frost
and buses, which glow like lamps,
luminous in the dark afternoon.

Karen McCarthy (2007)

EIGHT | 'Porno-nationalism' and the male subject

DIBYESH ANAND

Nationalism as a love of the self

> Nationalism has typically sprung from masculinized memory, masculinized humiliation and masculinized hope. (Enloe 1989: 44)

Cynthia Enloe's insight on nationalism offers an entry into challenging the simplistic and arbitrary distinctions conventionally made in terms of what counts as politics, whether personal, local, national or international. In this chapter, using Hindu nationalism in India as an example, I call for nationalism to be conceptualized as a political move to create, awaken and strengthen a masculinist-nationalist body which is always already vulnerable to the exposure of the self as non-masculine. Narcissistic nationalism is preoccupied with desires and concerns of (im)potency; I argue that this concern in certain cases (such as Hindu nationalism) is highly sexualized. I coin the term *porno-nationalism*, since no other existing term captures the centrality of sexualized (often what is deemed as 'abnormal' sexual practices) imagination in nationalism as an ideology and a lived collective political movement. Porno-nationalistic imaginings of the other facilitate politico-cultural mobilization of the self. This militarized/masculinized/nationalized self is, however, from its originary moment, fearful of its own fragility and seeks to expunge from within what it perceives as non-masculine, thus weak.

As expressions of collective politics, the international and the national cannot function without individual corporeal bodies that perform. Body is crucial to the nationalist project. Performativity is 'not a singular act; it is a repetition and a ritual, which achieves desired effects through its naturalization in the context of a body, understood, in part, as a culturally sustained temporal duration' (Butler 1999: xiv–xv; see also Butler 1993). These performative and performing bodies in the nation-politics are predominantly, though not exclusively, male-identified bodies, especially when conjured up as active agents. A focus on masculine bodies, as in this chapter, does not imply that feminine bodies are secondary since no conception of masculine can exist without a constitutive mirror opposite of the feminine. Peterson is right when she argues that 'it is *women's* bodies, activities and knowing that must be included if we are to accurately understand human life and social relations' (1992: 11). This chapter argues it is equally important that we reconceptualize political movements of dominance such as nationalism for what they first and foremost are – a construction/expression of masculinized bodies that assume biological 'maleness' as the main referent point. We cannot understand nationalism unless we see it as constituted primarily through, to modify Peterson, *men's bodies, activities and knowledge*, even while recognizing that categories of men and women are not biologically but socially constructed.

The masculinized-nationalized political bodies are collectively narcissistic since their very essence implies a love of the self: my nation, right or wrong! This chapter investigates Hindu nationalism in India – an ideological and political movement that seeks to convert India, a secular state with the majority of its population Hindu, into a Hindu nation – as a site of masculinist nationalism and nationalist masculinity. I analyse Hindu nationalism by conceptualizing it as a porno-nationalism. Nationalism, as a narcissistic ideology, has at its core a sexualized conception of sometimes the self and often the other; and at the level of *nationalized* corporeal bodies too, sexual desire and 'perversions' play a crucial role (see McClintock 1995 and Stoler 2002, 1995 on imperialism, nationalism and sexuality).

While the public aspect of *Hindutva* (Hindu nationalism) discourse is consciously asexualized, 'the Muslim' as a stereotyped imaginary (see Anand 2005) has a conspicuous dimension of porno-sexuality for the ordinary young Hindu male activists. Using jokes, slogans, gossip, private conversations, public speeches and pamphlets as ethnographic resources, the chapter will chart the framing of the hyper-sexed Muslim as a grave threat to India and explore the facilitative role played by such imagination in sociocultural mobilization and political organization along Hindu nationalist lines. It will argue that a pornographic imagining of Muslim men and women does not disrupt the asexual-but-virile self-understanding of Hindu nationalism since stereotyping allows for this displacement of desire and disgust on to the Muslim other.

The sexual dimension of the *Hindutva* discourse is relevant not only as an ethnographic curiosity but because it is politically salient. Such a porno-nationalist imagination of the Muslim other performs two moves at the same time: it assures the Hindu nationalist self of its moral superiority and yet instils an anxiety about the threatening masculine other. This anxiety threatens to destabilize the Hindu collective body *unless* it is awakened to the threats posed by the Muslim other. An awakened nation is also a violent nation (see Anand 2005, 2007). Hindu nationalism, despite claiming to represent the majority Hindu community, has at its core a deep masculinist anxiety which, it claims, will be solved through a masculinist, often bordering on militarized, awakening. This anxious awakening facilitates sociocultural mobilization and political organization in the name of protecting Hindu society and the Hindu nation.

This chapter analyses Hindu nationalism as a collective political movement, usually a forte of social science, using an ethnographic approach.[1] Traditional social scientific frameworks tend to ignore the self-understanding of the political actors themselves and privilege their own explanatory authority. The focus is usually on the political, economic and social factors behind the rise of Hindu nationalism as a political movement and the ways in which it transforms wider state–society relations in India. In this kind of analysis, the self-understanding of the Hindu nationalists themselves is underemphasized; the poetics and politics of their imaginations ignored. But the choice of ethnography as a method is not without its own problems.[2] In my case, it forced me to confront my own politics of scholarship: how do I conduct fieldwork among actors who indulge in politics I completely disagree with? Should I express my disgust and lose the opportunity to gather ethnographic material? Should I go along with their reading of me, which was evident during private conversations, as a natural sympathizer owing to my social identity as a Brahmin, Hindu, middle-class male, since this complicity with their reading allowed me to gain insights into the imaginative politics of Hindu nationalist male activists? A politicized feminist scholarship implies that I must confront the normative and extraordinary and the real and the epistemic violence played out in the name of my identities, even if it means being a traitor to my identity categories – gender, caste, religious and nationalist. Betrayal is a virtue when one's subjectivity is privileged (see also Dunn, this volume, on privilege and scholarship); and in the case of Hindu nationalism, my identity is privileged.

The tension between my roles as a researcher interested mostly in gathering research materials and as a human being, who sees majoritarian/masculinist nationalism as a grave danger to societies, could not be resolved. While conducting the ethnographic fieldwork, I privileged the former through an adoption of curious silence and pretended objectivity, always aware that this divide between researcher/human being is spurious and problematic. Conscience was a casualty as I listened to activists often boasting about raping Muslim women or joking about Muslim sexuality and moral depravity. While the Hindu nationalist men thought my interest was innocent and merely sexual like that of any other normal male, I was indeed interested in sexualized jokes and sex-talks as ethnographic sites. My silence was read as complicity by most of the Hindu activists with whom I interacted, even though they knew I was a researcher. The academic writing that followed my research also sought to impose its own discipline. One reviewer advised me to use neutral language and not be one-sided in my critique of Hindu nationalism, for an excessive politicization detracts from the objectivity of the work. Here, in the tradition of feminist and post-colonial writings, I have pushed the boundaries of academic writing to avoid a depoliticization of my subject and subjectivity[3] and maintain an ironic stance[4] towards that which I seek to engage. I do not endeavour to provide an authoritative overview of Hindu nationalism, nor a survey of the rich body of scholarship that already exists. I am very much present in my writing about a political movement that legitimizes itself in my name, in the name of my identities.

Potency and nationalism

Hindu nationalism is a majoritarian nationalism claiming to be a genuine representative of the Hindu majority population in India and equating India with Hindu society. Muslims and Christians, as religious minorities, are cast as foreign and/or those whose loyalty to India is suspect. Couching itself in cultural terms, Hindu nationalism is essentially a political movement seeking to purify culture and transform society. The capturing of the state is seen as a means to an end, to create a Hindu nation. The Hindu nationalist movement has been extensively studied in the context of its organization, communalism and relation with the officially secular Indian state (see Basu et al. 1993; Brass 2003, 1997; Brass and Vanaik 2002; Das 1990; Datta 1993; Hansen 1999; Jaffrelot 1999; Kakar 1996; Ludden 1996; Pandey 1993, 1990; Varshney 2002; Wilkinson 2005). Hindu nationalism is embodied within various political and cultural organizations, most of which are branded as being part of the *Sangh Parivar* (the Sangh family). While the Bharatiya Janata Party (BJP) is the main political party associated with the Sangh family, most identify the *Rashtriya Swayamsevak Sangh* (RSS or the *Sangh*) as the primary ideological source. Other members of the Sangh family include the *Vishwa Hindu Parishad* (VHP), *Bajrang Dal, Rashtriya Sevika Samiti, Durga Vahini*, and so on (see Jaffrelot 2005).

A conspicuous feature of Hindu nationalism, when it rose to political prominence in the 1990s, was the visibility of women as active participants; and several studies have analysed the relationship between women and the movement (Bacchetta 2004; Jayawardena and De Alwis 1998; Sarkar and Butalia 1995).[5] Very little scholarship has dealt with the masculinity of the movement, however, particularly in regard to its personnel, ideas and ethos (Bacchetta 1999; Banerjee 2006; Hansen 1996). Hindu nationalism is a gendered nationalism; and even though this gendering has masculine as well as feminine aspects, depending on the context (for instance, the representation of Mother India), overwhelmingly it is gendered masculine (where an awakened masculine nation is called to protect the feminine land). Hence, it is not very different from nationalist movements worldwide (see Anthias and Yuval-Davis 1992; Enloe 1989; Nagel 1998; Pettman 1996). Nationalism is conceptualized as an awakening of the Hindu nation, which is seen as being made possible by an awakening of the Hindu body, particularly the Hindu male body. As Dr Rameshwar Das Vaishnav Das, a Hindu nationalist religious figure, proclaimed in a public speech in Hardwar in December 2005, 'so long as we have potent [*punsat*] men, we will win the oncoming war against the Muslims and their allies' (Vaishnav Das 2005). These potent men are the ones who can protect Hindu female bodies, the Hindu nation and Mother India. But this potent masculinity (see also Munn and Conway, this volume) demands an awakened mind and an awakened body. In this context, the emphasis on physical exercises, outdoor sports and quasi-military drills is meant to make the Hindu male body physically strong. Brute physical strength is accompanied by an awakening of the mind, a mind that is able to recognize the enemies of the nation and is proud of Hindu history and culture. The concept of *shakti* (strength) combines physical ability and mental fortitude. What makes these men potent is not their ability to perform sexually as an individual body, but their willingness to sacrifice their individual desires to serve the higher cause of the collective Hindu body. The RSS, as Hansen argues, serves to 'encourage a systematic sublimation of sexual energy into ideologically purified services to the Mother – the nation' (1996: 148).

Thus, Hindu nationalism seeks to masculinize Hindu society. History is interpreted in terms of a pre-Islamic golden era, Hindi–Muslim antagonism for the past many centuries, emasculation of the Hindu body under Muslim rule, and selective masculine heroes who resisted alien Muslim rule,[6] thus providing an inspiration for contemporary Hindus. Religion is reinterpreted to purge its ambiguity, diversity and accommodativeness and to emphasize its martial and organizing potential. Prakashananda, a one-hundred-year-old religious figure, declared to an admiring crowd in Hardwar in December 2005 that the day Hindus awaken the universe will shake: *'bharat ke charno par brahmand jhukega'* ('the world will bow at the feet of India') (Prakashananda 2005). Contemporary Hindu nationalists imagine a masculinized Hindu society that is reproductively fertile, effectively organized, proud of its culture, and awakened to the dangers posed by enemies within the country. These enemies within, as articulated by the VHP leader Ashok Singhal in his public speeches and pamphlets, include the Muslim and Christian minorities, the communists, the secularists and the Westernized media. These inimical forces acquire their danger through their association with hostile foreign forces – Muslims are backed by the 'Muslim world', Christians by the Western/Christian world, communists by China, and the media by the West (Singhal 2005). The secularists are those weak Hindus who allow foreign and hostile domestic forces to denigrate the Hindu nation. Parmananda ji, a Hindu religious figure, attacked both the secularists for weakening Hindu society and the media for Westernizing innocent Hindu boys and girls through sexually permissive images. His statement, *'apne bache aur bachiyon ko kutta, kuttiya kyon banana chahte ho?'* ('Why do you want to make your sons and daughters into dogs and bitches?'), was met with loud applause during a public speech in Hardwar in December 2005 (Parmananda 2005).

The hope is that an awakened Hindu collective body will effectively challenge the political dominance of emasculated secularists. The awakening of the Hindu nation, however, requires sacrifices from at least some of the awakened Hindu male bodies – a sacrifice not of their masculinity but of their sexuality – and this sacrifice is deemed to be essential to the performance of that masculinity. This challenges Connell's emphasis on sexuality within hegemonic masculinity, including the argument that 'the most symbolically important distinction between masculinities is in terms of sexuality. Hegemonic masculinity is emphatically heterosexual, homosexual masculinities are subordinated ...' (2000: 102). While remaining convincingly heterosexual, Hindu nationalism extols chastity over sexuality and control over performance. Thus, the hegemonic masculinity within the Hindu nationalist imagination is not simply sexual, but ranges between asexuality and controlled (hetero)sexuality.

RSS enforces a discipline of 'a masculine community, which sublimates libido from sexual desire to devotion to the patriotic causes' (Hansen 1999: 108). 'The RSS degrades sexuality ... but does not expel [it] from the discourse altogether. Instead, it projects sexuality onto its Others' (Bacchetta 2004: 101). To be masculine is to perform heterosexual sex; yet the ideal Hindu masculinity does not perform or offer a *controlled* performance. It does so by denigrating sexuality and sexual acts as demeaning, distracting and weakening. The real men are those who control and/or transcend these bodily weaknesses. The activist in the RSS is 'enjoined to be a *brahmachari*; a self-less, celibate disciple whose devotion to the common good is in direct proportion of his self-control' (Alter 1994: 568). Thus, the ideal Hindu nationalist masculinity does not lend itself to an easy analysis in terms of virile heterosexuality, for the ideal masculinity is virile asexuality for the activists and controlled sexuality. Therefore, sex is not for pleasure but a means of producing Hindu children to proliferate the Hindu population (see Bacchetta 1999). Most senior Hindu nationalist leaders remain unmarried and celibate in the name of total devotion to the *mother*land.[7] Like religious ascetics, they see marriage as a distraction from the higher goals of life; but unlike them, the Hindu nationalists' goal is not religious but a nationalist salvation. The asexualized Hindu nationalist imaginary, however, goes hand in hand with a highly sexualized imagination of the inimical other, especially the Muslims, among the young male Hindu nationalists.[8] As became clear to me during my numerous conversations with young, male, Hindu nationalist activists in various places, a pornographic imagining of Muslim men and women does not disrupt their self-understanding of Hindu nationalism as asexual virility, since stereotyping allows for this displacement of desire, disgust and envy on to the Muslim other. Thus, the asexual Hindu nationalism allows for a porno-sexualized imagination among male Hindu nationalist activists.

Porno-nationalism

Asexualizing the Hindu self accompanies a porno-sexualizing of Muslim men and women. The imagined Muslim male body, with the female body being merely a fertile, passive recipient, is a repository of all the sexual desires/revulsions expressed by Hindu nationalist activists in their conversations. The hyper-sexuality of the Muslims is seen as common sense within Hindu nationalism. Muslims are believed to have rampant sex – many jokes, sayings, personal stories ('I do not know any Muslim myself, but someone I know knows a Muslim man who ...'), pornographic tales and serious analysis ('why are Muslims more dangerous than Christians?') take this sexualization of Muslim men for granted. The motif of 'overbreeding' Muslims is seen as proof of the hyper-sexuality of the Muslim male body. Jokes about the prolific, irresponsible, indiscreet and immoral sexuality of Muslims proliferate. Alternative sexual practices (homosexuality) are also imagined on to the Muslim other.[9] Muslim hypersexuality is ascribed to religion, diet, culture, physicality, living patterns and morality. Most of the views about Muslim sexuality (see also Kakar 1996) here have been gleaned from interviews and personal conversations I conducted during my fieldwork in 2005/06.

RD (name withheld),[10] a male photographer in his twenties from a provincial northern Indian town and a Hindu nationalist activist with the VHP, explained to me how he was an expert in identifying Muslim men just by looking at their eyes, since there was an essential untrustworthiness and *'vehshiyat'* (savage) lust in their eyes (Personal interview 2005a). In almost lyrical Hindi, he explained that Muslims engage in rampant open sex since they are children – *'Bachpan mein chuppan chuppai khelte samay, chudam chudai ho jaati hai'* ('While playing hide and seek during childhood itself, fucking takes place'). A small admiring crowd consisting of young male activists, a few older volunteers and half a dozen policemen gathered around us to see an awakened Hindu man (RD) enlightening a naive Hindu man (myself). Their smiles turned into laughter as RD narrated a joke about a typical Muslim family– *'Ek baap ne apni ladki ko akele paa kar pakad liya aur kahaa jo mazaa tujhme hai who their maa mein nahin. Ladki ne kahaa, haan bhaiya bhi yah kehte hain'* ('A father, finding his daughter alone, catches her and says, "You give more pleasure than your mother." The daughter replies, "Yes, elder brother says the same"'). RD brushed aside as ignorance my suggestion to him that the common view of Muslim families in India is of sexual repression as symbolized by Muslim women in burqa and not hyper-sexuality. His repartee played upon the pronunciation of the word burqa. This is veil in Urdu and Hindi; but when spoken aloud, it can sound similar to a pejorative expression for 'of cunt' – *'kehne ko moohn ka parda, kehlo to bur/qa* ('Supposedly a veil for the face, can be called burqa/of cunt'). A policeman (Personal interview 2005b), SS (name withheld), offered his own elaborate rationalization of supposed Muslim hyper-sexuality in multiple terms – their non-vegetarian diet (especially beef) increases body heat;[11] Islam as a religion encourages all forms of immorality; male circumcision or *khatna* increases sex drive; the public face of the repressive Muslim culture hides the oversexed practices inside the homes; and cramped living conditions (ghettoization) of Muslims in 'old' parts of many cities is a cultural preference and not an unavoidable response to discriminatory practices in the wider Indian society. SS revelled in attention as I noted down his hate-filled stereotypes, which he saw as common sense.

PT (name withheld), a young VHP activist in Nagpur in central India, narrated a story to support his claims about Muslim overpopulation, immorality, hyper-sexuality and cultural backwardness (Personal interview 2006). A police constable on his routine nightly round in a Muslim area noted a common practice and informed PT that because 'there are so many people in a single household they all cannot sleep together inside the house; so the young men and old men take turns to go inside and sleep'. This narration of a supposed observation has a sexualized connotation too; it hints at young men and old men having no discretion about whom they sleep with when they go inside. This became clear during my conversation with PT and half a dozen other male Hindu nationalist activists in the VHP office. Most explanations about the Muslim threat were filled with talk about sexual licence within Muslim families. I was informed that 'if a Muslim man gives triple *talaq* [divorce] to his wife and then regrets it, there is a way out – the woman can marry someone else and then get a divorce from the second person and come back to her first husband or more simply rectify the talaq by *sambhog* [sex] with another man'.

Such a porno-nationalist imagining of the Muslim other performs two functions at the same time. It assures the Hindu nationalist self of its moral superiority; yet, at the same time, it instils an anxiety about the threatening masculine other. This anxiety threatens to destabilize the Hindu collective body *unless* it is awakened to the threats posed by the other. Hindu nationalists take the protection of Hindu women, Hindu family and Hindu property as their responsibility. Individual anxieties about the 'protection' of Hindu female bodies metamorphose into a collective masculine anxiety about the security and welfare of the Hindu *samaj* (society), *dharma* (religion) and *sabhyata* (civilization). Sociocultural organization and political mobilization are answers to this anxiety. Hindu nationalism, despite being a majoritarian nationalism, has at its core a deep masculinist anxiety for which it claims to provide a solution through a masculinist awakening that sometimes borders on being militarized.

Mobilizing desire, desiring mobilization

How does a sharing of tacit knowledge about the other translate into political organization? Can a nationalist movement be built upon desire alone? The answers to these questions can never be simple for they will depend on the shifting and contesting dynamics within different contexts. In the case of Hindu nationalists, the porno-nationalist imagination of the hyper-sexualized Muslim other and anxious Hindu masculinity facilitate rather than cause sociocultural mobilization and political organization. That is, the imagination does not directly lead to political action; in this context, prejudices against Muslim minorities do not translate into automatic violence against them. Political action, including political violence, is a multifaceted phenomenon and imaginative practices are one of the many contributing dynamics. The anxiety generated by the threatening images of the inimical other is tapped by the Hindu nationalists to socioculturally mobilize supporters. Popular cultural resources and social practices, such as religious festivals, pilgrimages, songs, cheap CDs and VCDs, epics, and so on, are utilized to expand the support base for the Hindu nationalist movement. Homosocial bonding is clearly the biggest strength of the Hindu nationalist movement, probably more so than any other social/political movement in India. The *Sangh*'s practice of encouraging regular *shakhas* (branches) in different parts of India combining games, prayers, exercises and discussions facilitates bonding like no other political movement. The porno-nationalist imagination of the other, the claim to be the only protector of the vulnerable Hindu self, and the attractiveness of being part of a self-identified masculine nationalist project; these have proved effective means for mobilizing young Hindu boys and men, especially in small towns where there are limited alternatives.[12]

The image of hyper-sexed Muslim masculinity is tied in with the spectre of fast-breeding Muslims and vulnerable innocent Hindu femininity. These fears of demographic siege have more than a century of history. U. N. Mukherji's analysis of Hindus as a dying race in 1909, 'they count their gains, we calculate our losses' (in Elst 1997), was just the start.[13] This has led the Hindu nationalists to claim that Indian state family planning policies are anti-Hindu. The VHP leader Ashok Singhal declared in a speech in 2005, *'bacche badhakar lenge Hindustan'* ('We will control India by having more children'). By 2060, Muslims will be 50 per cent of the population; so we must end family planning and give the blessing of *Doodho nahaon, pooto phal* ('Bathe in prosperity, have plenty of children') (Singhal 2005). Such a declaration assumes reproductively inclined heterosexual male and female bodies. Suresh Das, a Hindu nationalist religious leader, explained to an admiring public in his speech in Hardwar in December 2005 that there is an Islamic conspiracy to turn India into another Pakistan using the twin strategies of religious conversion and demographic growth. According to him, Muslims are not bothered about how to take care of their numerous children. All they want is to increase their numbers so they can overtake Hindus, take over India, and then seize Hindu properties and women: *'roti, beti, zameen loot lenge'* ('We will loot your food, daughters and land'); so, 'each Hindu *bhai* [brother] should have at least six sons, two for the service of religion, two for protecting borders, and two for the economy' (Das 2005). Interestingly, in Das's vision of the Hindu nation awakened to the demographic danger posed by the duplicitous Muslims, there is no place for daughters or mothers, only sons and fathers.

A threat perceived by Hindu nationalists cutting across regional differences is that of Muslim men kidnapping Hindu girls. Stories abound of how such and such Hindu girls were kidnapped/misled by Muslim men and ended up being converted to Islam, abandoned or prostituted (for a historical analysis of the fear of vulnerable Indian women being attracted by demonic Muslim men, see Gupta 2001). The stories of kidnapping of women by the opposing community during the partition of India and their subsequent recovery (see Menon and Bhasin 1998) act as an important source of collective memory and resource for political mobilization. The kidnapped Hindu girls symbolize predatory Muslim masculinity and vulnerable Hindu femininity, and these are direct challenges to Hindu masculinity. The Hindu *nationalist masculinity* is a response to this challenge.

This sociocultural mobilization of Hindu nationalism, however, has not easily translated into political organization; hence, despite the widespread activities of the Hindu nationalist movement, politically it faces a strong challenge from other centrist, caste-based, regionalist and leftist forces. Even when the BJP, a Hindu nationalist party, came to power in the federal government, it did so by shunning most of the policy ideas that made it Hindu nationalist (see Adeney and Saez 2005). Political compulsion to secure support from various regional and centrist parties forced it to tone down its Hindu nationalist rhetoric and reach out to the minorities. My fieldwork suggests that the limited political gains of Hindu nationalists neither reflect more deep-rooted and widespread sympathies held towards the RSS among the Hindu population, nor indicate that the porno-nationalist imageries of the Muslim other are only confined to the Hindu nationalists. A medium-ranked Hindu nationalist activist, Mishra Ji, from Delhi, opined that '*muthi bhar musalman ke nak mein bhi aap nakel dal sakte hain*' ('we can easily control a handful of Muslims *if only we organize*'; Personal interview 2005c). The frustration of the Hindu nationalists with this *if only we organize* is deep and reflects a dislike of the weak self. This Hindu nationalist image of a supposed weak self, resulting in emotions ranging from uncomfortable anxiety to hatred, reminds us of earlier Indian nationalist reaction to the feminization of colonized subjectivity vis-à-vis colonial masculinity (see Sinha 1995).

Non-BJP Hindu nationalist activists and leaders today retain an ambiguous stance towards the BJP – they admire it for pursuing the Hindu nationalist agenda in states such as Gujarat but are highly critical of the BJP government at the federal level (1999–2004) for its betrayal and supposed appeasement of Muslim minorities for vote politics. The field of democratic politics is denigrated as essentially corrupt; hence, large sections of the Hindu nationalist movement, especially the RSS, define themselves as apolitical. At the same time, Hindu nationalism is essentially a political movement that seeks to organize Hindu society under its banner; and in this democratic politics, it is seen as an inescapable evil/ ally. While the state is criticized as pseudo-secular and the generic politician is branded as corrupt, the state institutions of police and military are hailed as potential allies. The capture of the state – the phallus par excellence – remains an unspoken but clearly evident goal of Hindu nationalists. Praveen Togadia, a senior VHP leader, warned religious men gathered for a public event in Hardwar in December 2005 against disillusionment with politics: 'disenchantment with politics will not help because without *Raja* [political ruler], *dharma* [religion] will perish' (Togadia 2005).

Violence becomes an integral part of the porno-nationalist asexualized masculinizing project that is Hindu nationalism. Violence against inimical others, especially the Muslims, is reactive, justified and demanded. As the maxim goes, '*Bhay bin hot na preet*' ('there is no love without fear'). Muslims understand only the language of violence. Suraj Pratap Singh, a Hindu nationalist leader, in a public speech narrated a story of a man with four sons, a lawyer, a doctor, a policeman and a judge. When someone slaps the father, the sons deliberate and discuss but take no action. The father laments; he wishes he had an illiterate son who would take action and avenge him. Singh cajoles the Hindu men to show their masculinity and to the accompaniment of loud claps declares, 'if your blood does not boil now, when will it boil? Slap those who humiliate you, there is no need to discuss' (Singh 2005). Ultimately, the Hindu nationalist violence is justified as reducing violence. SS, a policeman in the town of Ayodhya, rationalized the well-documented reports of sexual violence against Muslims with this comment: 'if rape did occur in Gujarat, so what, it is what they [the Muslims] did in the past, they did it to the Kashmiri [Hindu] women. Gujarat *kanda* [incident] in fact reduced rape by warning Muslims that the Hindus will respond in kind' (Personal interview 2005b).

Reconceptualizing nationalism as a fear of the self

Hindu nationalism's politics of imagination performs several apparently contradictory double moves: it abhors violence perpetrated by Muslims and their 'allies' but legitimizes violence in the name of the defence of the Hindu nation; it actively ropes in coercive branches of the state, especially the police, by appealing to shared religiosity while criticizing the state for being anti-Hindu; it depends on state complicity for committing anti-minority violence but absolves the state of any responsibility by claiming the violence to be a spontaneous outburst of long-suppressed Hindu *samaj* (society); the Muslim other is seen as a powerful enemy while at the same time a cowardly one in the face of the awakened Hindu body; it projects a militarized masculinity but cannot deny the anxiety of the feminine selves that inhabit the Hindu self. The fear of the hyper-masculine other is based ultimately on the hatred of the non-masculine within one's self and the fear that this non-masculine self will be exposed out of its closet. This argument has applicability beyond the example of Hindu nationalism on which this chapter focuses.

Therefore, nationalism as an ideological political movement can be conceptualized as a move to create, awaken and strengthen a masculinist-nationalist body, which is always already vulnerable to the exposure of the masculine as non-masculine. And the nationalists will use various social, cultural, political and military means to ensure that the mask is not pulled off their non-masculine core. Lives have to be lived, lives have to be hidden, lives have to be sacrificed, and lives have to be taken, all so the mask of masculine nationalism does not slip. This conceptualization of nationalism poses an important challenge with which feminist scholarship continues to grapple. How do we ensure that the self, masquerading as a defensive masculine self, sees this gesture of masquerading as abnormal, unhelpful and wrong?

Notes

1 The fieldwork among *Hindutva* activists and intellectuals was conducted in the northern and western Indian towns and cities of Ayodhya, Hardwar, Nagpur and Ahmedabad in December 2005 and January 2006. Several interviews, public speeches, and private conversations provided useful insights into the Hindu nationalist self-understanding. The trip was made possible thanks to the University of Bath's Centre for Public Economics. This research follows on from Anand (2005, 2007) and appears in greater detail in (2008). All translations from Hindi into English are my own. The chapter contains pejorative and offensive words; I have retained them because of the nature of the research and analysis undertaken.

2 Ethnography, the business of producing knowledge about human social groups, includes lively debates about the relations of power between the researcher and the researched (see Clifford 1986, Clifford and Marcus 1986 and Van Maanen 1995).

3 Feminist, postmodern and post-colonial writings have sought to push the boundaries of the politics of scholarship in various disciplines, including economics (Kaul 2007), social research (Letherby 2003), literary studies (Mohanty 2003) and international relations (Zalewski 2006).

4 Irony as a strategy recognizes the limits and that the struggle continues. As Ferguson points out, 'Irony is a way to keep oneself within a situation that resists resolution in order to act politically without pretending that resolution has come' (1993: 30).

5 Despite the existence of some high-profile Hindu nationalist women leaders, the attitude of Hindu nationalist male activists towards women as political actors remained pejorative. The comment made to me by an RSS local leader in Ayodhya about Uma Bharati, an ascetic Hindu nationalist politician who in 2005 was at loggerheads with her party's leadership, was illustrative – 'Uma Bharati ji is a typical woman ... despite being a *sadhavi* [female ascetic], she cannot give up her greed for power ... You know what women are like' (Personal interview 2005d).

6 Hindu nationalists recall Muslims as well as British rule as emasculating. Interestingly, in contemporary times, they focus overwhelmingly on the 'Muslim rule' as particularly contributing to the weakening of Hindu society.

7 Savarkar, an early proponent of Hindu nationalism with a strong admiration for European fascism, preferred to see India as a *pitribhumi* (fatherland/ancestral land) rather than a *matribhumi* (motherland) in

his ideological pamphlet of 1923
(Savarkar 1999).

8 For a theorization of this
apparent contradiction in terms of
Lacanian 'lack' and Zizekian *'jouis-sance'*, see Hansen (1996).

9 For a discussion of the shifting
relationship between heterosexuality, homosexuality and nationalist
groups, see Munn and Conway, this
volume.

10 Because of the sensitive nature
of the topic, names have been withheld unless the quote comes from a
publicly delivered speech.

11 For an interesting discussion
on meat, pornography and sexuality,
see Adams (2003).

12 It became clear during my
fieldwork that for many young boys
and men who participated in Hindu
nationalist activities, 'friendship' and
collective activities (such as games)
were very important pulling factors.
The *shakhas* (regular sessions held by
the *Sangh* volunteers) provide unique
opportunities to acquire pleasure
through friendship and games. Since
interactions between girls and boys
are frowned upon, same-sex friendships acquire greater significance as
a source of pleasure. This pleasure
of boys/men with male company
remains under-theorized within
scholarly studies on masculinity and
masculine political movements (for
an exception and a discussion of
'virile fraternity' within nationalism,
see Parker et al. 1992).

13 For analysis of demographic
politics of Hindu nationalism, see
Datta 1993; Dayal 2004; Rajalakshmi
2004.

References

Adams, C. J. (2003) *The Pornography of Meat*, New York: Continuum.

Adeney, K. and L. Saez (eds) (2005) *Coalition Politics and Hindu Nationalism*, London: Routledge.

Alter, J. S. (1994) 'Somatic national-ism: Indian wrestling and militant Hinduism', *Modern Asian Studies*, 28(3): 557–88.

Anand, D. (2005) 'Violence of security: *Hindutva* in India', *The Roundtable: The Commonwealth Journal of International Affairs*, 94(379): 201–13.

— (2007) 'Gendered anxieties: repres-enting Muslim masculinity as a danger', *British Journal of Politics and International Relations*, 9(2): 257–69.

— (2008) *Muslims as the Other: Hindu Nationalism in India and the Poli-tics of Fear*, New York: Palgrave Macmillan.

Anthias, F. and N. Yuval-Davis (1992) *Racial Boundary: Race, Nation, Gender, Colour and Class and the Anti-Racist Struggle*, London: Routledge.

Bacchetta, P. (1999) 'When the (Hindu) nation exiles its queers', *Social Text*, 17(4): 141–66.

— (2004) *Gender in the Hindu Nation: RSS Women as Ideologues*, New Delhi: Women Unlimited.

Banerjee, S. (2006) 'Armed masculin-ity, Hindu nationalism and female political participation in India', *International Feminist Journal of Politics*, 8(1): 62–83.

Basu, T., P. Datta, S. Sarkar, T. Sarkar and S. Sen (eds) (1993) *Khaki Shorts, Saffron Flags*, New Delhi: Orient Longman.

Brass, P. (1997) *Theft of an Idol: Text*

and Context in the Representation of Collective Violence, Princeton, NJ: Princeton University Press.

— (2003) *The Production of Hindu–Muslim Violence in Contemporary India*, New Delhi: Oxford University Press.

Brass, P. and A. Vanaik (eds) (2002) *Competing Nationalism in South Asia*, New Delhi: Orient Longman.

Butler, J. *Bodies that Matter: On the Discursive Limits of 'Sex'*, London: Routledge.

— (1999) *Gender Trouble: Feminism and the Subversion of Identity*, rev. edn, New York: Routledge.

Clifford, J. (1986) *The Predicament of Culture: Twentieth Century Ethnography, Literature, and Art*, Cambridge, MA: Harvard University Press.

Clifford, J. and G. E. Marcus (eds) (1986) *Writing Culture: The Poetics and Politics of Ethnography*, London: University of California Press.

Connell, R. W. (2000) *The Men and the Boys*, Los Angeles: University of California Press.

Das, S. (2005) Public speech during VHP *Dharma Sansad*, 13–14 December, Hardwar, India.

Das, V. (1990) 'Introduction: communities, riots, survivors – the South Asian experience', in V. Das (ed.), *Mirrors of Violence*, New Delhi: Oxford University Press.

Datta, P. K. (1993) '"Dying Hindus": production of Hindu communal common sense in early 20th century Bengal', *Economic and Political Weekly*, 19: 1305–19.

Dayal, J. (2004) 'Indian census: after xenophobia, the report card of the communities', *Countercurrents*, <www.countercurrents.org/comm-dayal120904.htm>, accessed 18 March 2006.

Elst, K. (1997) *The Demographic Siege*, New Delhi: Voice of India, Online, <koenraadelst.voiceofdharma.com/books/demogislam/index.html>, accessed 1 August 2006.

Enloe, C. (1989) *Bananas, Beaches and Bases: Making Feminist Sense of International Politics*, Berkeley: University of California Press.

Ferguson, K. (1993) *The Man Question: Visions of Subjectivity in Feminist Theory*, Berkeley: University of California Press.

Gupta, C. (2001) *Sexuality, Obscenity, Community: Women, Muslims, and the Hindu Public in Colonial India*, Delhi: Permanent Black.

Hansen, T. B. (1996) 'Recuperating masculinity: Hindu nationalism, violence and the exorcism of the Muslim "other"', *Critique of Anthropology*, 16(2): 137–72.

— (1999) *The Saffron Wave: Democracy and Hindu Nationalism in Modern India*, Princeton, NJ: Princeton University Press.

Jaffrelot, C. (1999) *The Hindu Nationalist Movement: 1925 to the 1990s*, New Delhi: Penguin.

— (ed.) (2005) *The Sangh Parivar*, New Delhi: Oxford University Press.

Jayawardena, K. and M. De Alwis (eds) (1998) *Embodied Violence: Communalising Women's Sexuality in South Asia*, London: Zed Books.

Kakar, S. (1996) *The Colors of Violence: Cultural Identities, Religion, and Conflict*, Chicago, IL: University of Chicago Press.

Kaul, N. (2007) *Imagining Economics Otherwise: Encounters with*

Identity/Difference, London:
Routledge.

Letherby, G. (2003) *Feminist Research
in Theory and Practice*, Milton
Keynes: Open University Press.

Ludden, D. (ed.) (1996) *Making India
Hindu: Religion, Community, and
the Politics of Democracy in India*,
New Delhi: Oxford University
Press.

McClintock, A. (1995) *Imperial
Leather: Race, Gender, and Sexu-
ality in the Colonial Context*,
London: Routledge.

Menon, R. and K. Bhasin (1998)
*Borders and Boundaries: Women in
India's Partition*, New Brunswick,
NJ: Rutgers University Press.

Mohanty, C. T. (2003) *Feminism with-
out Borders: Decolonizing Theory,
Practising Solidarity*, Durham, NC:
Duke University Press.

Nagel, J. (1998) 'Masculinity and
nationalism: gender and sexuality
in the making of nations', *Ethnic
and Racial Studies*, 21(2): 242–69.

Pandey, G. (1990) 'The colonial
construction of "communalism":
British writings on Banaras in
the nineteenth century', in V. Das
(ed.), *Mirrors of Violence*, New
Delhi: Oxford University Press.

— (ed.) (1993) *Hindus and Others:
The Question of Identity in India
Today*, New Delhi: Viking.

Parker, A., M. Russo, D. Sommer and
P. Yaeger (eds) (1992) *National-
ism and Sexualities*, London:
Routledge.

Parmananda (2005) Public speech
during VHP *Dharma Sansad*,
13–14 December, Hardwar, India.

Personal interview (2005a) Conversation with VHP activist RD (name
withheld) during the VHP Steering

Committee Meeting, 12 December, Hardwar, India.

— (2005b) Conversation with policeman SS (name withheld) guarding
a VHP leader during the VHP
Steering Committee Meeting, 12
December, Hardwar, India.

— (2005c) Conversation with VHP
activist Mishra Ji during the VHP
Steering Committee Meeting, 12
December, Hardwar, India.

— (2005d) Conversation with
Prakash Awasthi, an RSS leader
in Karsewak Puram, 5 December,
Ayodhya, India.

— (2006) Conversation with VHP
activist PT (name withheld) at the
VHP Office, 10 January, Nagpur,
India.

Peterson, V. S. (1992) 'Introduction',
in V. S. Peterson (ed.), *Gendered
States: Feminist (Re)Visions of
International Relations Theory*,
Boulder, CO: Lynne Rienner.

Pettman, J. J. (1996) *Worlding Women:
A Feminist International Politics*,
London: Routledge.

Prakashananda (2005) Public speech
during VHP *Dharma Sansad*,
13–14 December, Hardwar, India.

Rajalakshmi, T. K. (2004) 'The population bogey', *Frontline*, 21(20),
<www.frontlineonnet.com/fl2120/
stories/20041008006101600.htm>,
accessed 20 March 2007.

Said, E. (1983) *The World, the Text,
and the Critic*, Cambridge, MA:
Harvard University Press.

Sarkar, T. and U. Butalia (eds)
(1995) *Women and Right-Wing
Movements: Indian Experiences*,
London: Zed Books.

Savarkar, V. D. (1999) *Hindutva*, 7th
edn, Mumbai: Pandit Bakhle.

Singh, S. P. (2005) Public speech

during VHP *Dharma Sansad*, 13–14 December, Hardwar, India.

Singhal, A. (2005) Public speech during VHP *Dharma Sansad*, 13–14 December, Hardwar, India.

Sinha, M. (1995) *Colonial Masculinity: The 'Manly Englishman' and the 'Effeminate Bengali' in the Late Nineteenth Century*, New York: Manchester University Press.

Stoler, A. L. (1995) *Race and the Education of Desire: Foucault's History of Sexuality and the Colonial Order of Things*, Durham, NC: Duke University Press.

— (2002) *Carnal Knowledge and Imperial Power: Race and the Intimate in Colonial Rule*, Berkeley: University of California Press.

Togadia, P. (2005) Public speech during VHP *Dharma Sansad*, 13–14 December, Hardwar, India.

Vaishnav Das, R. D. (2005) Public speech during VHP *Dharma Sansad*, 13–14 December, Hardwar, India.

Van Maanen, J. (ed.) (1995) *Representation in Ethnography*, London: Sage.

Varshney, A. (2002) *Ethnic Conflict and Civic Life: Hindus and Muslims in India*, New Haven, CT: Yale University Press.

Wilkinson, S. I. (ed.) (2005) *Religious Politics and Communal Violence*, New Delhi: Oxford University Press.

Zalewski, M. (2006) 'Distracted reflections on the production, narration and refusal of feminist knowledge in IR', in B. Ackerly, M. Stern and J. True (eds), *Feminist Methodologies for International Relations*, Cambridge: Cambridge University Press.

NINE | Masculinity/ies, gender and violence in the struggle for Zimbabwe

JANE L. PARPART*

Much has been written about the struggle for majority rule in Zimbabwe,[1] particularly as a conflict over political and economic power, a challenge to colonial and settler authority and an assertion of racial equality and cultural autonomy (Alexander et al. 2000; Bhebe and Ranger 1995; Lan 1985; Ranger 1985). Gendered analyses of the conflict have focused almost entirely on women, initially uncritically accepting nationalist rhetoric about gender equality (Weiss 1986; Weinrich 1979), and more recently adopting a more measured, critical stance (Nhongo-Simbanegavi 2000; Ranchod Nilsson 2006). Very little, however, has been written about the role of masculinity/ies and male power in the conflict. Yet masculine discourse, authority and prerogatives have been at the heart of both the settler and the nationalist projects.

The struggles over power and legitimacy in Zimbabwe pitted competing notions of manhood and womanhood together in a complicated and often unforgiving history. This chapter explores this gendered process, deliberately including all racial and ethnic groups, on the assumption that Zimbabwe's past cannot be understood without addressing the experiences, beliefs and behaviour of all participants. The chapter draws on memoirs, literature and scholarly articles. Many are openly biased, some voices are rarely heard – particularly those of blacks, Coloureds and Asians in the Rhodesian forces – but the aim is not to discover the 'truth', but rather to explore the ways in which struggles over power shaped (and were shaped by) competing, interacting and often contested notions of manhood and womanhood in a period of violent change.

Asking the man question in Zimbabwe

While violence and conflict are shaped by economic, political and cultural contexts, they are also deeply gendered. As Cynthia Enloe argues, 'No person, no community, no national movement can be militarized without changing the ways in which femininity and masculinity are brought to bear on daily life' (1993: 20, 120). Indeed, militarization has tended to reinforce a masculine identity tied to protecting nation, women and children, while tolerating violence, and a femininity that requires both vulnerability and endurance (ibid.: 63). Nationalism is thus a highly gendered and often masculinist project (Giles and Hyndman 2004: 10; Enloe 1995).

Yet neither masculinity nor femininity is a settled or homogenous category, nor are they tied to sexed bodies. As Raewyn Connell (1995, 2005) argues, hierarchies among masculinities are produced and maintained by linking hegemonic masculinity to masculinist power while sidelining subordinate and marginalized masculinities as well as womanhood/femininity. Those who threaten the link between hegemony and masculinist power are expelled from the inner circle; women can enter, but only if they do not challenge the link with masculinist power (Hooper 2001; Wiegman 2001).

The need to consider post-colonial and colonial contexts as well as the intersectionality of factors such as race, culture and class on gendered practices has introduced some important caveats to the discussion of hegemonic masculinity (McCall 2005). In the African context, a number of scholars challenge Connell's notion of a singular hegemonic masculinity, arguing that in multiracial/ethnic societies, multiple hegemonic masculinities often contend and even complement each other. Moreover, particular historical conjunctures affect gendered identities (Cornwall and Lindisfarne 1994; Lindsay and Miescher 2003; Ouzgane and Morrell 2005).

These concerns are relevant to the chapter's exploration of the development of masculine and feminine identities in a multicultural, multiracial settler colony. The chapter focuses on the nationalist struggles (1952–80), but places them in the earlier colonial and pre-colonial contexts.[2] The aim is to explore the way gendered assumptions and practices framed, explained and legitimized the struggle, as well as how the struggle, and its historical antecedents, affected gendered identities, particularly the evolution and institutionalization of militant masculinism.

Manhood and womanhood in colonial Zimbabwe

Colonial Zimbabwe was characterized by a number of competing (and sometimes collaborating) notions of successful manhood and womanhood. The two dominant ethnic groups – the Shona, long-term inhabitants in the region, and the Ndebele, a splinter of the militant South African Zulu/Ngoni peoples, who conquered south-west Zimbabwe in the

1840s, tended to privilege senior men, particularly 'big men' with many dependants, who were regarded as the true embodiments of successful masculinity. Women in both societies had some power and influence, particularly in domestic and spiritual arenas, but control over women, as well as junior males and children, was considered a necessary condition for male success and a crucial element of true manliness (Schmidt 1992; Shire 1994; West 2002).

Tensions between the two groups over land, respect and power simmered below the surface, however, and were often cast in masculinist terms, with the Ndebele belittling Shona military skills, and the Shona reacting with resentment, while also sometimes appropriating the Ndebele language (SiNdebele) and warrior mythology/past when it enhanced their authority. As Shire points out, 'SiNdebele signified the epitome of a very physical masculinity: an ability to use the knobkerrie and the myths of the Zulu fighters like Shaka' (1994: 149). This framing of difference was exacerbated by the British preference for martial societies in the empire (Streets 2004). An 1886 settler diary, for example, described the Mashona as 'a dirty cowardly lot' while praising the Matabele (Ndebele) as 'bloodthirsty devils but a fine type' (Ranger 1979: 3).[3] These gendered myths of masculine martial abilities (and incapacities) continue to legitimize gender, ethnic and racial hierarchies today.[4]

The early European settlers generally identified with a muscular masculinity, linked to prowess at sport, physical toughness and the ability to deal with the challenges thrown up by the harsh African environment. There was a lot of 'hard living and drinking', as well as a sense of community developed through shared hardships (Jacobs 1995; Tredgold 1968: 21). This masculinized imaginary was reinforced by memories of the African uprisings in the 1890s (the first *Chimurenga*),[5] and the settler heroes who crushed them (Lovett 1977). Indeed, militarism was 'woven deep into the constructions of settler masculinity' (Morrell 2001: 139), reinforced by the celebration of white male heterosexuality, toughness and racial superiority played out in schools, on the sports field and in daily life (McCulloch 2000; Vambe 1976).

Colonial rule affected African masculinity/ies as well. Loss of land and political authority, as well as new opportunities in the urban areas, reduced many senior males' ability to attract and keep followers (Barnes 1999; Schmidt 1992). Racist practices – being forced off the pavement when a European passed by, prohibitions on speaking English to officials, being called 'boy' no matter one's age and doing 'women's work' as domestics in European homes – undermined male status and authority (Vambe 1976). Some senior males managed to secure an alternative form of 'big man' status by cooperating with native authorities or obtaining the education and employment needed to set up large households in town or at mission stations (Holland 2005; Ranger 1995; Summers 2002). For most, the road to respectable manhood was fraught with pitfalls. It had to be pieced together in rural homelands and the harsh circumstances of urban life, where 'respectable' Africans and local authorities sought to control and contain 'undesirable' men and women, especially youth (Barnes 1999, 2002; Maxwell 2006).

The economic expansion after the Second World War and the rise of liberal politics provided new models of manhood and womanhood. The Federation (1953–64) promised a multiracial, meritocratic future (someday), and encouraged interracial organizations dominated by liberal whites and educated African elites (Hancock 1984; Hughes 2003; Muzondidya 2005; Tredgold 1968). Liberal notions of respectable manhood (and womanhood), based on education, rationality and a commitment to modernity/progress and merit, offered an alternative to the frontier masculinity of early settler days – attracting many Europeans, as well as those black, Asian and Coloured elites who thought they had a chance to 'make it' under these conditions (Tosh 1999; Scarnecchia 1999). Formal education (particularly mission education), Western dress and food, and access to a modern/Western lifestyle became preoccupations of aspiring and established elites. Women joined this gendered quest, supporting their husbands' struggle for respectability and social status by running modern households, organizing key social events and producing 'properly' dressed children who studied hard and behaved like model citizens for a multiracial future (Barnes 1999: 93–123; Maxwell 2006; Muzondidya 2005; Ranger 1995; West 2002).

Those who saw little chance for themselves within this elite world tended to be more sceptical, and to remain wedded to local notions of masculinity, gender relations and respectability. Indeed, the privileges of patriarchal authority, particularly for senior men, must have been an attractive alternative to the limited rewards of Western 'civilization'. Despite widespread enthusiasm for some aspects of Western modernity, for the vast majority of African men control (or the appearance of control) over women, children and junior males remained a crucial marker of successful manhood. This requirement was increasingly difficult to achieve, particularly in towns, where women's increasing economic autonomy threatened male authority. The violent attack on a hostel for employed single women during the 1956 bus boycott, and the refusal to apologize for the rapes,[6] demonstrates the early nationalists' determination to place masculine concerns in the public domain and to sanction male hostility to independent (potentially defiant) women (Barnes 1999; Scarnecchia 1996, 1999; West 1997).[7]

The federal dream began to founder in the late 1950s – economic decline and racist legislation undermined hopes for genuine multiracial partnership. Urban riots, rural protests and growing sympathy for the nationalist cause reflected growing discontent, often expressed in gendered and class terms. The 1960 Bulawayo rioters, for example, burned down African businesses and threatened women without party cards (interview, Michael Hove, Bulawayo, 23 July 2005). The government's harsh response only hardened nationalist resolve. While some moderate Africans clung to the multiracial dream (Parpart 2008), a militant masculinist future became increasingly attractive to many, both white and black, as the right-wing Rhodesia Front (RF) triumphed in the segregated polls and set about creating the white-dominated settler state of Rhodesia, and the nationalists called for authentic African manhood to rise up and challenge that state (Caute 1983; Sithole 1977).

Manhood, masculinity/ies and gender in the struggle for power: 1964–80

Struggles over power, nation and nationalisms dominated the history of the new settler state. While clearly affected by economic, social and political forces, discourses and practices of masculinity/ies were central, framing the fighters (on all sides) as heroes/saviours of the nation and protectors of women and children (Kriger 1995). But this frame also defined womanhood in terms of unconditional loyalty to the cause, condemning defiant, critical women (and men) as 'sell-outs' and traitors. This section explores the way gendered discourses and practices were both used and contested during the struggle, and the consequences of these practices for constructions of masculinity/manhood and femininity/womanhood on all sides.

The conflict went through several phases. In the 1960s, the nationalists' military efforts made little impact. The leaders were jailed or banished and the government declared victory over the 'few communist extremists' causing the unrest (Tredgold 1968: 244–6). In the early 1970s, ZANLA adopted Maoist guerrilla tactics, while ZIPRA continued to rely on more formal Soviet-style warfare (Raeburn 1978: 97).[8] The war intensified as ZANLA expanded its operations, buttressed by well-trained ZIPRA defectors and new recruits. The Rhodesian regime responded by setting up counter-insurgency units and creating Protected Villages (PVs), but did little to endear themselves to the local African population, assuming that the nationalist forces were no match for Rhodesian power (Caute 1983; Kesby 1996; Reid-Daly 1999: 87).[9] Indeed, military efforts slowed in the mid-1970s, when the increasingly autocratic, inefficient and sexist practices of both military commands fuelled dissent and rebellions, particularly the Nhari rebellion within ZANLA. The brutal suppression of these revolts led to a period of instability, conflict and assassinations within the nationalist groups, which, along with several abortive peace negotiations, complicated and slowed military campaigns in the mid-1970s (Chung 2006; Kriger 1992; White 2003).

The war intensified dramatically after 1976 as a group of idealistic, more educated junior officers combined forces to prosecute the war and encourage debate on political freedoms and gender relations.[10] The senior (male) leaders' return soon put a stop to this, and they were jailed in 1977 (Chung 2006: 124–33; Moore 1995). The war grew more deadly, violent and ambiguous as the internal settlement pitted nationalists against each other in a struggle more over power than national liberation, which was now seen as inevitable. Indeed a third of total deaths occurred in 1979 (Kriger 1992: 92–3). Dirty tricks, such as poisoning water and clothes, increased, made worse by the government's introduction of the untrained, often criminal Security Force Auxiliaries (SFA) and Sithole's brutal Ugandan-trained forces (Alexander and McGregor 2005: 79; Caute 1983: 191–3, 142; Ellert 1989: 108–9; Nkomo 1984: 195). The nationalists were little better. They increased attacks on 'sell-outs' and suspected sorcerers/witches, attacking missionaries, abusing local women and abducting schoolchildren (Cowderoy and Nesbit 1987: 69, 130; Ellert 1989; Kriger 1992; Werbner 1991). Both sides adopted a 'shoot first and ask questions later' approach, with devastating consequences for civilians, who became increasingly desperate for peace and order (Cowderoy and Nesbit 1987; Fuller 2004). Throughout the struggle, gendered discourses and practices continued to frame, explain and legitimize contestants on all sides.

Claiming the nation; claiming manhood Both the Rhodesian regime and its opponents explained their right to rule/take power in masculinist terms. Despite women's crucial involvement in the anti-colonial struggle, the nationalist leaders (male) were 'intent on achieving a masculinist victory over the colonial state' (Barnes 1999: 149). The struggle for power was largely framed as an opportunity for 'real men' to end white/male domination and to complete the work of the first *Chimurenga*. Dominated by angry young men, who regarded violence as key for contesting state authority and political mobilization, nationalism became even more explicitly linked 'to a newly aggressive expression of masculinity ...' (Alexander 2007: 5–6). Despite socialist slogans about gender equality, the reassertion of male power framed much nationalist discourse. John Moyo, an early nationalist leader, rallied an attentive audience, declaring that 'We, the Sons of the Soil, have become foreigners in our own country', because of 'our unwillingness to fight like men ... It is high time that we acted like men to retrieve our stolen land' (Sithole 1977: 2). Such masculinist language litters the memoirs and documents produced by nationalists. Didymus Mutasa, for example, cited daily humiliations meted out to African men by the Rhodesian settlers as a factor in the belief that only violence could restore African manhood (1983: 95–6). Maurice Nyagumbo condemned a white official's refusal 'to treat him with the respect – and the manners – due to him as a man and a nationalist' (Alexander 2007: 7).

Tensions and disputes among rival camps were often cast in masculinist language. One young nationalist complained that ZAPU leaders were belittling the Shona as 'natural cowards' while trumpeting Ndebele bravery. Those who dared to challenge allegedly authoritarian and anti-intellectual commanders were condemned as 'sell-outs' and often met a brutal end (Tshabangu 1977: 12–13, 17; Raeburn 1978; White 2003). Rival nationalist factions condemned each other's judgement and military skills and strategy, often in highly masculinized language (Chung 2006; Tshabangu 1977). Indeed, Nyagumbo vilified his critics as men who had 'no interest in politics but [only] in women and beer' (1980: 146–8). Considering Nyagumbo's earlier days of drinking, womanizing and ballroom dancing in South Africa, this statement reveals both a self-critique and the very masculinist rhetoric and practice required of converts to the nationalist cause.[11]

Blacks who worked for the regime or believed in gradual, multiracial change were branded as 'sell-outs'/'quislings', 'loyal lapdogs', effeminate (and often homosexual), too cowardly to lay down their life for family, culture and nation (Alexander 2007; Chung 2006: 130; Nyagumbo 1980). They were accused of selling their souls for 'money, for women, for beer and for material possessions' (Sithole 1977: 127). Identifying and killing 'sell-outs' thus became a mark of loyalty to the nationalist movement and a sign that one was truly a nationalist warrior, unafraid and willing to kill even close kin for the cause. Indeed, *Chimurenga* battle songs urged people to crack the heads of 'sell-outs' and whites (Pongweni 1982). The label 'sell-out' thus became a means for disciplining one's own group, legitimizing violence, and all too often for grabbing property and getting rid of personal enemies – particularly attractive to poor young men (and women) bent on challenging senior males' authority (Chinodya 1989; Kaarsholm 2005; Kesby 1996; Kriger 1992; Staunton 1990).

The Rhodesian Front's claim to power was based on assertions of white (male) technical and martial superiority, and their self-proclaimed ability to protect both 'civilization' and their dependent women and children. The Rhodesian Front's determination to defy British opinion, as well as internal and external critics, fostered a belligerent, martial masculinity, emerging easily from a racist, macho culture centred on racial hierarchies, rugby, beer and *braais* (barbecues). Popular songs celebrated the 'men and boys [who] are fighting for the things that they hold dear'.[12] Popular culture and government propaganda fêted the Rhodesian heroes risking their lives to defend the nation from godless communism, terrorists and all enemies of civilized living standards (Hancock 1984; Moore-King 1988), and promised that the West would eventually see the justice of their cause (Cowderoy and Nesbit 1987: 71).

At the same time, given the small size of the white population, the discourse of militant white male triumphalism had to be moderated to attract black, Coloured and Asian supporters. With the warning that the nationalists would return the nation to the Stone Age, loyal citizens were congratulated for siding with modernity and progress, rather than communism, terrorism and African nationalism (Bull 1967: 141). These arguments initially appealed largely to moderate urban Africans put off by young nationalists' excesses, as well as some rural patriarchs who enjoyed government support. As the violence intensified, however, many beleaguered patriarchs (and weary civilians) longed for peace – and voted in large numbers (64 per cent) for a multiracial compromise in 1978 (Ellert 1989: 1–2; Kriger 1992; Muzondidya 2005: 100–101; Skimin 1977: 97).

Like the nationalists, the Rhodesian regime vilified their enemies as weak, effeminate, failed men – whether white or black (Ellert 1995: 89–91). Garfield Todd, a former prime minister, was confined to his ranch and condemned as a turncoat who cared nothing for nation or family

(Weiss with Parpart 2001). The nationalists were dismissed as a small, incompetent group of thugs intent on terrorizing an otherwise peaceful African population. Their rather inept early nationalist military incursions encouraged a cocky belief in the superiority of white military prowess, often expressed in masculinist and racist terms. The army chief of staff, for example, dismissed the early attacks as the work of 'garden boys' (Fuller 2004), referring to a widespread colonial discourse suggesting that Africans lacked the intellectual capacity, stomach and skills needed to successfully prosecute a war. Government security forces described the conflict as 'a jolly good war', one that provided opportunities to brag of martial exploits, openly ridicule black men and flirt with black waitresses at popular watering holes like the Makuti Motel, while vehicles with dead guerrillas waited outside (Ellert 1989: 13; Raeburn 1978: 66–8). These insults to African manhood not surprisingly fuelled opposition to the regime and support for war (Sithole 1977). They also prolonged the war, leading Rhodesian leaders to 'tragically wrong assessments of enemy capacity and determination, especially among the supposedly effeminate Shona' (Cowderoy and Nesbitt 1987: 210–11).

War makes the man Participants on both sides celebrated war as a means for making 'real' men. The Rhodesian regime told the young Rhodesians sent to fight that the war 'was a glorious adventure, an easy test of manhood, a war that was right and always honourable, a war where the good were white and the evil were black, a war as simple as that' (Moore-King 1988: 3, 51, 77). Indeed, the war was represented as the quintessential arena for turning boys into men. The men in the armed forces were compared to the European heroes of the 1890s uprisings; they were celebrated in songs, novels and the media (Chennells 1995). Most men felt the war was a test of their manhood – 'this kind of thing makes a man of you' (Weiss 1994: 52). Recruits were guaranteed masculine status – after all, 'It's a man's job to protect God's own country' (Bond 1977: 124). The infamous Selous Scouts appealed to masculine pride – 'we are looking for men to do men's work – very tough men' (Reid-Daly 1999: 58). When soldiers went to town, they would harass civilians, telling young men, 'Get a fucking haircut, you civvies. When are you going to join the army, you wanker?' (Cocks 1988: 23). Men who refused to join the war were ridiculed as failures. Women joined the chorus (ibid.: 15). Thus the discourses of war reinforced both the manliness of those who fought and the lack of manly qualities among men who refused.

Moreover, sexualized, masculinized language among soldiers differentiated those who knew how to fight and had been hardened by war and
those who had not. New recruits were accused of being '"little cunts"
or "fucking fairies". Inexperienced soldiers in the field were razzed by
the experienced fighters, who asked them "What are you fuckin' fresh
puss doing here – eh?" The experienced soldiers compared themselves
with the newcomers by reminding them that "This prick's fucked more
chicks than you *okes* have had hot breakfasts!"' (ibid.: 9, 23, 36). African
recruits in the Selous Scouts were egged on during intense, difficult
training, with threats that 'only women would fail to complete such an
easy course' (Reid-Daly 1999: 58–60). Such images surface repeatedly in
soldiers' memoirs, reminding us just how gendered and sexualized the
performance of war often is.

The trauma of war, the deaths and the killing of the 'enemy' were also
framed in antiseptic and masculinist terms. Soldiers described the war
as 'a fine punch up'. Fighting was a 'contact' and killing was sanitized as
'scribbling', 'culling', 'slotting', 'drilling', 'wasting', 'snuffing', etc. Those
killed were dismissed as 'munts', 'gooks', 'Affs' or 'terrs', all fighting for
godless communism (Fuller 2004: 59–60). Killing became a numbers
game – the more 'terrs' killed, the greater the celebration (Lovett 1977).
Moral scruples were for women and weak men, not the fighting men
of Rhodesia. As one former soldier said, 'We were all mad in that war.
That's why we were so fucking good' (Fuller 2004: 66).

Intense bonding also developed. As one soldier wrote, 'It is easy to
feel forgotten in the bush, not only for the chap who has no family or
girlfriend. All of us at times ... feel alone and scared.' Letters from home
and parcels from the Loyal Women's Guild helped (MacBruce 1983: 37),
but the daily camaraderie at base and during combat was a crucial survival
strategy (Lotter 1984). Some of the units even developed their own language. Most partied hard. The Rhodesian Light Infantry (RLI) had regular
parties which did not end till every officer's stiff-front shirt had been
torn off (Bond 1977: 90, 151). The nature of guerrilla warfare no doubt
intensified bonding – the Selous Scouts downplayed racial and political
loyalties, demanding only loyalty to 'a band of brothers and comrades
called the regiment ...' (Reid-Daly 1999: 107). Long periods of sitting
around, waiting and worrying, were broken up with sporadic, deadly
encounters with the enemy. Soldiers dreamt of home, but the daily reality
facing most Rhodesian forces (and the increasing number of reservists
on rotation duty) was framed by an intense, homoerotic environment

which inspired life-long friendships and emotional ties (Cowderay and Nesbit 1987: 161). Indeed, as Cocks reminisced, 'comradeship took the place of everything outside the RLI ... even families and lovers ... and would save the lives of many of us later on' (1988: 22).

The nationalists demonstrated a similar belief that war would restore dignity and manhood to African men who had become emasculated subjects under settler rule. Didymus Mutasa, citing Fanon (1963), argued that 'A time will come when men will not fear guns, interrogation cells, police informers, or the Gonakudzingwa detention camp; they will cross the Zambesi to return home greater men, determined, disciplined and equipped to penetrate into their country not as terrorists but as liberators' (1983: 95–6). Memoirs of ZIPRA forces struck a similar chord. Nicholas Nkomo, a ZIPRA commander, 'came to the conclusion that violence was the only language the colonialists could understand'. For him, leaving the country, 'to become a man and a fighter', was a logical response to colonial oppression (Alexander and McGregor 2004: 84–5). All recruits were assured that the war would transform them into warriors fighting a just cause. Indeed, this began with the assignment of war names, often highly masculinist labels such as Comrade Danger, Comrade James Bond or Comrade Cast out the Boers (ibid.: 87; Lan 1985: 125).

Training for the nationalist forces generally took place outside the country. Political indoctrination accompanied military training, but the entire experience was framed by the goal of producing warriors – 'Sons of the Soil who would rise up and fight' (Lan 1985: 172). The arduous, often harsh training was regarded as necessary to produce hardened fighting men, who could cope with the 'rough and masculine world' of bush combat and challenge the assumption that killing was the preserve of whites (Alexander and McGregor 2004; Nhongo-Simbanegavi 2000: 44; Sithole 1977: 111). It was 'very tough and brutal, more punishment and reprimand than praise and encouragement' (Tshabangu 1977: 21). Internal as well as external threats fostered an authoritarian leadership style in both armies which brooked no dissent, celebrating ruthless, loyal warriors, while punishing critics (especially the educated) with death, torture and exile. Tongogara was particularly noted for his harsh discipline and ruthless extermination of enemies (Chung 2006; Tshabangu 1977).

The training invoked past heroes in struggles against the whites, claiming that the guerrillas were warriors of the past returned in a new guise. Drawing on the power of spirit mediums adept in the art of killing, the nationalist forces adopted many of the mediums' rules of war, including the prohibition on sex while on duty (Lan 1985). This 'regulation' was often ignored. Indeed, the ZANLA high command was known for its promiscuity and its 'feudal' attitudes towards women (Chung 2006: 124–33), and ZIPRA leaders were accused by some of enforcing 'a draconian code while … observing no morals' (Tshabangu 1977: 8). The prohibition no doubt was partly invoked to placate rural leaders' frustrations with rebellious young men (and women) and their desire to maintain established gender hierarchies (Kesby 1996; Kriger 1992: 195). The fact that some people blamed the failure of Muzorewa's troops and Tongogara's death on their sexual transgressions suggests, however, that the link between sexual discipline/control and warrior status had some purchase (Chung 2006: 139; Lan 1985: 158).

Divisions within and between the nationalist fighters were often framed in masculinist terms as well. ZIPRA memoirs celebrate their military skills, discipline and training, while condemning the treacherous, untrustworthy character of ZANLA fighters. As one former ZIPRA soldier recalled, 'We had no time to organise bush rallies and singing in the mountains [i.e. the *pungwes* popular with the ZANU forces] … The men with whom I served were highly trained in both modern warfare and guerrilla warfare, they were soldiers not armed politicians' (Caute 1983: 22; Alexander and McGregor 2004). ZANLA forces condemned Nkomo as a rich capitalist 'sell-out', criticized ZIPRA's military strategy and massacred ZIPRA soldiers when the opportunity presented itself (Caute 1983: 18; Chung 2006: 147–8).

Women and womanhood in war: supporters/dependants/enemies Just as war strengthened militant forms of masculinity, it also affected notions and practices of womanhood. Scholars have celebrated the 'new' women and men emerging from the cauldron of violence in nationalist struggles (see Nhongo-Simbanegavi 2000: 1–12). Indeed, on both sides of the conflict some women began to carry guns, defend farms and villages, and even kill – traditionally masculine undertakings. Women in the nationalist forces were given aggressive names, such as Joyce Mujuru's title as Cde. Teurai Ropa (Spill Blood). A few women moved up the ranks in the nationalist forces, gaining some authority and respect. Indeed, Joyce Mujuru's celebrated downing of a Rhodesian chopper legitimized her rise in the ranks of the nationalist forces. Some young women (and men) took the opportunity to experiment with new gender identities and practices, challenging the authority of senior males, parents and local authorities, sometimes by joining the nationalists and sometimes by selling critics out to government or guerrilla forces (Cowderoy and Nesbit 1987: 54; Kesby 1996; Kriger 1992).

While acknowledging the importance of women's support, military and civilian authorities sought to contain these challenges to masculinist authority. Both sides celebrated warrior males as 'protectors', and women and children as the 'protected', legitimizing male authority and reinforcing 'traditional' gender hierarchies. Joyce Mujuru's marriage to a leading ZANLA commander, and the rarity of women in the high command, suggests that her advance did little to challenge the link between masculinity and warrior status. Neither the Rhodesian nor the ZIPRA commands favoured women on the front line (Alexander and McGregor 2004: 90). ZANLA allowed women in battle only after 1978, and even then, when an area became a hot zone, a situation 'for real men', 'women were automatically cleared from this male space'. ZANLA commanders 'were far from convinced that women could face the enemy in battle' – even if they had the same training as men (Nhongo-Simbanegavi 2000: 82–3). Nationalists applauded women 'warriors' for turning their cooking sticks into weapons of war, and the Rhodesians celebrated the bravery of women defending farms from attack, but the dangerous nature of this work, particularly in the rural areas, did little to challenge gender hierarchies. Even the nationalists' early attempts to halt domestic violence faltered as the leaders concentrated on reining in unruly young men (and women) and pleasing disgruntled rural patriarchs (Kriger 1992: 195; Nhongo-Simbanegavi 2000).

Moreover, the messy realities of a guerrilla war complicated gender relations, even among allies. Officials turned a blind eye to the sexual antics of the Rhodesian forces, including the Selous Scouts' 'Roman villa cum harem' mess/eating place in Bindura (Ellert 1989: 26, 116). The nationalist commanders set a poor example with their multiple wives and girlfriends. Indeed, Tongogara regarded sexual favours as a rightful reward of battle (Chung 2006: 82, 125). Female comrades were often raped or seduced and then banished to camps for unwed mothers if they became pregnant. Women who complained were brushed aside – they must have been asking for it! (Caute 1983: 18; Nhongo-Simbanegavi 2000). The Rhodesian 'guards', and later the Auxiliaries, routinely demanded sexual favours from young women in the protected villages (Ellert 1989: 26; Kesby 1996). Similarly, the nationalist forces often breached established social norms by kidnapping, seducing and raping local women, despite pleas of frustrated and frightened parents, and many unwanted pregnancies (Staunton 1990: 49–50; Werbner 1991). Thus even supportive women were not immune from the violence of war.

Women seen as enemies met no mercy; both sides exerted ruthless, deadly revenge. Long-established norms of respect for women, for seniority, for education and for the young crumbled in the onslaught. The Rhodesian forces routinely stripped naked, raped and threatened to drown African women suspected of collaboration. Sometimes, hot porridge, flames or sharp objects were inserted into their vaginas, often with deadly effects (Fuller 2004: 62–3; MacBruce 1983: 99). Guerrilla forces were no better, systematically torturing and killing women identified as collaborators, no matter how flimsy the evidence. Women teachers at the Elim Pentecostal Mission were raped and killed. On both sides, killing women, even older respected members of the community, became an everyday occurrence, often unremarked and unacknowledged (Ellert 1989: 117–18; Kriger 1992; Nhongo-Simbanegavi 2000).

Violence, gender and social change The final violent years of the struggle complicated and intensified conflicts within and between warring groups, undermining established hierarchies of age, wealth, race and gender. The chaos provided a cover for grabbing property, challenging elders' authority, settling scores with 'enemies' and obtaining sexual favours on both sides (Alexander and McGregor 2005: 79; Ellert 1989: 117; Kriger 1992). Seniority and wealth counted for little if someone could make an accusation of disloyalty stick. Young men and women brandishing arms declared their independence, threatening to identify parents as 'sell-outs' if they refused to cooperate (Kesby 1996). Respect for women fell by the wayside as women and girls experienced sexual harassment and worse from government and nationalist forces, particularly the Auxiliaries, 'many of them resembling villains in B movies, sporting pendants, hats wrapped in animal skins, fancy shirts, bandoliers of copper-typed cartridges coiled round their bodies like sharks' teeth' (Caute 1983: 270; Kesby 1996; Nhongo-Simbanegavi 2000).

Racial divisions and hierarchies began to crumble as well. The internal settlement brought blacks into power (albeit with serious constraints). Race increasingly failed to define either enemies or friends as former nationalist allies fought each other in a vicious and desperate battle over power. Government forces were increasingly multiracial – the Selous Scouts were five-sixths black in 1979. Small groups of black and blacked-up white soldiers fought for weeks in the bush, returning to base to relax together at evening *braiis* where they drank and sang *Chimurenga* songs (Ellert 1989: 95; Reid-Daly 1982: 66).[13] White reservists up to the age of sixty spent half the year in the bush. Crowded urban hospitals put white and black patients side by side (MacBruce 1983: 45) These embodied transgressions of supposedly fixed racial, cultural and ideological divides suggest the possibility that long-held 'certainties' about race, manliness and courage were being disturbed by the struggle, at least in certain quarters (White 2005).

At the same time, willingness to brook opposition and tolerance for dissent crumbled even further as it became increasingly apparent that political power was going to be won through the gun. The government centre of power shifted from politicians to the military, with the ruthless Brigadier-General Peter Walls effectively running the country (Cowderoy and Nesbit 1987: 177). Josiah Tongogara's authority grew, as did that of the ZIPRA leadership. Militant masculinity ruled the day; enemies were vilified as failed men – dangerous unprincipled thugs or effeminate weaklings. Muzorewa denounced his former nationalist allies, ZANU and ZAPU, as 'terrorists' and thugs, while Sithole condemned ZANLA as 'a bunch of murderers' (Caute 1983; Chung 2006: 112, 234). ZANU and ZAPU leaders ridiculed Muzorewa and Sithole as weak and indecisive clients of Smith, neither capable nor worthy of leading the nation (Chung 2006: 230). Critics on all sides were swiftly and ruthlessly silenced. Those who questioned such behaviour were ridiculed as weaklings who lacked the stomach for war. Executions became commonplace, as poorly disciplined soldiers attacked 'sell-outs', 'prostitutes' wearing Western clothes and supposed (often female) 'witches' (Caute 1983; Chung 2006; Lan 1985: 129).

Both sides promised to restore law and order to a traumatized populace. The war had left deep scars on civilians and soldiers. Violence and death had become daily occurrences, always possible, always unpredictable, always at close quarters. People had grown weary of war and sceptical of the fighters, some of whom, made mad by guns, had become 'almost like animals' (Staunton 1990: 130; Werbner 1991: 158). Everywhere, the longing for peace and order intensified, especially the need to bring young men and women under control (Kriger 1992: 143–53). Support for the internal solution had not worked, and threatened by ZANLA and a few ZIPRA forces lobbying in the war zones, the candidate with the largest military presence won (Alexander 1998: 152–3; Kriger 2005: 4–6). Militarism thus defined victory and set the ground rules for Zimbabwe's future, as had colonial occupation in 1890 and earlier ethnic conflicts. Mugabe promised compromise, progress and order for all, and no doubt many believed him. Some, however, remembered the past, feared the future and just hoped for the best – as an older black woman exclaimed at a 1980 Harare prayer meeting, 'Mugabe has killed many in my village, please give him a change of heart' (Spring 1986: 17: Nhongo-Simbanegavi 2000: 125–33).

Conclusion

In the end, the war turned out to be a triumph for masculininist author-ity and long-established gender hierarchies (Nhongo-Simbanegavi 2000). The evidence suggests that the militant masculinist imaginary that framed so much of the war fostered a vision of masculinity that prized physical toughness, the ability and willingness to use violence, loyalty to the cause and protection of dependants. Enemies were feminized, while success in war and the unflinching use of violence became the litmus test of man-hood. The presence of a few women 'warriors' did not destabilize the link between militant masculinity and power, as long as most women accepted their role as 'protected' dependants. The escalation of violence during the struggle reinforced and reshaped patterns of gendered domination, paternalism and violence that had existed throughout the colonial period. While the power relations between participants had changed, the natural-ized link between militant masculinity and power remained unscathed, even if significantly more multiracial. This vision of masculinist authority resonated with many war-weary citizens across the country, who voted for Mugabe in the hope that he would bring peace and a return to established (and predictable) hierarchies, particularly the right to bring young men and women under control. Thus, while shaped by specific racial, cultural and class forces, and deeply influenced by past injustices and gendered practices, a hegemonic masculinist project emerged with the new state.

It is easy to assume this gender regime was an inevitable consequence of violence and conflict. Indeed, the link between violent nationalist struggles and the resurgence of militant masculinist power is depress-ingly commonplace (Enloe 1995; Giles and Hyndman 2004). On the surface, Zimbabwe seems to have been just one more example of this prac-tice. The ruling party's violent attacks on independent women (branded prostitutes), on homosexuals and on critics of the system – no matter what their race, ethnic identity or class – demonstrated a preference for violent solutions (Ranchod Nilsson 2006). The rhetoric of inclusion and tolerance disappeared as the ruling party systematically wrote 'enemies' out of history (Ranger 2004; White 2003), legitimized attacks on critics and muzzled an independent press, organizational life and political opposition (Nhongo-Simbanegavi 2000). The rhetoric of war continues as Mugabe brags of his 'degrees in violence' and promises to protect the nation from the opposition – branded as 'tea-drinking lackeys/sell-outs' of Blair and Bush. Thus the purchase of militant masculinist language and practices continues, legitimizing atrocities and defining who has the right (or not) to power and rule.

At the same time, it is important to remember that gendered practices are not fixed; they are contested and fluid. The rebellions against the military command in ZIPRA and ZANLA not only demanded greater tolerance and debate, they also launched vitriolic critiques of their leaders' sexual excesses. Moderate blacks and whites continued to call for peaceful, multiracial solutions. Different circumstances might have allowed those voices to flourish. An earlier resolution to the conflict might have undermined militarist power, offering more space for negotiated, democratic processes. The current crisis is inspiring much path-breaking scholarship on nationalism, citizenship, democracy and gender. Challenges to the present system are possible, but they have to interrogate the way militant masculinism and its feminine counterpart have explained, reinforced and maintained male privilege and autocratic power in Zimbabwe. Challenges that ignore that process, and its historical antecedents, will surely fail.

Notes

* I would like to thank Theresa Barnes, David Moore, Brian Raftopoulos, Stephan Chan, Daniel Conway, Jocelyn Alexander, Robert Muponde, Guy Thompson, Moses Chikowero and Gary Kynoch among others for their constructive and helpful comments.

1 The British South Africa Company ruled the colony from 1890 to 1923; Responsible Government in Southern Rhodesia (SR) was established in 1923; SR joined Northern Rhodesia and Nyasaland in the Federation of Central Africa (1953–64), after which Rhodesia became a settler-dominated state. In 1980 Zimbabwe declared independence.

2 A succession of nationalist organizations were established and banned from the 1950s. The Zimbabwe African Peoples' Union (ZAPU) emerged in 1961, led by Joshua Nkomo. In 1963, the Zimbabwe African National Union (ZANU) broke away, initially led by Ndabaningi Sithole and later by Robert Mugabe. ZAPU's seeming identification with the Ndebele and ZANU with the Shona exacerbated ethnic rivalries. The more moderate African national Congress (ANC),

led by Abel Muzorewa, with Sithole (ZANU-Sithole) and Chief Chirau, negotiated an internal settlement with the Rhodesian regime in 1977. Muzorewa was elected in 1978, but the conflict continued and in 1980 he lost power to ZANU-PF and Robert Mugabe (Ndlovu-Gatsheni 2005).

3 The question of Indian and Coloured masculinities has largely been ignored by scholars (Muzon-didya 2005).

4 Mugabe often reverts to SiNdebele when making a particularly threatening point (interview, Pathisa Nyathi, Oxford, UK, 15 June 2007).

5 *Chimurenga* means struggle in Shona and has been associated with battles for African independence since the 1890s.

6 Sixteen women were raped, but these 'tea-drinking sell-outs' were blamed for inciting the rapes (Barnes 2002; Scarnecchia 1996).

7 For a different assessment, see West (2002). While the attack on these women may have aimed to build support for the nationalist cause, the nature of the attacks clearly demonstrates a strong gender/masculinist bias (personal communication, Moses Chikowero, November 2007).

8 ZANLA was the military wing of ZANU and ZIPRA of ZAPU. Josiah Tongogara, a ruthless, patriarchal but very capable leader, headed ZANLA (Chung 2006).

9 The Rhodesian forces included police, army, air force and counter-insurgency units such as the Selous Scouts (SS) and the Rhodesian Light Infantry (RLI). Africans played an important role in all forces (in 1979 over half the front-line fighters were black), except the all-white RLI and the air force. White officers led an otherwise all-black Rhodesian African Rifles. Coordinating this complex structure was an ongoing and contested enterprise (Bond 1977; Cowderoy and Nesbit 1987; Ellert 1989).

10 They established the joint Zimbabwe Peoples' Army (ZIPA) and set up a college for debating issues, including the treatment of women in the nationalist forces (Chung 2006; Moore 1995).

11 Personal communication, Moses Chikowero, November 2007.

12 This is from a ballad by John Edmonds and Clem Tholet, 'The Story of Rhodesia', pointed out to me by Ian Taylor. It begins: 'They can send their men to murder and they can shout their words of hate. But the cost of keeping this land free will never be too great.'

13 The impact of such socializing and sharing of 'enemy' songs needs much deeper analysis as it suggests the possibility of cultural interaction that was largely derailed after 1980.

References

Alexander, J. (1998) 'Dissident perspectives on Zimbabwe's post-independence war', *Africa*, 68(2): 151–82.

— (2007) 'Political prisoners' memoirs in Zimbabwe: passages in the meta-narrative of nationalism', mimeo.

Alexander, J. and J. McGregor (2004) 'War stories: guerrilla narratives of Zimbabwe's liberation war', *History Workshop Journal*, 57: 79–100.

— (2005) 'Hunger, violence and

the moral economy of war in Zimbabwe', in V. Broch (ed.), *Violence and Belonging*, London: Routledge.

Alexander, J., J. McGregor and T. Ranger (2000) *Violence and Memory: One Hundred Years in the 'Dark Forests' of Matabeleland*, Oxford: James Currey.

Barnes, T. (1995) 'The heroes' struggle: life after the liberation war for four ex-combatants in Zimbabwe', in N. Bhebe and T. Ranger (eds), *Soldiers in Zimbabwe's Liberation War*, Oxford: James Currey.

— (1999) *'We Women Worked So Hard': Gender, Urbanization and Social Reproduction in Colonial Harare, 1930–1956*, Portsmouth, NH: Heinemann.

— (2002) '"We are afraid to command our children": responses to the urbanisation of African women in colonial Zimbabwe, 1930–44', in B. Raftopoulos and R. Yoshikuni (eds), *Sites of Struggle: Essays in Zimbabwe's Urban History*, Harare: Weaver Press.

Bhebe, N. and T. Ranger (eds) (1995) *Society in Zimbabwe's Liberation War*, Oxford: James Currey.

Bond, G. (1977) *The Incredibles: The Story of the 1st Battalion, the Rhodesian Light Infantry*, Salisbury (Harare): Sarum Imprints.

Bull, T. (1967) *Rhodesian Perspective*, London: Michael Joseph.

Caute, D. (1983) *Under the Skin: The Death of White Rhodesia*, London: Penguin.

Chennells, A. (1995) 'Rhodesian discourse, Rhodesian novels and the Zimbabwean liberation war',

in N. Bhebe and T. Ranger (eds), *Society in Zimbabwe's Liberation War*, Oxford: James Currey.

Chinodya, S. (1989) *Harvest of Thorns*, Harare: Baobab Books.

Chung, F. (2006) *Re-living the Second Chimurenga*, Harare: Weaver Press.

Cocks, C. (1988) *Fireforce: One Man's War in the Rhodesian Light Infantry*, Alberton, SA: Galago.

Connell, R. (1995) *Masculinities*, Cambridge: Polity Press.

— (2005) 'Change among the gatekeepers: men, masculinities, and gender equality in the global arena', *Signs*, 30(3): 1801–25.

Cornwall, L. and N. Lindisfarne (eds) (1994) *Dislocating Masculinity*, London: Routledge.

Cowderoy, D. and R. Nesbit (1987) *War in the Air: Rhodesian Air Force, 1935–1980*, Alberton, SA: Galago.

Ellert, H. (1989) *The Rhodesian Front War: Counter-insurgency and Guerrilla War in Rhodesia, 1962–1980*, Harare: Mambo Press.

— (1995) 'The Rhodesian security and intelligence community 1960–1980', in N. Bhebe and T. Ranger (eds), *Soldiers in Zimbabwe's Liberation War*, Oxford: James Currey.

Enloe, C. (1993) *The Morning After: Sexual Politics at the End of the Cold War*, Los Angeles: University of California Press.

— (1995) 'Feminism, nationalism and militarism: wariness without paralysis?', in C. R. Sutton (ed.), *Feminism, Nationalism and Militarism*, New York: American Anthropological Association.

Fanon, F. (1963) *Wretched of the Earth*, New York: Grove Press.

Fuller, A. (2004) 'Letters from Zimbabwe: the soldier', *New Yorker*, 1 March, pp. 54–67.

Giles, W. and J. Hyndman (eds) (2004) *Sites of Violence: Gender and Conflict Zones*, Berkeley: University of California Press.

Hancock, I. (1984) *White Liberals, Moderates and Radicals in Rhodesia, 1953–1980*, New York: St Martin's Press.

Holland, K. (2005) 'The troubled masculinities in Tsitsi Dangarembga's *Nervous Conditions*', in L. Ouzgane and R. Morrell (eds), *African Masculinities*, London: Palgrave Macmillan.

Hooper, C. (2001) *Manly States: Masculinities, International Relations, and Gender Politics*, New York: Columbia University Press.

Hughes, R. (2003) *Capricorn*, London: Radcliffe Press.

Jacobs, S. (1995) 'Gender divisions and the formation of ethnicities in Zimbabwe', in D. Stasiulis and N. Yuval-Davis (eds), *Unsettling Settler Societies*, London: Sage.

Kaarsholm, P. (2005) 'Coming to terms with violence', in R. Muponde and R. Primorac (eds), *Versions of Zimbabwe*, Harare: Weaver Press.

Kesby, M. (1996) 'Arenas for control, terrains of gender contestation: guerrilla struggle and counter-insurgency warfare in Zimbabwe 1972–1980', *Journal of Southern African Studies*, 22(4): 561–84.

Kriger, N. (1992) *Zimbabwe's Guerrilla War: Peasant Voices*, Cambridge: Cambridge University Press.

— (1995) 'The politics of creating national heroes: the search for political legitimacy and national identity', in N. Bhebe and T. Ranger (eds), *Soldiers in Zimbabwe's Liberation War*, Oxford: James Currey.

— (2005) 'ZANU (PF) strategies in gender elections, 1980–2000', *African Affairs*, 104(414): 1–34.

Lan, D. (1985) *Guns and Rain, Guerrillas and Spirit Mediums in Zimbabwe*, Oxford: James Currey.

Lindsay, L. and S. F. Miescher (eds) (2003) *Men and Masculinities in Modern Africa*, Portsmouth, NH: Heinemann.

Lotter, C. (1984) *Rhodesian Soldier and Others Who Fought*, Alberton, SA: Galago.

Lovett, J. (1977) *Contact*, Harare: Galaxie Press.

MacBruce, J. (1983) *When the Going was Rough: A Rhodesian Story*, Pretoria, SA: Femina Publishers.

McCall, L. (2005) 'The complexity of intersectionality', *Signs*, 30(3): 1771–800.

McCulloch, J. (2000) *Black Peril, White Virtue: Sexual Crime in Southern Rhodesia, 1902–1935*, Bloomington, IN: Indiana University Press.

Maxwell, D. (2006) *African Gifts of the Spirit*, Oxford: James Currey.

Moore, D. (1995) 'Democracy, violence and identity in the Zimbabwean war of national liberation', *Canadian Journal of African Studies*, 29(3): 375–402.

Moore-King, B. (1988) *White Man Black War*, Harare: Baobab Books.

Morrell, R. (2001) *From Boys to Gentlemen: Settler Masculinity in Colonial Natal*, Natal: University of South Africa.

Mutasa, D. (1983) *Black behind Bars:*

Rhodesia 1959–1974, Harare: Longman.

Muzondidya, J. (2005) *Walking a Tightrope: Towards a Social History of the Coloured People of Zimbabwe*, Trenton, NJ: Africa Research and Publications.

Ndlovu-Gatsheni, S. (2005) 'The last days of Rhodesia and the politics of transition to independence in Zimbabwe, 1977–1980', Mimeo.

Nhongo-Simbanegavi, J. (2000) *For Better or Worse? Women and ZANLA in Zimbabwe's Liberation Struggle*, Harare: Weaver Press.

Nkomo, J. (1984) *The Story of My Life*, London: Methuen.

Nyagumbo, M. (1980) *With the People: An Autobiography from the Zimbabwean Struggle*, London: Allison and Busby.

Ouzgane, L. and R. Morrell (eds) (2005) *African Masculinities*, New York: Palgrave Macmillan.

Parpart, J. (forthcoming) 'Silenced visions of citizenship, democracy and nation: African MPs in Rhodesian parliaments, 1963–1978', in S. Ndhlovu-Gatsheni and J. Benjamin (eds), *Re-thinking and Re-Imagining Nationalism in 21st Century Africa*.

Pongweni, A. (ed.) (1982) *Songs that Won the Liberation War*, Harare: College Press.

Raeburn, M. (1978) *Black Fire*, London: Julian Friedmann.

Raftopoulos, B. (1999) 'Nationalism and labour in Salisbury, 1953–1965', in B. Raftopoulos and T. Yoshikuni (eds), *Sites of Struggle*, Harare: Weaver Press.

Ranchod Nilsson, S. (2006) 'Gender politics and the pendulum of political and social transformation in Zimbabwe', *Journal of Southern African Studies*, 32(1): 49–67.

Ranger, T. (1979) *Revolt in Southern Rhodesia 1986–7*, London: Heinemann.

— (1985) *Peasant Consciousness and Guerrilla War in Zimbabwe*, Harare: Zimbabwe Publishing House.

— (1995) *Are We Not Also Men?: The Samkange Family and African Politics in Zimbabwe 1920–64*, Oxford: James Currey.

— (2004) 'Rule by historiography: the struggle over the past in contemporary Zimbabwe', in R. Muponde and R. Primorac (eds), *Versions of Zimbabwe: New Approaches to Literature and Culture*, Harare: Weaver Press.

Reid-Daly, Lt Col. R., as told to Peter Stiff (1982) *Selous Scouts Top Secret War*, Alberton, SA: Galago.

— (1999) *Pamwe Chete: The Legends of the Selous Scouts*, Weltevreden Park, SA: Covos-Day.

Scarnecchia, T. (1996) 'Poor women and nationalist politics', *Journal of African History*, 27(2): 283–310.

— (1999) 'The mapping of respectability and the transformation of African residential space', in B. Raftopoulos and T. Yoshikuni (eds), *Sites of Struggle*, Harare: Weaver Press.

Schmidt, E. (1992) *Peasants, Traders and Wives: Shona Women in the History of Zimbabwe, 1870–1939*, Portsmouth, NH: Heinemann.

Shire, C. (1994) 'Men don't go to the Moon: language, space and masculinities in Zimbabwe', in A. Cornwall and N. Lindisfarne (eds), *Dislocating Masculinity*, London: Routledge.

Sithole, N. (1977) *Roots of a Revolu-*

tion, Oxford: Oxford University Press.

Skimin, R. (1977) *The Rhodesian Sell-out*, New York: Libra Publishers.

Spring, W. (1986) *The Long Fields: Zimbabwe Since Independence*, Basingstoke: Pickering and Inglis.

Staunton, I. (ed.) (1990) *Mothers of the Nation*, Harare: Baobab Press.

Streets, H. (2004) *Martial Races: The Military, Race and Masculinity in British Imperial Culture, 1857–1914*, Manchester: Manchester University Press.

Summers, C. (2002) *Colonial Lessons: Africans' Education in Southern Rhodesia, 1918–1940*, Portsmouth, NH: Heinemann.

Tosh, J. (1999) *A Man's Place: Masculinity and the Middle Class Home in Victorian England*, New Haven, CT: Yale University Press.

Tredgold, R. (1968) *The Rhodesia that was My Life*, London: George Allen and Unwin.

Tshabangu, O. M. (1977) *The March 11th Movement in ZAPU*, York: Tiger Papers.

Vambe, L. (1976) *From Rhodesia to Zimbabwe*, London: Heinemann.

Weinrich, A. K. H. (1979) *Women and Racial Discrimination*, Paris: UNESCO.

Weiss, R. (1986) *The Women of Zimbabwe*, London: Kesho.

— (1994) *Zimbabwe and the New Elite*, London: I.B.Tauris.

Weiss, R. with J. Parpart (2001) *Sir Garfield Todd and the Making of Zimbabwe*, London: British Academic Press.

Werbner, R. (1991) *Tears of the Dead: The Social Biography of an African Family*, Edinburgh: Edinburgh University Press.

West, M. (1997) 'Liquor and libido: "joint drinking" and the politics of sexual control in colonial Zimbabwe, 1920s–1950s', *Journal of Social History*, 30(3): 645–67.

— (2002) *The Rise of an African Middle Class: Colonial Zimbabwe, 1898–1965*, Bloomington: Indiana University Press.

White, L. (2003) *The Assassination of Herbert Chitepo*, Cape Town: Double Storey Books.

— (2005) 'Precarious conditions: a note on counter-insurgency in Africa after 1945', in S. D'Cruze and A. Rao (eds), *Violence, Vulnerability and Embodiment*, Oxford: Blackwells.

Wiegman, R. (2001) 'Object lessons: men, masculinity and the sign women', *Signs*, 26(2): 355–88.

How a Long Way Off Rolled Itself Up

Once, there was a place called A Long Way Off –
it was too far away to contemplate.

All that was known
was that the grass was a strange texture,
the trees grew upside down, and the houses
appeared to have been turned inside out.

So people were unprepared
when A Long Way Off rolled itself up
and edged a little nearer, and kept on
moving, until it had ventured so close
you could smell it, and breathe in
its otherness.

People laughed uneasily. A Long Way Off
was close enough to singe their hair.

Moniza Alvi (2005)

Afterword

For a long time I did not see men. I saw people who were men, but somehow it slipped my notice that they were *men*. What I saw during all those years when I was trying to make sense of political tensions – some of which burst into armed conflicts – were prime ministers, presidents, movement mobilizers, colonels, guerrillas, nationalists, colonial officials, party leaders, youths and intellectuals. I saw Chinese, Malays and Tamils; I saw peasants and landlords; I saw corporate executives and workers. The canvas seemed pretty crowded. The patterns of relationships between them seemed densely complex. The analytical task appeared daunting enough.

Even farther from my notice in those benighted years was masculinity – not to mention its plural. Of course, I saw that most of these people 'who happened to be men' crafted quite disparate styles of acting in public and of discursively justifying their actions. Also, I could scarcely miss their occasional odd-bedfellow alliances, their frequent rivalries with each other and their respective efforts to construct hierarchies of value of a sort that would put them and their aspirations on the top of the heap.

As I tried to take all this in – not just in a single country, but in several dozen countries – I thought I was immersing myself in the messy, intriguing practices of international politics. I thought I was becoming a moderately skilled practitioner of international relations. What I didn't know was how shallow my immersion was and how truly modest my skills then were. I didn't know how much I had underestimated the types of power wielded nationally and internationally. I had little clue how far I was from grasping the causes of state-organized and state-licensed violence.

Only now, especially after reading – slowly – these eye-opening, stretchy chapters on men and masculinities, have I realized how much deeper the ocean of international politics actually is and, therefore, how much more subtle our collective investigatory and theoretical skills need to be if we are to create an IR enterprise that can grapple effectively with those too often deadly politics.

As I have read along over several days, I have appreciated anew how valuable a *book* is, and what intellectual daring and downright stamina it takes to think up and then create this miracle called a book. For what Marysia Zalewski and Jane Parpart have done here is create a feminist conversation among political theorists and field research analysts, a conversation I could eavesdrop on over days, and return to later and reread in an entirely different order, sparking fresh insights. It is a feminist conversation about men and masculinities – and about the masculinized dynamics that have shaped the discipline of IR – in the sense that patriarchy has been visible and problematic from the scholarly enterprise's outset. Between these covers and in the minds of the editors and each of these contributors patriarchy – the social ordering that both privileges masculinized authority and serves to perpetuate it – is the subject of utterly serious interrogation. It may have been possible to create a conversation about men and masculinities that left patriarchy the unnamed elephant in the parlour. This is not that book.

Every edited book – every thoughtful conversation between bindings – is created, published and read at a distinctive moment in political history. *Rethinking the Man Question* comes at a time when the means for crafting destructive models of, and presumptions about, manliness are formidable. Moreover, we are all reading *Rethinking the Man Question* at a time when the militarizations of patriarchy are jeopardizing the well-beings of myriad peoples. The stakes are high.

These provocative chapters, singly, but particularly when read together, expose the depths to which we collectively must dig (or dive) to grasp the sources of masculinized ideals, presumptions and practices. We need to reread Hobbes with fresh eyes. We need to bone up on Hindu and Calvinist myths. We need to delve into Shona and Balkan histories. Doing the former may seem comfortably within the bailiwick of conventional IR, though if the theorists of masculinities here are taken as seriously as they deserve to be, such a rereading will likely provoke considerable, though productive, discomfort. The latter scholarly activities have not been on the agenda of most IR analysts at all.

Second, and at first glance paradoxically, these essays and studies reveal how precarious is any particular masculinized norm and any given pyramid of unequally valued masculinities. That is, as I read here, I was struck again at all the effort that has gone into sustaining a certain set of ideas about what constitutes the warrior ideal, the economic rational man, the nationalist manly hero, the courageous manly resister.

It will take more thinking, more diving, more sharing of findings to make sense of how certain masculinized ideals and particular hierarchies of masculinities can be so stubbornly entrenched yet simultaneously so in need of daily propping up. Or to put our joint conundrum another way: is the drill sergeant, shouting feminized insults at his raw male recruits in the hope of turning them into violence-wielding 'manly' soldiers, evidence of masculinity's deep entrenchment or of its precarious contingency – or, as I am now suspecting, of both?

Cynthia Enloe, Clark University

Notes on contributors

Dibyesh Anand is a Reader in International Relations at the Centre for the Study of Democracy in Westminster University, London. His research and teaching interests lie in the areas of international relations, post-colonialism, security, nationalism, and identity politics. He is the author of: *Geopolitical Exotica: Tibet in Western Imagination* (University of Minnesota Press), *Poetics and Politics of Imagination* (Routledge South Asia) and *Hindu Nationalism in India and the Politics of Fear* (Palgrave Macmillan). He is currently working on a comparative study of state–majority–minority relations in China and India. Taking masculinity seriously as a conceptual category and challenging the uses of masculinity for purposes of violence are a central focus of his politics and scholarship.

Terrell Carver is Professor of Political Theory at the University of Bristol, UK. He has published widely on Marx, Engels and Marxism, and sex, gender and sexuality, particularly in the context of international relations. Using methods derived from post-structuralist philosophy and semiotics, he has written at the nexus of feminist theory and the sociology of masculinities. His articles have appeared in *Review of International Studies*, *International Affairs* and *International Studies Review*, and his latest book is *Men in Political Theory* (Manchester University Press, 2004). Currently he is finishing a co-authored monograph and co-edited volume (both with Samuel A. Chambers) on the political theory of Judith Butler.

Raewyn Connell is University Professor at the University of Sydney, formerly teaching sociology at the University of California and Macquarie University. She is author, co-author or editor of twenty-one books, including *Masculinities*, *Ruling Class Ruling Culture*, *Making the Difference*, *Gender and Power*, *Sustaining Safe Sex*, *The Men and the Boys* and the recently published *Southern Theory*. A frequent contributor to research journals in sociology, education, political science, gender studies and related fields, she has also been a long-term participant in the labour and peace movements in Australia. She is currently writing on the social dimensions of neoliberalism; global power processes, especially corporate elite masculinity; and the changing role of intellectuals on the global periphery.

Daniel Conway studied at Exeter, Bristol and Rhodes Universities. He is a Lecturer in Politics at Loughborough University. His main research interests relate to the intersections between masculinities, sexuality, militarization and whiteness. The chapter in this volume draws from his PhD research on masculinities, citizenship and political objection to conscription in apartheid South Africa. This research has been further developed in his role as an Economic and Social Research Council (ESRC) Post-Doctoral Fellow in the Department of Politics, University of Bristol. He is currently interested in narratives of whiteness and the masculinity of white South Africans who have migrated to the UK since 1994 and in contemporary debates about whiteness and masculinity in the Republic of South Africa itself.

Kevin Dunn is Associate Professor of Political Science at Hobart and William Smith Colleges. His monograph *Imagining the Congo: The International Relations of Identity* was published by Palgrave in 2003. He has also co-edited *Africa's Challenge to International Relations Theory* (with Timothy M. Shaw, 2001), *Identity and Global Politics: Theoretical and Empirical Elaborations* (with Patricia Goff, 2004) and most recently *African Guerrillas: Raging Against the Machine* (with Morten Bøås, 2007). He has published articles on Africa, international relations theory and punk rock in numerous academic journals.

Cynthia Enloe is Research Professor of International Development and Women's Studies at Clark University in Worcester, Massachusetts, USA. She is on the boards of several journals, including *The International Feminist Journal of Politics, Signs, Minerva: Journal of Women and War* and the *American Political Science Review*. Among her books are: *Bananas, Beaches and Bases: Making Feminist Sense of International Politics, Maneuvers: The International Politics of Militarizing Women's Lives* and *The Curious Feminist: Searching for Women in a New Age of Empire*. Her most recent book is *Globalization and Militarism: Feminists Make the Link*.

Kimberly Hutchings is Professor of International Relations at the London School of Economics. She works in the fields of international ethical, political and feminist philosophy and theory. She is the author of *Kant, Critique and Politics* (Routledge, 1996), *International Political Theory: Rethinking Ethics in a Global Era* (Sage, 1999) and *Hegel and Feminist Philosophy* (Polity, 2003). Her current work is focused on theorizing time in world politics (see *Time and World Politics*, Manchester, 2008) and on feminist international ethics.

Cristina Masters is a lecturer in politics at the University of Manchester. She is the co-editor of *The Logics of Biopower and the War on Terror: Living, Dying, Surviving*. She has published a number of articles including 'Cyborg soldiers and militarized masculinities' in the *International Feminist Journal of Politics*. She is researching and writing on the new frontiers of homeland security, the war on terror and the bio-politics of death.

Jamie Munn is a freelance international development consultant. He has held lectureships at the City University in London and the University of the West of England. His research interests encompass gender and citizenship, ethnic conflicts, nationalism, and masculinities in politics. His work has appeared in several journals, most recently in *Nationalities Papers*, *Parliamentary Affairs* and *Men and Masculinities*.

Jane L. Parpart is Professor Emeritus at Dalhousie University in International Development Studies, Gender and Women's Studies and History (Africa). She is currently visiting professor at the Centre for Gender and Development Studies at the University of West Indies, Trinidad and Tobago. She has co-edited a number of volumes, including *The 'Man' Question in International Relations* (1998), *Gender, Conflict and Peacekeeping* (2005) and *Rethinking Empowerment* (2002). She has written extensively on gender and development, gender, development and violence and urban history in southern Africa. Her most recent writings explore the limits of empowerment, gender and development in an increasingly insecure world along with work on masculinities and violence in Zimbabwe and southern Africa.

Sandra Whitworth is a Professor of Political Science and Women's Studies at York University in Toronto, Canada. She is serving currently as the Graduate Program Director in Political Science, and as the home base editor for the *International Feminist Journal of Politics*. In addition to articles and chapters in edited anthologies, her publications include *Feminism and International Relations* (Palgrave Macmillan, 1994 and 1997) and *Men, Militarism and UN Peacekeeping: A Gendered Analysis* (Lynne Rienner, 2004 and 2007).

Marysia Zalewski is Director of the Centre for Gender Studies at the University of Aberdeen. Her research and teaching interests include theories of feminism and gender, critical international relations theory and masculinity studies. She is the author of numerous chapters, articles and books, including *The 'Man' Question in International Relations* (Westview Press, 1998), *Feminism after Postmodernism* (Routledge, 2001), *International Theory: Positivism and Beyond* (Cambridge University Press, 2004, 4th edition, co-edited with S. Smith and K. Booth) and *Intervening in Northern Ireland: Critically Re-thinking Representations of the Conflict* (Routledge, 2007, co-edited with John Barry). She is currently working on a monograph on feminism and its critics to be published by Routledge in 2009.

Index

Lightning Source UK Ltd.
Milton Keynes UK
UKHW03f0856270318
319957UK00010B/94/P